Music and Cultural Theory

... music itself [is] the supreme mystery
of the science of man, a mystery
that all the various disciplines come up
against and which holds the key to their progress

Claude Lévi-Strauss

Music and Cultural Theory

John Shepherd
and
Peter Wicke

Polity Press

Copyright © John Shepherd and Peter Wicke 1997

The right of John Shepherd and Peter Wicke to be identified as author of this work has been asserted in accordance with the Copyright, Designs and Patents Act 1988.

First published in 1997 by Polity Press in association with Blackwell Publishers Ltd.

2 4 6 8 10 9 7 5 3 1

Editorial office:
Polity Press
65 Bridge Street
Cambridge CB2 1UR, UK

Marketing and production:
Blackwell Publishers Ltd
108 Cowley Road
Oxford OX4 1JF, UK

Published in the USA by
Blackwell Publishers Inc.
350 Main Street
Malden, MA 02148, USA

ISBN 0–7456–0863–9
ISBN 0–7456–0864–7 (pbk)

A CIP catalogue record for this book is available from the British Library and the Library of Congress.

Typeset in 10½ on 12pt Palatino
by Wearset, Boldon, Tyne and Wear.
Printed in Great Britain by TJ International Ltd, Padstow, Cornwall

This book is printed on acid-free paper.

Contents

Preface

This book has been the product of seven years' work made possible by an exchange agreement between Carleton University, Ottawa, and the Humboldt University, Berlin. Although university-wide, this agreement was negotiated initially between the then Department of Music at Carleton (now part of the University's School for Studies in Art and Culture) and the Centre for Popular Music Research at the Humboldt. The agreement was signed in 1987, when the Humboldt University was part of the German Democratic Republic, and was the first agreement of a cultural or scientific nature concluded between Canada and the GDR. Events in 1989 and the years which followed altered dramatically the situation of the Humboldt University and its Centre for Popular Music Research. Progress on the book was as a consequence slowed while the future of the Centre in the unified Germany was assured. We would both like to extend our sincere thanks to Dr D. R. F. Taylor, Assistant Vice-President (International) and Director of Carleton International, for his unstinting and skilful support of the exchange agreement during a most difficult period. Without this support, it is entirely conceivable that the agreement would not have lasted and that this book would not have been finished. We would also like to thank Dr Bruce McFarlane, Acting Director of Carleton International in the period leading up to the signing of the agreement. We wish to thank as well the authorities of the Humboldt University as well as the University's former Directorate of International Relations which, although experiencing frequent changes of personnel, continued to support the agreement with energy and commitment.

We would like to thank Georg Knepler, Veit Erlmann, Philip Tagg, Alan Gillmor, Don Wallace and Alan Stanbridge, all of whom read earlier versions of the manuscript and discussed with us the ideas contained therein. We would also like to extend our thanks and appreciation to John Thompson at Polity, who was for seven years the epitome of a patient and understanding editor, as well as to Gill Motley, who was so helpful as our project neared completion. Our deepest gratitude, however, goes to our wives, Gisela and Norean, who have tolerated with good grace absences both physical and spiritual, and whose support and understanding have made this long and difficult project enjoyable.

Berlin and Ottawa
August, 1996

Acknowledgements

We are grateful to Richard Middleton and the Open University Press for permission to quote from *Studying Popular Music* (1990) and to Princeton University Press for permission to quote from Victor Zuckerkandl, *Sound and Symbol: Music and the External World*, © 1956 Bollingen Foundation Inc (Princeton University Press, 1956, 1969, 1973).

Introduction

The purpose of this book is to feed musicology into cultural theory, to consider the implications for cultural theory of a viable theory for the social and cultural constitution of music as a particular and irreducible form of human expression and knowledge. Our motivation in writing this book is musicological. While we assume music to be socially and culturally constituted, and fundamentally so, we cannot subscribe to the trend we see as dominant in cultural studies, which is to discuss music in much the same way as any other cultural artefact: in terms of theoretical and methodological protocols whose development has not been affected at all by cultural theoretical treatments of music. The result of this, in our view, is that it is not really music that is being discussed. The object of study as often as not is the linguistic discourses that are constructed around musical practices. As Jenny Taylor and Dave Laing observed some eighteen years ago, 'popular music remains a poor relation in cultural theory' (1979, p. 43). As musicologists who have worked in the related fields of popular music studies and the sociology and aesthetics of music during this period, we hold the view that nothing, essentially, has changed.

Our initial task in this book is therefore to interrogate those forms of cultural theory which have been central to its development since the late 1950s, and which either have been or could conceivably be brought to bear in a useful way on the question of how music is constituted and signifies socially and culturally.

Our purpose in undertaking this interrogation in the first four chapters of the book is to determine where the application of cultural theory has had some success in grasping affect in music as socially and culturally constituted, where problems have been encountered, where the social and cultural character of music has been misunderstood by cultural theory, and to identify the lacunae that need to be addressed if cultural theory is to be of genuine assistance in understanding music. However, to move directly from such an assessment to some kind of reformulation of cultural theory in the light of a full understanding of music as a signifying practice that is socially and culturally constituted would imply that a viable theory for the social and cultural constitution of music as a particular and irreducible form of human expression and knowledge actually exists. It is our view that – the work of scholars such as Middleton (1990) and McClary (1991) notwithstanding – no such theory exists. The work of such scholars has achieved a great deal in establishing the viability, legitimacy and necessity of examining music in the light of much recent cultural theory. However, a careful examination of such work (see, for example, Shepherd, 1991a, and Wicke, 1991) reveals that, as such, no theoretical protocol exists for underwriting the 'link' beween the sounds of music and the social and cultural affects, the social and cultural identities – whether individual or collective – to which they give life and substance. This situation persists, we argue, because of the lacunae identified during the course of the first four chapters.

Our task in the four chapters which follow this interrogation therefore becomes that of developing a viable theory for the social and cultural constitution of music as a particular and irreducible form of human expression and knowledge. If the overall purpose of the book is to feed musicology into cultural theory, then the task of these next four chapters is to feed cultural theory into musicology by thinking of music in ways unprecedented within musicology. The latter in fact becomes a prerequisite for the former. However, this feeding is in spirit rather than substance, in that the cultural theory necessary for thinking of music in these ways remains at this point undeveloped. These chapters take their lead from structuralist and semiological accounts of language in considering how music as a distinctive and irreducible signifying practice can be thought of as a structure with features distinct from those of language, as well as of 'communicating' semiologically in ways which are quite different from those of language.

It is in chapter 9 that we are able as a consequence to turn our attention to the central issue of the book. In addressing it, we argue that sound in music functions in a manner distinct from sound in language. We develop a detailed account of music as an asemantic yet material structure whose role it is to impart the principles of symbolic structuring to society, language and other forms of human expression. Considerable stress is placed on the body as the site through music for the mediation of social and symbolic processes. We argue that music is in this way as fundamental as language to the formation and persistence of human societies. Music's social character therefore flows as much from its unique contribution to social processes as it does from its capacity to symbolize them. Music is an activity central rather than peripheral to people and society.

Cultural studies have customarily insisted that the only legitimate way to examine music as a signifying practice is to examine specific musical practices in the circumstances of their historical contingency. To examine music in any other way is to invite the charge of essentialism if not idealism, sins which have more than once quite correctly been laid at the door of musicology. This line of argument is frequently advanced by scholars who apparently experience little difficulty in embracing theories for signification through language which have been developed independently of any consideration of the relations possible between language as a signifying practice and historical contingencies. This inconsistency of approach then results in music as a signifying practice being treated as if there were no alternative but to assume that it signifies, in the circumstances of its historical contingencies, as if it were language (which it clearly is not). This particular critique of cultural theory as frequently applied to music is one of the central themes of the book. Music is no different from language in that it is a signifying practice with its own particular characteristics that, as a socially and culturally constituted form of human expression and knowledge, gives rise to affects and meanings specific – and indissolubly so – to particular sets of historical contingencies. There is thus no intention, in thinking of music as a distinctive signifying practice, of essentializing it. Indeed, the symbiotic relatedness of language and music that is argued for in chapter 9 – in terms of which

both language and music are understood to *share* the same signifying potentials of sound, but in distinctively different permutations and combinations – leads to the realization that 'language'
and 'music' are themselves but discursive constructs arising
from the cultural use by people of the various signifying potentials offered up by sound as a material phenomenon. In this
sense the principal purpose of the book, to feed musicology into
cultural theory, leads to a sociology of sound, a theme taken up
in the book's concluding chapter.

The musicology we contemplate is clearly quite different
from that which predominates in the academic world. It is
important to make this point, because the tendency of academic
musicians in approaching the issue of affect and meaning in
music – the issue of the characteristics of aesthetic experiences
as occasioned by music – has been to argue from the particular
to the general. In this, they mirror the tendency of cultural studies scholars who are prepared to discuss the same issues only in
the context of the examination of specific musical practices as
historically contingent. The difference with the musicological
approach is that there is customarily scant sense of any historical contingency in social terms. The musicological approach we
take is different in that we are attempting to understand the
characteristics of music as a distinctive signifying practice that is
nonetheless constituted socially and culturally. We are thus
occasioning a fundamental break with one of the principal para-
digms of musicology in thinking of music as a signifying practice based in sound rather than as a totality of singular works.
We contend that the manner in which music signifies cannot be
understood successfully if music is thought of only as a totality
of individual works.

It is for this reason that the book does not undertake the
musical analysis of individual pieces as such, although we have
been at pains to illustrate the points we are making by reference
to musical examples where this has proved feasible. It is in this
sense that musical analysis as customarily conceived has to be
beyond the scope of this book. To move from the particular to
the general would inevitably have been to trap ourselves in
many of the received assumptions of academic music, and in
this way to prevent ourselves from achieving our objective. It is
with the greatest of respect for the work of these scholars that
we nonetheless contend that it is this tendency that results in a

certain theoretical impoverishment in the ideas of Middleton and McClary. In the end, Middleton (1990) treats music and subjects as discrete absolutes. The notion of music remains unproblematized, individual pieces are discussed in traditional academic terms, and the notion of the subject retains the fixities of the French psychoanalytic tradition. Both music and subject remain ultimately outside the scope of the social and cultural processes that purportedly constitute them. McClary (1991) also engages in the traditional analysis (from a technical, musical–theoretical point of view only) of individual pieces of music, in this case in the service of feminist criticism. However, there is scant indication of the cultural–theoretical ground necessary to establish the legitimacy of the relations posited between music analysis and feminist criticism.

Music cannot be conceived in this way as a phenomenon generalizable from individual pieces of music. To the contrary, individual pieces of music have to be thought of as particular instances of a signifying practice. It is understanding this signifying practice which, as we argue in chapter 6, points to the traps and impoverishments of traditional music theory and music analysis, and sets the stage theoretically for different kinds of music analysis, kinds for which the work of scholars such as Cusick (1994 and 1997) and Brett (1997) is prophetic. If cultural theory has grown to an appreciable extent from linguistics and the particular relationships it has had to the study of literature, then there is surely the room, if not the necessity, for an equivalent undertaking in musicology, if not a new discipline equivalent to that of linguistics.

Although motivated by concerns that are essentially musicological, this book for the reasons indicated takes an approach to understanding music that is unconventional within musicology. We believe, however, that this kind of undertaking is critically important for musicology. In this regard, and before we engage a text of a primarily cultural–theoretical character, we wish, as musicologists, to say something to our colleagues. We cannot allow the initiative in the development of theoretical protocols to understand the social constitution of cultural forms to be developed with virtually no input from musicology. Where music is concerned, it is musicology which must set the agenda by posing to other disciplines such as sociology and communication and intellectual trajectories such as cultural studies the questions for which answers are required in understanding music as a social and cultural form. It is a matter of urgency that musicology formulates and puts these questions, and that other disciplines take such questions seriously. This urgency occurs because musicology – as we intend to make clear in this book – is the only discipline through which it is possible to access certain processes vital and fundamental to human societies. It is only through musicology that these processes and their effects upon individuals can be rendered public for understanding and critical discussion. If musicology is not successful in formulating and putting the appropriate questions, and if other disciplines do not become engaged seriously in answering them, then these vital and fundamental aspects of human life will remain privatized and mythologized.

Musicology as a discipline and musicologists as academic practitioners are at present hardly well placed for such an undertaking. Like one or two other 'minority' disciplines, musicology has hardly been affected by, and has hardly begun to contribute to, the many important intellectual developments that have occurred within the humanities and social sciences since the late 1950s. Making these contributions, and making them sooner rather than later, is of the utmost importance for musicology. What musicology *should* and, indeed, could contribute to the arts, the humanities and the social sciences is important for an understanding of everyday life *as a whole*. That musicology should undertake the initiatives we have suggested is also important to the future, if not the survival, of the discipline as a viable intellectual enterprise. It is in this way that we urge a renewed, invigorating *and important* role for musicology within the arts, the humanities and the social sciences.

1

The Problem of Affect and Meaning in Music

This book is about processes of affect and meaning in music. It is also – and as a consequence – about insights into processes of affect and meaning as they operate in wider cultural contexts that can be gained through an examination of music. Methods of analysing affect and meaning in music have hardly kept pace with the increased diversity and currency of musical genres in everyday life. Musicology is the discipline within the academic world which, unlike other disciplines such as sociology and communication, has as its principal object the study of music. Yet musicology has been remarkably unsuccessful in putting forward concepts and theories capable of explaining the attraction of music for people in their everyday lives, and the power and influence it appears to have over them. Musicology has frequently avoided questions of affect and meaning altogether, claiming that its proper purpose is the establishing of facts about music and its history. When, however, it has considered questions of affect and meaning – either implicitly or explicitly – it has tended to do so in a manner which isolates musical processes from their embeddedness in social and cultural processes and the everyday lives of people.

Musicology: The Question of Context and Text

To think of music as a cultural process is to imply that social or cultural elements are contained within or passed through its sonic components. These elements must as a consequence have an origin and existence that are at least in part extrinsic to the musical experiences to which they contribute. The relationship between 'extra-musical' and 'musical' elements has previously been formulated within musicology in terms of received wisdoms concerning the character and function of music. That is, music has been taken to appeal autonomously to the autonomous awareness of the individual. This tendency can be traced to the way in which the traditional emphasis on positivism that has characterized the study of music since the late 1950s has resulted in the question of the relationship between musical processes and processes of subjectivity being studiously and sometimes consciously avoided. We cannot forget, argues Palisca, 'that musical aesthetics is not musical scholarship; it is musical experience and musical theory converging upon a philosophical problem. Aesthetics does not rest on documentary or similar evidence but on philosophical and psychological principles tested by experience' (1963, p. 110). This avoidance has in turn been entrenched by the way in which an emphasis on positivistic tasks has precluded a meaningful dialogue between the disciplines of historical musicology and music theory. As Leppert and McClary (1987a, p. xiii) have observed, 'the disciplines of music theory and [historical] musicology ... cautiously keep separate considerations of biography, patronage, place and dates from those of musical syntax and structure.' The concentration of musicologists 'on limited positivistic tasks', argues Kerman (1985, p. 72), has 'had the decided effect of side-stepping "the music itself" '. He continues, 'if the musicologists' characteristic failure is superficiality, that of the analysts is myopia ... by removing the bare score from its context in order to examine it as an autonomous organism, the analyst removes that organism from the ecology that sustains it' (1985, p. 72).

This separation of contextual from textual matters resonates in a less stringent and more constructive manner within the disciplines of ethnomusicology and popular music studies. The history of ethnomusicology has been characterized by debates between anthropologically or contextually oriented scholars such as Alan P. Merriam and musicologically or textually oriented scholars such as Mantle Hood. Although these debates have been played out since the late 1950s in increasingly complex and nuanced ways, it is only more recently that ethnomusicology has witnessed the treatment of musical sounds as cultural texts in the work of Blacking (1973), Keil (1979), Ellis (1985) and, most notably, Feld (1982 and 1988). Popular music studies, established as a separate undertaking since the late 1970s, have likewise experienced some not unhealthy tensions between sociological and musicological approaches to their subject matter (Shepherd, 1991b, pp. 189–212).

The tendency within disciplines such as sociology and communication has been to look to the lyrics of songs in dealing with questions of affect and meaning in popular music. This 'content analysis' approach to popular music has been particularly evident in journals such as *Popular Music and Society*. The problem here is that 'the sounds of music themselves' go unexamined. The analysis of affect and meaning is grounded exlusively in an examination of language decontextualized from sounds recognized as 'musical'. Musicological approaches to the analysis of popular music have tended to manifest the opposite tendency. The sounds of music are analysed in terms of methods and vocabularies derived from the analysis of European artmusic by the disciplines of music theory and music analysis. Although there is much to recommend in his work, this tendency is evident in Allan F. Moore's book, *Rock: The Primary Text* (1993). The more general problems of attempting to approach questions of affect and meaning in music – the aesthetic experiences occasioned by music – by using the traditional methods and vocabularies of music theory and music analysis – problems unavoidably highlighted through the analysis of popular music (Shepherd, 1991b, pp. 189–212) – are discussed in chapter 6.

The analysis of popular music reveals that there are in fact many levels of meaning having to do with music, lyrics, images and movement as negotiated by individuals with specific social and cultural biographies (Shepherd, 1991b, pp. 174–85). These levels can frequently act in contradictory ways. Frith and McRobbie (1979), for example, have pointed to the apparently contradictory messages contained in the lyrics and vocal timbre of the song 'Stand by Your Man' as performed by Tammy Wynette: the lyrics reinforce a traditional gender role for women, the hard, unrelenting voice seems to betray that this is a woman 'not to be messed with' (for a critique of Frith and McRobbie, see Taylor and Laing, 1979; for an analysis of voice-types in popular music, see Shepherd, 1991b, pp. 152–73). Tagg (whose work is discussed in chapter 5) has identified another level of meaning in his analyses of the theme music from the television series *Kojak* and the Abba hit, 'Fernando the Flute' (Tagg, 1979 and 1991). Particular melodic, harmonic, rhythmic and timbrel configurations are equated with particular moods, emotions and cultural meanings in a manner drawn from the analysis of language.

All three levels of meaning can be discerned in a song such as 'Yesterday' by the Beatles. The lyrics conform to the principle of nostalgia fundamental to the sentimental ballad as a musical genre, the use of the string quartet backing can be understood to signal that this song 'aspires to the condition of art', the use of the acoustic guitar can be understood to impart a 'serious', 'folky' feel, and the more formal melodic, harmonic, rhythmic and timbrel features of the sounds as music can be interpreted in ways that are not yet clear to underscore the feeling of loss occasioned by the song. It is this clever synthesis of different cultural reference points in the history of music (for example, 'classical', 'folk', 'mainstream popular' and – although not in this particular song – 'rock') which does much to explain the Beatles' phenomenal success (for similar arguments with respect to Elvis Presley, see Middleton, 1990, pp. 18–21). As Chambers has observed, the Beatles 'did not dramatically tear up Tin Pan Alley and previous popular music. Their music was described as "fresh" and "exciting", not "alien" and "offensive". Masterfully working through black and white pop traditions, they offered a novel, synthetic focus: an altered perspective, not a foreign landscape' (1985, p. 63).

The part of this equation in the generation of affect and meaning through music that has never been properly understood is the role played by 'the sounds of music themselves': the melodic, harmonic, rhythmic and timbrel configurations that lead us to recognize music as 'music'. A central problem in understanding significance in music has been that, in their 'abstract' (by which we mean 'non-denotative') manifestations, the sounds of music do not obviously refer outside themselves to the world of objects, events and linguistically encodable ideas. In terms of the way in which symbols are commonly understood to have meaning, this 'abstract' aspect of music emerges either as having 'no meaning', or as having a meaning that is quite distinct and apart from all other forms of meaning. Communication, as Duncan ironically observes, 'must be explained by everything but communication ... it must have, as we read so often, a "referent" ' (1968, p. 31). This difficulty has served to perpetuate and entrench within musicology the assumption that, if music can be accepted as in some way having meaning, then this meaning must be intrinsic or *immanent* to music's sounds. It is this difficulty which has allowed the appearance of the autonomous character of music (by which, in this context, is nearly always meant 'serious' or 'classical' music) to persist. The tensions that have existed between the study of the 'extra-musical' and the 'musical' have as a consequence been perpetuated in no small measure by the genuine intellectual difficulty of understanding how the two may relate.

Only one music theorist, Leonard B. Meyer, has consistently confronted this difficulty in terms of received wisdoms concerning the character and function of music. Meyer, remarks Kerman (1985, p. 107), 'has always kept his distance from other [music] theorists'. As 'a genuine polymath of music ... [he] has more or less systematically worked his way through the central problems of aesthetics, theory, modernism, criticism [and] history.' Meyer argues that embedded in much music theory is the idea that 'the meaning of music lies specifically ... and ... exclusively ... in the musical processes themselves' (1956, p. 33). Meaning in music is in other words assumed to be immanent to music's sounds, and music thus reducible to their condition. However, continues Meyer, there has been a failure 'to state with either clarity or precision ... in what sense these [musical] processes are meaningful'. This failure, continues Meyer, 'has led some critics to assert that musical meaning is a thing apart, different in some unexplained way from all other kinds of meaning'. This, he concludes, 'is simply an evasion of the real issue'.

The real issue seems to lie in confusing a form of human expression that does not obviously refer outside itself to the world of objects, events and linguistically encodable ideas with one which makes no appeal beyond itself in the process of generating and evoking meaning. While it can be accepted that music falls within the former category, it cannot sensibly be said to fall within the latter. It is this distinction which allowed Meyer to argue that musical processes appeal directly to the logic and flux of mental and psychological processes. The purpose of Meyer's influential study, *Emotion and Meaning in Music* (1956), was 'to establish and explain the general causes and conditions for the affective aesthetic response to music' (p. 197). These affective experiences, argued Meyer, 'result from a direct interaction between a series of musical stimuli and an individual who understands the style of the work being heard' (p. 256). Both the individual and the music thus have a role to play in the generation of the aesthetic response. The mind of the individual is governed by general laws in its organization of the stimuli impinging on it: 'The organisation which the mind imposes upon the separate stimuli which are constantly "bombarding the system" is not an accidental or arbitrary one. The mind in its selection and organisation of discrete stimuli into figures and groupings appears to obey certain general laws. These ... account, in part, for the way in which the mind organises musical stimuli' (p. 87). However, 'because the forces shaping such an experience are exclusively musical, the form of the affective experience will be similar to the form of the musical work which brought it into play' (p. 256). The aesthetic experience, therefore, arises within limits of tolerance imposed by the laws of psychology, the form of the music in question, and the competence of the listener in the tradition of the music being heard. Within these limits a formal congruence between music and the mind must obtain for an aesthetic response to occur. Musical meaning is as a consequence taken to originate and be located within 'psychological constants' (Meyer, 1973, p. 14) presumed to be innate in humans. There is consequently no need to entertain the notion that music invokes the external, 'objective' world. The ability of music to evoke meaning is facilitated through a conformity between the structures of music and the structures of the human mind.

Meyer's position is allied to that of Langer, who has argued that the 'inner life' has 'formal properties similar to those of music – patterns of motion and rest, of tension and release, of agreement and disagreement, preparation, fulfilment, excitation,

sudden change, etc.' (Langer, 1942, p. 228). This similarity, concludes Langer, allows music to act in relation to the emotional
world in the same way that language acts in relation to the
propositional world of objects, events and ideas – symbolically:

> If music has any significance, it is semantic, not symptomatic. Its
> 'meaning' is evidently not that of a stimulus to evoke emotions, nor
> that of a signal to announce them; if it has an emotional content, it
> 'has' it in the same sense that language 'has' its conceptual content –
> *symbolically*. It is not usually derived *from* affects nor intended *for*
> them; but we may say, with certain reservations, that it is about
> them. Music is not the cause or cure of feelings, but their *logical
> expression*. (1942, p. 218)

While Langer's work has been philosophical, Meyer's has rested
on detailed and persuasive analyses of music in the tradition of
'classical' music. Meyer has demonstrated that the 'best' music
in this tradition works according to the principle of 'deferred
gratification' (Meyer, 1959). A piece of music creates expecta-
tions that it will proceed to fulfil, but not directly. While the
most fundamental of its architectonic (harmonically, melodically
and rhythmically architectural) levels will, indeed, move
sequentially towards a satisfying conclusion, other, higher levels
will engage in deviations that detract from the inevitable. The
technical characteristics of the music keep the listener in a state
of meaningful suspense: meaningful, because fulfilment is not
so directly achieved as to render the music banal, and the deviations not so compelling as to render it anarchic and without a
sense of direction. In this way the harmonic, melodic and, to a
lesser extent, rhythmic elements of this architectonic tradition
speak symbolically to the ebb and flow of the inner life.

Meyer has undoubtedly contributed important insights into
the structural rather than referential principles according to
which music evokes meaning. However, because Meyer's work
does not take into account the social ecology that sustains it,
these insights do not stretch to an explanation of the mechanisms through which musical processes and processes of subjectivity are involved with one another. Musical processes and
processes of subjectivity speak meaningfully to one another
because they are grounded in, informed by, and constituted
through similar sets of social mediations. The substance and
logic of the inner life flow from these mediations rather than

from 'psychological constants' presumed innate in people. As a consequence, it is difficult to see how Meyer's insights could stretch to provide an adequate theorization of the substance of musical meanings. Meyer's analyses of 'classical' music are compelling only because the consequences of social mediations to this tradition are revealed intuitively and through omission. What Meyer identifies as psychological constants appealed to by a particular tradition of music are, in fact, psychological processes specific to particular social and historical circumstances. It is for this reason that Meyer's views on music outside the tradition of 'classical' music (or music effectively influenced by that tradition, for example, 'real jazz' (Meyer, 1959, p. 33)) have at times been ethnocentric and dismissive. Judged in terms of criteria drawn from the aesthetic and technical characteristics of 'classical' music rather than from the social and cultural circumstances of their creation and appreciation, traditional and popular music have emerged, inevitably, as less valuable than music in the 'classical' tradition. According to this logic, a song such as the Beatles' 'Yesterday' emerges as inherently inferior to Schubert's *Lieder* because it is understood to have less complex harmonies and as a consequence to lead to forms of gratification which are less elevated and less enriching. If Meyer theorizes an 'extra-musical' significance for music in a manner which circumvents the traditional problem of referentialism, therefore, he does so without challenging the view that both music and the individual awareness to which it appeals are ultimately autonomous in relation to social and cultural processes. The complete autonomy of music which is presumed to exist as a consequence of the assumption that meaning in music is immanent to music's sounds is in Meyer's case transferred to the dual autonomy of music and individual awareness.

Sound in Music: Fixity and Negotiation of Meaning

If musicology has had little to say on the question of music's meanings in their social and cultural circumstances, then other disciplines have had little to say on the role of music's sounds in generating and articulating social and cultural meanings. The study of the meanings and affects of various forms of contemporary culture and mass communication within everyday life has taken place in disciplines such as sociology and communication, and within intellectual trajectories such as cultural studies. Music has certainly formed part of such studies (see, for example, Bradley, 1992; Chambers, 1985; Hebdige, 1979; Goodwin, 1992; Kaplan, 1987; Schwichtenberg, 1993). However, because the tendency has been to consider questions of affect and meaning without reference to music's central characteristic, its sounds, affect and meaning in music have almost without exception been located in processes that are 'extra-musical'. This implies that the sounds of music are of little or no consequence to questions of affect and meaning, and that musical affects and meanings are driven by forces that are largely or entirely social and cultural.

It would seem that dominant approaches to questions of affect and meaning in music from musicology, sociology, communication and cultural studies have in common a concept of music as a 'thing'. Either music contains meaning in its material qualities as a phenomenon autonomous in relation to social and cultural processes, or it acts more or less as a cipher, an inscrutable black box, the role of whose internal characteristics in the transmission or creation of social and cultural meanings is neither considered nor understood. In terms of this contrast, musicology would typically make much of the role of the motor rhythms of Beethoven's Fifth or Seventh Symphonies in generating immanent meaning, while sociology and communication would typically pay scant attention to the possibility of the prominent bass guitar riff in the Rolling Stones' 'Satisfaction' (another example of motor rhythm) playing a significant role in the generation of the social and cultural meanings customarily associated with this song: 'an explicit sexual strategy intent on dismantling the prevalent sentimental and romantic ties that dominated pop and Tin Pan Alley' (Chambers, 1985, p. 68). Musicology has in this way tended to conceive music's meanings as phenomena extrinsic to social and cultural forces: social and cultural forces are seen either as immaterial to music's meanings or as external forces capable only of 'influencing' a central aesthetic, musical core (Meyer, 1956). Here, there is a tendency to reduce music's meanings to the condition of music's sounds. Sociology, communication and cultural studies, on the other hand, have tended to conceive music's sounds as phenomena extrinsic to social and cultural forces and the affects and meanings they generate. Both approaches tend to keep separate music's sounds from the social and cultural processes that are of consequence for them. Neither approach seems capable of discussing a *relationship*, a set of *processes* between music's sounds and music's meanings wherein sounds are significant, but meanings are the consequence of the socially and culturally mediated character of this relationship. Neither approach, in other words, can adequately understand *processes* of affect and meaning through music.

This tendency on the part of sociology, communication and cultural studies flows from the received wisdom on how sound in language signifies, a wisdom derived from the work of Ferdinand de Saussure. According to Saussure, it is important to distinguish between a word in language, and the object or concept invoked by the word. Saussure argued that the behaviour of a word in a language was influenced irrevocably by the context of that language. The meanings of words could not as a consequence be fixed by external reality. Neither could they correspond simply to the phenomena presumed to be present in external reality. As Saussure concluded, it was necessary to distinguish between the *value* of a word *in language* and the *signification* achieved by the word in relation to some aspect of external reality. Thus, for example, the word 'bird' exists and functions within the structure of the English language as a sign achieving signification independent of any necessary, *a priori* influence flowing from the characteristic behaviour of birds in the real world. While the problem of 'naming birds' in a sense 'results' in the creation of the word 'bird', the qualities of the word and its behaviour in the English language have nothing to do with birds or their qualities and behaviour in the real world.

This understanding of the relationship between words, language and external reality led Saussure to draw a critical distinction between the 'signifier' or amalgam of sounds recognized by the structure of the language – and by people with a competence in the language – as being meaningful in their differences, and the 'signified' or mental concept traditionally associated through the structure of the language with that amalgam of sounds. 'The linguistic sign', said Saussure, 'unites, not a thing and a name, but a concept and a sound-image' (1966, p. 66). 'The linguistic sign is then a two-sided psychological entity', continued Saussure. 'The two elements are intimately united, and each recalls the other' (p. 66). It is important to know that by the term 'signifier', Saussure did not mean the sounds of the word itself, but the psychological image of the sounds constituted in the experience of an individual. It is equally important to know that the meaning of the term has shifted somewhat since Saussure's time to mean more often the inherent characteristics of the sounds which constitute a word. This issue of the respective roles of sounds as matter and of the sensory sound-image that is the physical imprint of 'sounds as matter' in processes of signification is one to which we will return in discussing the role of sounds in *music* in processes of signification.

It is important to stress also that the signified or mental concept is not the same thing as an object or concept as it might be imagined to exist in the real world. The signified 'bird' traditionally and conventionally invoked by the amalgam of sounds or signifier ('sound-image') 'bird' may have a certain relation to birds as they might be imagined in the real world, but, as a mental concept, it is quite distinct and separate from them. Because the relationship between signifier and signified becomes so heavily conventionalized within the structure of any language, what in fact is a purely arbitrary relationship (there is nothing inherently 'bird-like' about the signifier 'bird') comes to appear as seamless, natural and 'given' in reality. In everyday life and everyday reality the sign, achieved through the arbitrary yet seamless coming together of signifier and signified, seems naturally to invoke reality and to reflect it. The sign signifies or gives rise to signification, in other words, *because* of this arbitrary yet seamless join. To understand how signs generate meaning ('the science of semiology') is thus potentially subversive of conventional realities, knowledge systems and therefore social structures *because* there is nothing given or fixed in processes of signification. However, while languages actually change organically through time, they tend, in their everyday and conventional manifestations, to act as a *conservative* force in reproducing knowledge and reality for individuals within cultures and societies.

If – in contrast to the position musicology customarily adopts – the meanings of music are assumed *not* to be immanent in the materials of music, then the established semiological model of how sounds in language signify becomes very attractive *because* of the arbitrary connection of the signified to the signifier. However, to apply this model to an understanding of how sounds in music signify inevitably renders music as a special, but, unfortunately, inferior case of language. This, as we shall see, is the direction taken by French poststructuralist thinking on music. The nature of this choice is hinted at strongly by Simon Frith in an article which examines the role of discourse in assigning value to music. Frith argues that – in constituting an object of study according to the assumption that the meaning of music is immanent in music's sounds – musicologists constitute in popular music an object of study to which few people listen. 'What I have been trying to suggest', says Frith,

> is that arguments about the value of particular pieces of music can only be understood by reference to the discourses which give the value terms concerning their meaning. Arguments about music are less about the qualities of the music itself than about how to place it, about what it is in the music that is actually to be assessed. After all, we can only hear music as having value, whether aesthetic or any other sort of value, when we know what to listen to and how to listen for it. Our reception of music, our expectations from it, are not inherent in the music itself – which is one reason why so much musicological analysis of popular music misses the point: its object of study, the discursive text it constructs, is not the text to which anyone listens. (1990, pp. 96–7)

'Ordinary' listeners are not concerned about the question of the supposedly immanent meanings of music, in other words. They are concerned about what music means to them. What Frith seems to be suggesting is that if the meaning and value of music are not located in the materials of music themselves, then the only reasonable alternative is to locate them within the discourses through which people make sense of and assign value to music. In his article Frith engages in a sociological analysis of the contradictory ways in which value comes to be assigned to music. If the nature of this assigning is so contradictory, he concludes, 'if the meaning of "good music" is so unstable how can we possibly assign it to the notes alone?' (1990, p. 101).

The scholar whose work has revolved most clearly around this conundrum is Jean-Jacques Nattiez (1975, 1987 and 1990). Nattiez's work draws on that of Jean Molino (1975 and 1978) in proposing a tripartite semiological scheme involving producers, a symbolic form and 'receivers'. Production or creation results in the 'poietic dimension' (Nattiez, 1990, p. 11) or the level of intentionality in respect of the musical work. 'Reception' accounts for the 'esthesic dimension'. Here, however, the term 'reception' is misleading because 'we do not "receive" a "message's" meaning ... but rather *construct* meaning' (1990, p. 12). Music, therefore, does not *simply* convey the intended 'message' of the composer to the listener. However, in its physical or material, which is to say symbolic form, music nonetheless carries a *trace* of intended meaning:

> the symbolic form is embodied physically and materially in the form of a *trace* accessible to the five senses. We employ the word *trace* because the poietic process cannot immediately be read within its lineaments, since the esthesic process (if it is in part determined by the trace) is heavily dependent upon the lived experience of the 'receiver'. Molino proposed the name *niveau neutre* ... or *niveau matériel* ... for this trace. (1990, p. 12)

In one sense Nattiez's work possesses the *potential* to dispense with the notion of immanent meaning in music (at the 'level' of the 'neutral') by allowing for the construction of meaning on the part of the 'receiver' in a manner related to but distinct from this *niveau neutre* (because this process of meaning construction is 'heavily dependent upon the lived experience of the "receiver" ', and only 'in part determined by the trace'). Yet in another sense Nattiez retains a *certain* notion of immanence (the trace) in quite rightly refusing to allow that just any meaning can be passed through or assigned to musical materials themselves. However, this notion of immanence seems to depend, not on the musical materials themselves, but on the perpetuation within them of a trace of the poietic dimension responsible for their configuration, a trace which then proceeds in part to determine the esthesic dimension. Although meaning is constituted by the 'receiver', it is constructed – it would seem – not simply according to the possibilities inherent in the *niveau neutre*, but in addition according to the trace of the poietic dimension which remains immanent at this level. In retaining a notion of immanence in this *particular* way, Nattiez's work unfortunately retains strong resonances of traditional high culture positions on questions of meaning and value in music. A careful reading of Nattiez reveals that the notion of the *niveau neutre* is handled ambiguously – it is constructed according to the context of its use. As a consequence, Nattiez frequently experiences difficulty in not assuming that meaning and value reside, immanently, in music's 'neutral level'. It is for this reason that Nattiez's analyses of music – which draw on the principles of established modes of music analysis and do not deviate from them – can sit quite comfortably within his semiological analysis. This problem with the *niveau neutre* occurs precisely because Nattiez is unclear on the question of the relations of music's sounds as material phenomena to music as a process of creation and 'reception'. Nattiez's work as a consequence throws little light on the question of resolving the tension between the opposed poles of the arbitrary and the immanent.

According to the traditional semiological model of how sounds in language signify, sounds in music would be taken to signify in fundamentally the same way as sounds in language, but with one notable difference. Sounds in music are understood to work differently from sounds in language in the sense that they do not invoke or call forth signifieds coterminous with the world of objects, events and linguistically encodable ideas. There is little disagreement, in other words, on the question of music's 'non-denotative' effects. According to this traditional semiological model there is therefore little alternative but to understand sounds in music as occasioning a ground of physiological and affective stimulation which is subsequently interpellated into the symbolic order of language. It is at this point that the sounds of music are taken to enter the social world and take on significance. Meanings in music are in this way taken to be discursively constituted, *and exclusively so*. Sounds in music are thus taken to be equally as arbitrary in their relationship to processes of signification as are sounds in language, except that, to the extent that sounds in music depend upon the arbitrary signifying processes of language in order to take on meaning, they are more distanced from and not as immediately implicated in processes of meaning construction as are sounds in language. Sounds in music could thus be said to float even more free in their relationship to processes of signification than do sounds in language, because they are not as directly burdened by the conventions of traditional associations between signifiers and signifieds. There is more of a sense, according to this understanding of signifying processes in music, in which sounds in music can take on meanings assigned to them arbitrarily than can sounds in language.

According to this understanding of processes of signification through sounds, music becomes an empty sign in the sense that its sounds can be taken to be completely polysemic in nature, capable of all meanings because, in and of themselves, they are capable of none. In its nascent state music can thus stand for the 'nothingness and being' taken by poststructuralists to be characteristic of the subject before entry into language. Therefore, while the sounds of music could never be 'innocent' in the sense of existing apart from any imaginable meanings, they could never carry any responsibility for their own 'guilt'. The inherent characteristics of the sounds of music could never be implicated in the meanings they facilitate. The only limitations placed on the construction of meaning through the sounds of music are therefore taken to derive from the social and cultural contexts in which the music is situated. This is the reasoning that seems to lie behind Julia Kristeva's position on significance in music when she says that

> while the fundamental function of language is the *communicative* function, and while it transmits a *meaning*, music is a departure from this principle of communication. It does transmit a 'message' between a subject and an addressee, but it is hard to say that it *communicates* a precise *meaning*. It is a combinatory of differential elements, and evokes an algebraic system more than a discourse. If the addressee hears this combinatory as a sentimental, emotive, patriotic, etc., message, that is the result of a subjective interpretation given within the framework of a cultural system rather than the result of a 'meaning' implicit in the 'message'. (1989, p. 309)

As Kristeva concludes, 'the musical code is organized by the *arbitrary* and *cultural* (imposed within the frameworks of a certain civilization) difference between various local values: *notes*' (p. 309).

There is a sense in which we would argue that the 'linguistic', discursive approach to understanding meaning in music, and approaches more typically taken by musicologists, both retain a certain validity. On the one hand, it is clear that meanings ascribed to musical processes are very significantly influenced by the nature of the discourses constructed around them. On the other hand, the fact that people not infrequently argue intensely about meaning and value in music (Frith, 1990) would seem to suggest that there is more at stake than this. There must, in other words, be something to argue *about*, something which is powerful yet 'imprecise' enough (in respect of language) for radically different views to be instigated by the same piece of music (or, to be more precise, the same sonic event). It seems likely that the lack of precision obtains in the interface between the character of the musical experience (as socially structured and structuring through sound), and the character of language inevitably brought into play through the constitution of linguistic discourses.

Feld (1984) has argued that it is the difficulty of translating the simultaneously multidimensional character of the musical experience into the essentially linear medium of language that leads people to become 'inarticulate' and 'confused' in discussing music while at the same time retaining demonstrably strong feelings about it. Speech about music can thus only become effective through a context of frames provided by the speaker that is shared by others. It is in this way that people use words to convey what words, as such, *cannot* convey. People

> *locate* and *categorize* musical experiences in relation to similar or dissimilar experiences. They *associate* musical experiences with experiences of other types. They *reflect* on how an experience relates to like or unlike imagery. And they *evaluate* the experience by relating it to their particular preferences. When people say, 'It's different from . . . ', 'It's a kind of . . . ', 'It sort of reminds me of . . . ', and things of this sort, they are creating locational, categorical, and associational features. When they say, 'Well, if I had to name it . . . ', 'I mean on some level . . . ', 'For me at least . . . ', 'I really can't say but, do you know what I mean?' they are not necessarily tongue-tied, inarticulate, or unable to speak. They are caught in a moment of interpretive time, trying to force awareness to words. They are telling us how much they assume that we understand *exactly* what they are experiencing. In fact, we do understand exactly what they are experiencing. We take it as socially typical that people talk this way about music, stringing together expressives, and we assume that this confirms what we are all supposed to know: that at some level, one just cannot say with words what music says without them. (Feld, 1984, p. 14)

Language is thus incapable of pinning meaning in its customary manner. In referring to music's powerful yet 'imprecise' effects, the German linguist Manfred Bierwisch has argued in a similar vein when he says that

A musically encoded gesture is related in a constitutive manner to a variable but not arbitrary cognitive content of experiences ... This fact plays a fundamental role in the relationship between the meanings of musical signs and non-musical factors. This relationship can be paraphrased in terms of two apparently opposing statements: it is practically impossible to fix the thoughts or notions which are evoked by music; and, the connections between musical configurations and non-musical thoughts and notions are by no means arbitrary. (1979, p. 57)

According to Bierwisch, therefore, not just *any* meaning can be associated with music's sounds.

The Move to Structuralism

A way forward in resolving the conundrum of fixity and negotiation in music's meanings is suggested by way of the more structuralist dimensions of Saussure's work. Saussure's important contribution to linguistic (and subsequently, through the ways in which his work was taken up by others, cultural) analysis can best be approached through a description of the concept of a 'structure' as exemplified in this tradition. This description is drawn from the work of Piaget (1971), as summarized by Hawkes (1977). For Piaget, says Hawkes (1977, p. 16), 'structure ... can be observed in an arrangement of entities which embodies the ... fundamental ideas ... of wholeness ... transformation ... [and] self-regulation'. By wholeness, argues Hawkes,

is meant the sense of internal coherence. The arrangement of entities will be complete in itself and not something that is simply formed of otherwise independent elements. Its constituent parts will conform to a set of intrinsic laws which determine its nature and theirs. These laws confer on the constituent parts within the structure overall properties larger than those each individually possesses outside it. Thus a *structure* is quite different from an *aggregate*: its constituent parts have no genuinely independent existence outside the structure in the same form they have within it. (1977, p. 16)

By transformation is meant the process whereby a structure is dynamic and active rather than merely passive. It is the process 'whereby new material is constantly processed by and through it'. Finally, a structure is self-regulating if 'it makes no appeals

beyond itself in order to validate its transformational procedures. The transformations act to maintain and underwrite the
intrinsic laws which bring them about, and to "seal off" the system from reference to other systems' (1977, p. 16).

In conceptualizing language as a self-maintaining structure,
Saussure provided an initial model of how any symbolic system
or structure could act. In this way, he laid the foundations for
'the science of semiology'. He revolutionized the discipline of
linguistics by critiquing the dominance of philology, both historical and comparative, in its development (1966, pp. 1–5). He thus
dispensed with the idea that languages were constituted exclusively by aggregates of words – however organized grammati-
cally – with meanings flowing directly from and grounded
ineluctably in real objects or concepts in external reality, and
replaced this conception with a notion of language as a structure
composed both of individual entities and the relations obtaining
between them: 'signs and their relations are what linguistics
studies', said Saussure (1966, p. 102). For Saussure, there was
thus a crucial distinction to be drawn between the diachronic
dimension of language, which he termed *parole* (loosely translatable as 'speech'), and the synchronic dimension of language,
which he termed *langue* (loosely translatable as 'language').
Language (*langue*) behaved like a structure, whereas speech
(*parole*), which *langue* made possible and which gave *langue* life,
did not. It was *langue* which made language – in the diversity of
the physical, physiological and psychological aspects of speech
– possible as a social institution. It was *langue* that lent order to
speech, and thus made possible the scientific study of language
as constituted both by *langue* and *parole*. If *parole* referred to
actual, concrete speech, the way in which words are articulated
through time and their meanings constantly negotiated and
re-negotiated, then *langue* referred to the rule system, never
concretely articulated, according to which actual speech would
be generated at any one time.

It is the capacity to develop language as opposed to speech
which is specific to human societies, argued Saussure. At any
one time, the *langue* of a language is complete, whole, self-
regulating and transformational. A crucial characteristic of language is that it lives, thrives, regulates and maintains itself with
only an indirect relationship to the world to which it is taken to
refer (but a relationship nonetheless). If the qualities and behav-

iour of a word do not flow simply and directly from the qualities or behaviour of the object or concept in the external world
which it nonetheless signifies, then the sounds of a word have
meaning or signify, not because they have meanings inherent to
them which flow from their actual sonic characteristics, but
because they are maintained in certain relationships by the
structure of the language. If the qualities or behaviour of an
object or concept do not influence in a direct or simple manner
the qualities and behaviour of a word, there can be no necessary
connection between the *sounds* of a word and what the word is
taken to name or 'signify'. In other words, the 'meanings' of
words are in no way intrinsic to the sounds of words. In fact,
argued Saussure, we only recognize sounds as meaningful in
terms of their relationship of difference *from other sounds* recognized as likewise meaningful by the structure of the language.
In reproducing knowledge and reality in this way language acts
as a structure which is whole, transformational and self-regulating. The structural character of language as a social institution
thus gives it a certain distance both from society as a whole and
from the individual in society. Language is in other words relatively autonomous in its relationship to both.

Saussure's work offers specific possibilities for the analysis of
music. As evidenced in the work of Meyer, significance, affect
and meaning in music have been assumed by music theorists
and music analysts to be generated through the way in which
discrete sonic events relate to one another through time and
space. This way of thinking does not seem so far removed from
Saussure's argument that the sounds of a word have meaning
and signify, not because they have meanings inherent in them
which flow from their actual sonic characteristics, but because
they are maintained in certain relationships by the structure of
the language. It is this structural and relational character of language which guarantees language its distinctiveness *vis-à-vis*
society and the individual, while at the same time allowing for a
relationship with them. In thus 'echoing' the structural and relational character of the thinking typical of music theorists and
music analysts such as Meyer, Saussure's work moves beyond
the idealism, essentialism and 'immanence' customarily characteristic of such thinking in opening the way for a structural and
relational form of signification with ramifications beyond the
closed circuits of its articulative practices.

The ability of Saussurean thinking to move beyond that characteristic of music theory and music analysis does, however, point to an incipient tension between the two lines of thought. It is a condition of the structural and relational character of Saussurean thinking that the sounds of words can have no necessary or logical connection to their customary meanings. Only in this way can language act as a structure independent of the world it names and thereby constitutes. This line of thinking does little, however, to guarantee music a similar status. This is because the character of the relations possible between music and the world extrinsic to it are at best unclear. It is, in other words, unclear how mechanisms of signification in music might enable it to produce this world while at the same time remaining independent of it as a structure. The principle of the arbitrary which in the case of language guarantees it independence as a structure can in the case of music constitute a threat to its integrity. If the principle is applied to music in a situation where the character of processes of signification in relation to the extrinsic world remains unclear, then the possibility exists for music *to be conceptualized* as being 'blueprinted' by forces external to it. Lack of an understanding of how sounds in music produce meaning and signification can in other words leave a vacuum only too susceptible to conceptual occupation through the positing of meanings extrinsic to the sounds which are placed in an arbitrary relationship with them.

It is against a presumed centrality for the principle of the arbitrary in more general theories of signification that the idealism, essentialism and 'immanence' of much thinking in musicology can be thought to be pitched. Most musicians and musicologists experience difficulty with the idea that music's meanings are somehow arbitrary in their relationship to music's sounds. To them, as well as to us, this idea seems to lead to the inevitable conclusion that music is somehow the *product* of processes and forces extrinsic to it. This is especially the case given the tenuous state of understanding where the relatedness of music's sounds to the isolatable and isolated elements of the world extrinsic to music are concerned. Music seems 'defenceless' in the face of the arbitrary. More specifically, the imposition of the principle of the arbitrary seems to reduce music to the condition of language and thus to make impossible the very thing guaranteed for language by Saussure, namely, a distinctive and specific status *vis-à-vis* other social institutions. In the context of a lack of understanding as to how exactly the sounds of music produce meaning and signification, the presumed immanence of music's meanings to music's sounds becomes an effective mechanism in defending the integrity of music as a distinct form of human expression and signification. If music is true only to itself, then its integrity cannot by definition be compromised by processes and forces extrinsic to it. This tension between the opposed poles of the arbitrary and the immanent in relation to significance in music constitutes one of the central difficulties to be addressed in this book.

2

Music and Cultural Theory

A crucial step in resolving this tension between the arbitrary and the immanent is to find a way of reconciling the principles of structural analysis evident in the work of Meyer – consistent as they are with an acceptance of music's presumed autonomous character – with the principles of structuralism evident in the work of Saussure, principles which assume that language as a structure is linked in an indissoluble though irreducible manner to social processes and processes of subjectivity. A framework for thinking of music as both structural and social in character can be derived from the tradition of British subcultural theory as well as from the work of Raymond Williams which preceded it.

Subcultural Theory and the Question of Style

English subcultural theory can be traced to a seminal article by Phil Cohen (1972) which analyses the radically changed circumstances of working-class young people in Britain after the Second World War. Cohen notes that social and economic changes in post-war Britain resulted in two sets of altered circumstances for the working classes: firstly, urban redevelopment resulted in the dissolution of many characteristic features of working-class culture; secondly, new technologies and new industries were causing traditional occupations to disappear. Unlike previous American work in the sociology of youth and the sociology of deviance, Cohen's does not theorize subcultural behaviour in terms of general and historically unspecific reactions on the part of working-class young people to a world dominated by the middle classes and middle-class values. It demonstrates how specific social and economic changes obtaining *throughout* British society during and after the 1950s received particular expression *within* the working classes and therefore occasioned subcultures and subcultural behaviour which were as specific to working-class life as they were to the overall circumstances of that society. As a consequence, Cohen argues that 'the latent function of subculture ... [is] to express and resolve, albeit "magically", the contradictions which remain hidden or unresolved in the parent culture.' Mods, parkers, skinheads, crombies, continues Cohen, 'all represent in their different ways, an attempt to retrieve some of the socially cohesive elements destroyed in the parent culture, and to combine these with elements selected from other class factions, symbolising one or other of the options confronting it' (1972, p. 23).

The notion of an individual's or group's behaviour emanating from their lived experience of the world, a somewhat ungrounded concept as it derived from work on deviance within the American tradition of symbolic interactionism, came, in Cohen's work and that which followed it, to be marked by an awareness that lived experience was both contradictory and culturally specific. Behaviour was understood in terms of contradictions imposed on and experienced by young people in terms of specific social locations mediated by class. As Cohen suggests, 'sub-culture is ... a compromise solution, between two contradictory needs: the desire to create *autonomy and difference* from parents ... and the need to maintain ... the *parental identifications* which support them' (1972, p. 26). It was only later that mediations brought on by questions of ethnicity and gender entered the picture, and in this sense, early work on youth within the tradition of English cultural studies displayed both an ethnic and gender bias. An important point, however, was that theories for explaining the behaviour of young people were beginning to match the contradictions and complexities implicit in such behaviour, and were making problematic the very relationship of behaviour as a cultural practice to objective social conditions.

A concern with cultural practices as the matrices from which behaviour emanated quickly expanded to include the question of style as a cultural manifestation. The focus of English subcultural theory was on subcultures regarded as spectacular, not only in terms of supposed behaviour, but also in terms of the visual styles developed by subcultural groups to identify and demarcate themselves in relation to other groups and the greater society (see, for example, Hall and Jefferson, 1976, and Willis, 1977 and 1978). An additional question which came to be addressed was that of theorizing the characteristics of these styles in relation to the institutionalized set of practices constituting the subcultures from which they emanated (see Hebdige, 1979). Subcultural theory argued that elements of a particular style were typically drawn both from the parent culture and from mass-mediated culture, the culture of those with power and influence. Frequently, these elements were divested of their traditional meanings and invested with altered or new ones as part of a process of stylization. As well as mapping their relatedness to different cultures by reference to stylistic elements drawn from various locations in the overall social configuration, therefore, subcultures lent these elements their own special significance through a process by which they made them their own:

> The various youth sub-cultures have been identified by their possessions and objects: the boot-lace tie and velvet-collared drape jacket of the Ted, the close crop, parker coats and scooter of the Mod, the stained jeans, swastikas and ornamented motorcycles of the bike-boys, the Chicago suits or glitter costumes of the Bowieites, etc. Yet, despite their visibility, things simply appropriated and worn (or listened to) do not make a style. What makes a style is the activity of stylisation – the active organisation of objects with activities and outlooks, which produce an organised group-identity in the form and shape of a coherent and distinctive way of 'being-in-the-world'. (Hall and Jefferson, 1976, p. 54)

A particular relationship was therefore seen to exist between this process of stylization and the outlooks and activities of the group:

> important were the aspects of group life which these appropriated objects and things were made to reflect, express and resonate. It is this reciprocal effect, between the things a group uses and the out-

looks and activities which structure and define their use, which is the generative principle of stylistic creation in a sub-culture. This involves members of a group in the appropriation of particular objects which are, or can be made, 'homologous' with their focal concerns, activities, group structure and collective self-image – objects in which they can see their central values held and reflected. (1976, p. 56)

It was the French-language concept of the structure which gave rise to this notion of stylization and thus made possible the concept of the 'structural homology'.

Raymond Williams and the Social Character of Art

However, in approaching this question of the significance of subcultural styles, English subcultural theorists also had recourse to the earlier work of Raymond Williams. In a passage which has since become classic, Williams argued that to conceive of the social character of an art-work in terms of the art-work's *relationship* to its social context is to engage in a misleading fiction. 'Since we realised how deeply works or values could be determined by the whole situation in which they are expressed', he said, we have got into the habit 'of asking about these relationships in a standard form: "what is the relation of this art to this society?" ' But 'society', he concludes, 'is a specious whole. If the art is part of the society, there is no solid whole, outside it, to which, by the form of our question, we concede priority' (Williams, 1965, p. 61). If art is social, in other words, its social character need not lie outside itself in some reified notion of society as a thing apart from the cultural and symbolic forms through which it is manifest to people. It can be constituted through art's very practice in the sense that the practice of art is at one and the same time an essentially *social* practice. Art, like any other human activity, is *constituted* through its social character. An understanding of art as a social practice need only refer outside artistic practice in grasping the manner in which this *one* practice (artistic and social at the same time) resonates and is in tension with other social, but non-artistic practices.

It is important to understand what this line of thinking means for the analysis of music as a cultural practice. It is, of course, possible to conceptualize the cultural character of music in a number of different ways (see, for example, Grenier, 1990). Not surprisingly, there are two significant trends in these conceptualizations which reflect and grow largely out of the two sets of disciplinary approaches (musicological and sociological) identified in the previous chapter. The first is that while cultural contexts are of relevance to the forms and styles of different musical genres, they do not affect the central aesthetic core of music itself. Meyer has, for example, argued that

> the explanations [for meaning in music] furnished by reference to political, social and cultural history tell only part of the story. For stylistic changes and developments are continually taking place which appear to be largely independent of such extra-musical events. Although an important interaction takes place between the political, social and intellectual forces at work in a given epoch, on the one hand, and stylistic developments on the other, there is also a strong tendency for a style to develop in its own way. If this is the case, then the causes of these changes must be looked for in the nature of aesthetic experience, since for composer and listener style is simply the vehicle for such an experience. (1956, p. 65)

According to this view, the *musicality* of music cannot be explained ultimately by reference to anything other than music and its central aesthetic core.

The second trend is based on the assumption that the sounds of music are in some way extrinsic to culture (an assumption which, as we have noted, is ironically similar to the one operating in musicology). That is, sounds are assumed – usually through omission – to be of questionable relevance in understanding the cultural meanings and cultural affects articulated through music. This trend is evident, for example, in the work of Lawrence Grossberg. Music in Grossberg's writings is conceived not so much as a cipher in reflecting social, cultural and subjective processes. It is conceived more as an instigator in their production, but an instigator whose inherent material qualities, its sounds, seem to be of little or no consequence (apart from their 'brute' presence) to the particular character of the processes articulated. Grossberg's position thus seems remarkably close to the one which we argued in the previous chapter flows from the work of Saussure. This position sees the sounds of music as little more than a ground of physiological and affective stimulation which can take on meaning only after being interpellated into the world of language. Grossberg has argued more than once that meanings in rock music cannot be read from the surface of rock's 'text', which we assume to mean the 'music itself': '... rock and roll cannot be approached by some textual analysis of its message. Rock and roll, whether live or recorded, is a performance whose "significance" cannot be read off the "text" ' (1984, p. 233). Rather than begin with questions of meaning and affect in music, therefore, Grossberg concentrates on processes which we would regard as more distant from – but certainly most relevant to – these questions: 'In order to understand the relationship between rock, youth, and fan, I propose to look at the ways in which rock and roll organizes not the meaning we give to the world, but the ways we are able to invest and locate energy, importance, even ourselves, in those meanings' (1987, p. 182).

There is therefore a sense in which music's importance is displaced from the centre of gravity of its affective power – its sounds – and located elsewhere. By describing it as a formation, argues Grossberg, 'I want to emphasize the fact that the identity and effect of rock depends on more than its sonorial dimension.' Speaking of rock as a formation 'demands that we always locate musical practices in the context of a complex (and always specific) set of relations with other cultural and social practices; hence I will describe it as a cultural rather than a musical formation' (1993, p. 41).

A common omission with such views is a failure to entertain the possibility that the articulation of affect and meaning through music cannot be explained solely by reference to 'the cultural', and that characteristics of music's signifying practices specific to itself constitute an important and inescapable part of social and cultural processes. This is a view which appears to be consistent with the position argued by Williams on the social character of art. In line with the spirit of Williams's argument, it can be argued that *no* aspect of music is capable of being understood independently of the wider gamut of social and cultural processes (social and cultural processes, it should be remembered, which include *as part of themselves* processes typically thought of as 'musical'). Yet, *because* of this, it is possible that there are *aspects* of social and cultural processes which are revealed *uniquely* through their musical articulation. The *necessity* of referring to the wider gamut of social and cultural processes in order to explain 'the musical' does not in other words amount to a *sufficiency*. There are aspects of affect and meaning *in culture* that can only be accessed through an understanding of the specific qualities of the signifying practices of music as a cultural form: that is, its sounds. As Philip Tagg has observed, a viable understanding of culture requires an understanding of its articulation through music just as much as a viable understanding of music requires an understanding of its place in culture:

> any discussion of mass culture or mass society in general will need to include analyses of musical meaning, for it is in the non-verbal forms of symbolic representation that emotional levels of social, cultural, political and ideological meaning are to be found ... if cultural theorists, sociologists, linguists, etc. are not prepared to take music into consideration in their discussion of symbolic production in contemporary society and if musicians and musicologists are not prepared to shoulder the responsibility this lays on them to demystify their art and its hieroglyphics, we will be left with little or no viable cultural theory of our own times. (1991, p. 144)

The Structural Homology and the Analysis of Music

Williams's line of thinking was suggestive to English subcultural theorists in terms of understanding the significance of subcultural styles not only in relation to other elements of subcultural practice, but in relation also to the objective social conditions which inform the contradictions and experiences of subcultural practice. For Williams, the study of culture became 'the study of relationships between elements in a whole way of life'. A key-word in such analysis, continued Williams, 'is pattern: it is with discovery of patterns of a characteristic kind that any useful cultural analysis begins, and it is with the relationships between these patterns ... that general cultural analysis is concerned' (1965, p. 63). For subcultural theorists, 'patterns of a characteristic kind' developed into the identification of parallels of structure between the characteristics of styles, behaviours and objective social conditions. The notion of the 'structural homology' was born, and it was taken to explain meaning and signifi-

cance in style in terms of the way in which the structural manifestations of style mirrored and were mirrored by the structural
manifestations of the behaviours and objective social conditions
in which style was embedded and of which it was taken to be
symptomatic. As Willis explains, 'essentially it [the homological]
is concerned with how far, in their structure and content, particular items parallel and reflect the structure, style, typical concerns, attitudes and feelings of the social group. Where
homologies are found they are best understood in terms of
structure' (1978, p. 191). Meaning and significance in style could
thus be understood as one particular dimension of cultural practice through which the negotiation of social spaces experienced
as problematic and contradictory could occur and be rendered
meaningful. In this way, the English-language notion of the
structural homology came to differ quite radically from the
concept of the structure as played out in much French-language
linguistic, social and psychoanalytic theory, a difference that
will become clear in the discussions which follow.

The notion of the structural homology was particularly suggestive for the analysis of music in its social and cultural set-
tings. It perpetuates the methodology implicit in Meyer's work,
but allows for the social character of music by providing a theoretical protocol through which the structures of music can be
put into a meaningful relationship with the social and cultural
practices (assumed by social and cultural analysts to be charac-
teristically structural) in which music is embedded and from
which it emanates. According to this logic, for example, a structurally homologous relationship could be taken to exist between
the formal structural characteristics of the motor rhythms of the
bass guitar riff in the Rolling Stones' song 'Satisfaction', and the
formal structural characteristics of the particular kind of sexuality – *machismo* as socially and culturally constituted – which the
song is customarily understood to evoke. The problem of referentialism, which before the 1970s had proved intractable
(although, for example, addressed by Adorno, 1984, and
Dahlhaus, 1985) in terms of assigning social and cultural meanings to music, was thereby circumvented. This circumvention
was prefigured in the work of the ethnomusicologist John
Blacking (1967 and 1973). 'If music expresses attitudes', said
Blacking, 'we should expect correlations between the different
attitudes and the patterns of sounds with which they are

expressed' (1973, p. 56). Social and cultural processes were of pre-eminent importance for Blacking in understanding attitudes, music and the relations between them. The social and the musical were thus intimately linked. Blacking, for example, made the following observation in discussing the music of the Venda of South Africa: 'Changes in musical style have generally been reflections of changes in society ... various styles of Venda music reflect the variety of its social groups and the degree of their assimilation into the body politic. Musical performances are audible and visible signs of social and political groupings in Venda society' (1973, p. 76). Another ethnomusicologist, Charles Keil, arrived at a similar conclusion some six years later in his important work on the music of the Tiv of Nigeria: 'What snapped into place', says Keil, 'was a sense that in trying to describe how songs fit in with "everything else" in a cultural pattern, I was also discovering that "everything else" was as simple as roof structure and compound layout, as basic as everyday conversations and social interactions, as direct and urgent as the struggle for classless society' (1979, p. 7).

The development of this kind of thinking within ethnomusicology bore a quite different character from that which developed within English subcultural theory. It was markedly more consensualist, and was informed by a more traditional, anthropological concept of culture as a system of shared assumptions, beliefs and behaviours. There was little room for differentiation or conflict. Straw has contrasted different approaches to conceptualizing musical cultures drawn from cultural anthropology and ethnomusicology on the one hand, and cultural studies on the other. The distinction is between the older notion of a musical community – which 'may be imagined as a particular population group whose composition is relatively stable ... and whose involvement in music takes the form of an ongoing exploration of a particular musical idiom said to be rooted organically in that community' – and that of a musical scene ('the most appropriate term for designating centres of musical activity today'), which is 'that cultural space within which a range of musical practices co-exist, interacting with each other within a variety of processes of differentiation and according to widely varying trajectories of change and cross-fertilization' (Straw, 1991, p. 373). It is possible that the concept of the musical scene as described by Straw has always been the more appropriate for 'designating centres of musical activity' in the sense that there have always been migrations of peoples and the constant mixing and cross-fertilizations of the world's musics. There is a hint of this line of thinking in Straw's observation that cultural theorists like himself 'encountering ethnomusicological studies for the first time after an apprenticeship in the hermeneutics of suspicion may be struck by the prominence within them of notions of cultural totality or claims concerning an expressive unity of musical practices' (1991, p. 369).

It was, however, other work (Willis, 1978, and Shepherd, 1977 and 1982a) which established the notion of the structural homology within the tradition of English subcultural theory as a protocol for elucidating the 'relations' between music and society. This work had more room conceptually for the conflict and the complexity which can be discerned in these relations. In each instance the authors drew parallels between the internal, structural characteristics of music's melodies, harmonies and rhythms, and structural features deemed characteristic of the social locations in which the music was practised. However, Willis's observations on both progressive rock and early rock 'n' roll resonate with a common assumption that popular music is empowering of individuals, and unexceptionally so. The technical, stylistic features of rock music in Willis's analyses are understood to be oppositional in character, rather than negotiating spaces within received and dominant structures, both social and musical. It is on these grounds possible to disagree with some of the more politically progressive aspects of Willis's claims for rock. Willis argued, for example, that rock 'n' roll 'opened up "new" possibilities because it ... avoided being trapped by the received conventions concerning rhythm, tonality and melody' (1978, p. 76). It is possible to agree with Willis that the continuous pulse of much early rock music articulates a temporal flow of consciousness, an emphasis on the ever-unfolding immediacy of the here and now essentially denied through the spatialized time of 'classical' music (on the spatialized time of 'classical' or functional tonal music see Shepherd, 1977), and that earlier rock music 'was not caught up in the end of the possibilities of harmony' (Willis, 1978, pp. 76–7) or, for that matter, in the harmonic teleology of extended emotional structures. However, it is not possible to agree with Willis that the rhythms of early rock music 'escaped from the determinations of the bar structure' to 'subvert the bar form' (1978, p. 76) or that 'the normal rules of progression, and forms of cadence, are replaced in rock 'n' roll by a kind of anarchy' (p. 77). It can be argued that while rock's *more* even pulse (as compared to some jazz and blues, as well as to functional tonal music) and its 'simple' chord structures allowed for a strong emphasis on the temporal flow of the subjective here and now, they at the same time constituted a largely neutral and apolitical reproduction of the musical framework derived from functional tonality. There was, to be sure, a 'timelessness' in early rock music, but it was a 'timelessness' (so-called: representing the abnegation simply of a spatialized or mechanical sense of time, which itself squeezes out the true flow of temporality – see Shepherd, 1977) of a social and musical framework that is taken for granted and largely unquestioned (Shepherd, 1982a, pp. 169–70). This essential tension is caught in Willis's description of the time-sense of one of the subcultures to espouse early rock music, the bikeboys:

> In one way, and concentrating on its oppositional aspects, the whole motor-bike culture was an attempt to stop or subvert bourgeois, industrial, capitalist notions of time – the basic experiential discipline its members faced *in the work they still took so seriously*. The culture did not attempt to impute causality or logical progression to things. It was about living and experiencing in a concrete, essentially timeless, world – certainly timeless in the sense of refusing to accept ordered, rational sequences. (1978, p. 78, our italics)

It is however possible to argue a position more perceptibly influenced – in its analysis of musical style – by the broader spirit of subcultural theory in discerning reference points within processes of musical stylization drawn from society as a whole, the parent culture (in this case their emphasis on the enjoyment of leisure time outside the temporal discipline of the workplace), and the subculture itself. These reference points, as subject to processes of stylization, constituted a terrain of negotiation (see Shepherd, 1977 and 1982a). For the first time, a theoretical protocol existed through which the social and cultural meanings of music, as articulated through music's internal, technical characteristics, could be grasped and understood within the framework of cultural analysis.

The Structural Homology and its Problems

There are, however, a number of significant difficulties with the ways in which the notion of the structural homology has been conceived and put into operation, both generally, and with specific reference to music. Firstly, and most importantly, the way in which the notion of the structural homology was applied to the analysis of music's social and cultural significance in the 1970s and early 1980s assumed a certain immanence of structure with regard both to social practices and musical forms. There was a failure to problematize the term 'structure' as applied to social practices on the one hand and musical forms on the other, and thereby to discern whether there was, or could be, a significant difference in the ways in which the term was applied in both instances. Because the term 'structure' *could* successfully be employed in both instances, in other words, it was assumed that similar, if not identical, processes were being addressed. This was an assumption made on the part of analysts. Such an assumption therefore ignores the role of the analyst (or, indeed, reader) in constructing meaning or significance around a particular set of practices. It is clear that, although the material facts of social practices and musical forms constrain, limit and, indeed, shape possibilities for reading various structures into them, they are not themselves determining of such readings. The presumed immanence of structure with regard to both social practices and musical forms was, in other words, a creation of the minds of analysts. It does not follow from this that such an immanence occurs.

The second difficulty with the concept of the structural homology is, that despite the admonition of Williams, there has been an implicit assumption within English subcultural analysis that cultural styles, including those of music, do in actuality 'give expression' to something outside themselves. We are here, it would seem, in the realm of a commonsense assumption concerning the ability of popular music to empower individuals, and so to express authentically the 'purity' of political opposition. This shift in emphasis from Williams's original position occurred, perhaps, because many subcultural analysts were themselves fans and consumers of the cultural styles they were analysing. As a consequence, they tended to buy into the notion that 'good music', as Frith has put it, 'is the authentic expression of something – a person, an idea, a feeling, a shared experience' (1987, p. 136). They tended, in other words, to keep alive a certain 'high culture' notion of the aesthetic as intensively subjective. Frith has been critical of this assumption as it has constituted 'the sociological common sense of rock criticism'. In his view, 'the myth of authenticity is, indeed, one of rock's own ideological effects.'

Thirdly, the role of the individual in creating or appreciating the meanings of cultural styles is conceptualized overwhelmingly in terms of the individual's membership of a social group. This is curious, given the undoubted stress in both American and English subcultural theory on the way in which individuals and groups act in a relatively autonomous manner in terms of the meanings that the world holds for them. Dominant meanings are taken to encourage certain forms of behaviour, but they are not taken to determine them. If individuals (or subjects) are constituted socially, in other words, they are constituted socially in a manner which is relatively autonomous within the context of wider, non-subjective, that is to say, objective social processes (for the distinction between subjective and objective social realities, see Berger and Luckmann, 1967). Yet, despite this orientation of subcultural theory, there has been little conceptual space created for a theorization of the private, internal world of an individual's awareness of existence and self, of the way that an individual may deal in a relatively autonomous and creative way with this awareness, and of the way in which this world may connect to the external public world of shared cultural meanings. The principle of the structural homology speaks almost exclusively to an analysis of this shared public world.

This vacuum in subcultural theory creates a real difficulty in analysing music as a socially constituted cultural form, a difficulty highlighted by one of the most powerful, commonsense assumptions concerning the significance of music. It has, of course, been a feature of traditional thinking about music that it appeals to the internal world of private emotions. This appeal was the object of Meyer's early work, and of the groundbreaking work of Langer (1942). This emphasis on the world of internal, private emotions has constituted and underpinned in a very large measure the idealism of traditional musicological approaches towards understanding music. If, however, important forms of cultural analysis have assumed that individuals are relatively autonomous in the face of 'wider social forces', then the traditional stress placed within musicology on the internal world of private emotions cannot be dismissed simply as an exigency and vagary of idealist thought. It points to the necessity of theorizing the individual as relatively autonomous in relation to 'musical', and 'wider social processes'. This world is not one that can therefore be ignored in attempting to understand how music generates affect and meaning.

Music, Structuralism and Semiology

In view of our discussion of the ways in which the notion of the structural homology can be applied to the analysis of music, two related problems need to be addressed. Firstly, there is the question of how the 'musical' and 'non-musical' processes of the external world precisely relate to one another. That is, the question remains as to how the *social* character of the musical and non-musical processes of the external world resonate meaningfully with one another. Secondly, there is the question of how musical processes and processes of subjectivity intersect with one another. However, if one subscribes to the view that both music and subjects *are* socially constituted (which has certainly been the position in principle of English cultural studies), then the two related problems become a composite one: how, as different and relatively autonomous, yet complementary aspects of wider social processes, musical processes and processes of subjectivity relate to one another. While specifically musical social processes occur in the context of wider social processes, and are informed and, indeed, partially constituted by them (as these processes are imbricated in specifically musical social processes), these musical social processes nonetheless remain irreducible conceptually to wider social processes. It is this *musical* sociality which concerns us in this book. *That* sociality is constituted uniquely and ineluctably at the intersection of musical processes and processes of subjectivity.

The question of this intersection focuses attention much more sharply on the interplay between a socially constituted cultural and symbolic phenomenon and various aspects of human awareness and cognition as socially constituted. As we have seen, initial trajectories of English cultural studies had little to say on this question. There was an almost complete failure to theorize the concept of 'the subject'. Trajectories of French-language linguistic, cultural and psychoanalytic theory have on the other hand provided concepts and ideas which are more suggestive in terms of addressing this question. The tradition of French-language linguistic, cultural and psychoanalytic analysis is a rich and complex one reaching back to the work of Saussure in the early years of this century. It has made two major contributions to understanding the relationships between symbolic and cultural systems on the one hand, and the development of human awareness and consciousness on the other. Firstly, it has established that linguistic and symbolic systems do not simply name or reflect pre-existing realities. To one degree or another (and depending on the scholar in question), they are taken to constitute, to shape and structure them, and therefore to play a vital role in giving meaning to external realities. Equally, these systems are taken – not to reflect the meanings that individuals are assumed to express through them – but actually to constitute, shape and structure such meanings, and thus consciousness itself.

It was Claude Lévi-Strauss and Roland Barthes who took respectively the principles of structuralism and semiology established by Saussure and applied them to entire cultural or mythical systems. By 'myth' is meant the systems of cultural knowledge through which societies make sense of the worlds in which they exist. This application involved the development of Saussure's theories into 'two-level' models whereby language as understood by Saussure facilitated and came to be contained by structural systems of myths and semiological systems of myths. The chief proponent of the idea that culture and, indeed, the entire field of social behaviour might not only constitute an act of encoding similar to that of language, but might, indeed, *be* a language, was Lévi-Strauss. Lévi-Strauss's work revolutionized the field of cultural anthropology, and occupies a position in relation to it not dissimilar to that of Saussure in linguistics. In a seminal article ('The Structural Study of Myth'), Lévi-Strauss argued that Saussure's theories on their own could not explain the structural character of myth. 'In order to preserve ... [the]

specificity [of myth]', said Lévi-Strauss, 'we must be able to show that it is both the same thing as language, and also something different from it' (1972, p. 209). Myth therefore has in common with language the property of being a structural system, but a system that subsumes language at a lower level. Myth's 'gross constituent units' are as a consequence to be located at a level higher than those of the units (phonemes, morphemes or sememes) understood to constitute language. They are, for Lévi-Strauss, to be found on the level of the sentence. However, as with the basic constituent units of language, the significance of those of myth lies not in their isolated existence, but in the relations obtaining between them. Further, since the structural character of myth – like language – lies not in its actual articulation through time, but in a synchronic *langue*, it is manifest, not in individual relations occurring diachronically, but in bundles of relations as manifest both synchronically and diachronically. Myth in this way goes further than language in manifesting an additional time referent that is both synchronic and diachronic, and it is this which guarantees myth's relative autonomy in relation to language.

Myth does not reveal the external world any more than language does. In acting as, or in a manner similar to, language, myth encodes, structures and makes sense of material reality and thus renders it as a mapping or notational device for cultures as lived. The important point for the arguments we are to develop in relation to music is that Lévi-Strauss extends the principles of structuralism as established by Saussure to indicate the possibility of 'purely abstract' structures which transcend both the level of language *and its principles of articulation*. However, myth as theorized by Lévi-Strauss remains nonetheless language-dependent. This principle of language-dependence is a principle espoused unambiguously by Barthes in his semiological analysis of myth.

Barthes's major contribution to the development of semiology is contained in his book *Mythologies* (1973). Within the realm of semiology as distinct from structuralism, Barthes argued that 'in myth, we find again the tri-dimensional pattern . . . the signifier, the signified and the sign.' However, he continued, 'myth is a peculiar system, in that it is constructed from a semiological chain which existed before it: it *is a second-order semiological system*. That which is a sign (namely the associative total of a

concept and an image) in the first system, becomes a mere signifier in the second' (Barthes, 1973, p. 114). Because semiologists
of myth need to know only the role of the sign at the first level
as signifier in the second, they do not need to know how the
sign signifies at the first level. Language and pictures can thus
be treated in the same way from the point of view of the analysis of myths: what is retained from them 'is the fact that they are
both *signs*, that they both reach the threshold of myth endowed
with the same signifying function, that they constitute, one just
as much as the other, a language-object' (1973, p. 115). While
structuralism developed into a set of theories about the character and processes of human cultural systems, semiology developed into a set of analytical tools in terms of which it was
thought possible to analyse the generation of meaning ('signification') through any human symbolic system, including, presumably, music. The important point is that the principles of
structuralism and semiology as established by Saussure became
capable of being applied to complete mythological and cultural
systems. That is, theoretical and methodological protocols
existed in terms of which, *in principle*, the meanings of any signifying system could be analysed within the context of their mythical or cultural relevance.

As we have seen in discussing the work of Willis, Blacking,
Keil and others, principles of *structuralism* can be usefully
applied to understanding music. In fact, these principles seem to
have a special relevance for understanding its processes of signification because, to paraphrase Lévi-Strauss's words, 'if there is
meaning to be found in music [myth], it cannot reside in the isolated elements which enter into its composition, but only in the
way those elements are combined' (Lévi-Strauss, 1972, p. 210).
Lévi-Strauss at one point in his work referred to music as a concrete example of how it might be that entire mythological systems work. Myth and music, he said, both share the
characteristic of 'being languages which, in their different ways,
transcend articulate expression' (1969a, p. 15). Music shares with
myth the ability to be simultaneously diachronic and synchronic,
to gather up and reveal through the unfolding present the significance of elements variously and diachronically deployed:

> Below the level of sounds and rhythms, music acts upon a primitive
> terrain, which is the physiological time of the listener; this time is

irreversible and therefore irredeemably diachronic, yet music transmutes the segment devoted to listening to it into a synchronic totality, enclosed within itself. Because of the internal organisation of the
musical work, the act of listening to it immobilizes passing time; it
catches it and enfolds it as one catches and enfolds a cloth flapping in
the wind. (1969a, p. 16)

In making this comparison between myth and music, Lévi-
Strauss is, however, careful to respect music's integrity as a signifying system. Indeed, it is the integrity and specific character
of music that attracts Lévi-Strauss in his desire to identify in
myth vital elements of its own structural integrity that transcend the articulate expressive qualities of language, even as
these qualities manifest characteristics traceable *only* to their
presence in myth:

> since ... music stands in opposition to articulate speech, it follows
> that music, which is a complete language, not reducible to speech,
> must be able to fulfil the same functions on its own account. Looked
> at in the round and in its relation to other sign systems, music is
> close to mythology. But, so far as the mythic function is itself an
> aspect of speech, it must be possible to discover in musical discourse
> some special function that has a particular affinity with myth. (1969a,
> p. 29)

As Lévi-Strauss concludes, 'mythology occupies an intermediary position between two diametrically opposed types of sign
systems – musical languages on the one hand and articulate
speech on the other' (1969a, p. 27).

Through a comparison with the non-denotative medium of
music, Lévi-Strauss was striving to grasp myth at a certain level
in its specific character as incorporating principles of structuralism which go beyond those of myth *as linguistically manifest*.
Music can, indeed, be understood as if it were a mythical system, which in some ways it is. Lévi-Strauss has elsewhere
likened music to myth (rather than using music as an illustration of how myth works). Music, he says, is 'a myth coded in
sounds instead of words'. Lévi-Strauss thus accepts a distinction
between music *as myth* and myth as he customarily analyses it.
As sounds, continues Lévi-Strauss, 'the musical work furnishes
a grid of signification, a matrix of relationships which filters and
organizes lived experience; it substitutes for experience and
produces the pleasurable illusion that contradictions can be

overcome, and difficulties resolved' (1971, p. 5). In this context, it is interesting to refer to Meyer's observations with respect to the difficulty of fixing connotation in music: 'the flexibility of connotations in music is a virtue', says Meyer, 'for it enables music to express what might be called the disembodied essence of myth, the essence of experiences which are central to and vital to human experience' (1956, p. 265). This confluence of views from a cultural anthropologist and a music theorist seems to indicate that music's centrally structural character is in some way related to its ability to speak to myth (or culture) in a particular way. We have already referred to examples of this kind of thinking as applied to entire musical systems, to the musical *'langue'* as opposed to *'parole'* of functional tonality (Shepherd, 1991b, pp. 96–127), various genres of popular music (1991b, pp. 128–51; see also Wicke, 1990a), Venda music (Blacking, 1973) and Tiv song (Keil, 1979). In this sense, principles of structuralism as embodied in the work of Lévi-Strauss seem forward-looking and helpful in developing the arguments we wish to make.

Principles of structuralism, together with the associated concepts of *langue* and *parole*, therefore seem promising for understanding music. However, those of the 'signifier' and 'signified' are much less so. This is particularly the case as they have been reinterpreted by Barthes into a two-level analytical model for myth in which it is presumed to be unnecessary to understand the character of signifying processes at the first level of primary signification in order to be able to understand the relevance of the 'mythical signifier' thus generated for the second level of secondary or connotative signification. The temptation as a consequence is to ignore primary but non-denotative processes of signification as they occur through the structural elements of music – elements which in this way are of clear importance to the manner in which music generates 'significance', but difficult to understand without some direct experience of, or formal training in, music-making or music analysis – and to replace them with an account of connotation alone. This is the direction in which Barthes goes. Barthes, in fact, hardly discussed music during his earlier, 'semiological' period, the period for which *Mythologies* stands as such an important emblem. The issue of music and of the character of its signifying processes did, however, become crucial for Barthes when he later turned his attention to questions of textuality. Barthes's thinking on questions of textuality and the role of music in that thinking were influenced significantly by the work of Kristeva. The approaches of both Kristeva and Barthes to the issue of music and its signifying processes are in many respects remarkably similar. Barthes's position will therefore be discussed later in our treatment of poststructuralist analyses of music. Suffice it to say that, because music does not display elements of denotation, it was assumed by Barthes to lie outside the realm of first-order semiological systems (in which Barthes saw language as occupying a privileged position) and not, therefore, to engage at all in processes of primary signification. For this reason, it was not susceptible to analysis in terms of what Barthes termed a 'first semiology' (although Barthes certainly saw technical analyses of music as opposed to analyses of musical experience as constituting an *attempt* at a 'first semiology'). While Barthes did *not* conceive of the importance of music's significance in terms of its capacity to be interpellated into language, a distinction he later drew between music's 'innocence' and 'purity' in being constituted by signifiers alone and music's capacity to be endowed with the ideology of language is nonetheless consistent with the view that music's *relationship* to the world of meaning is constituted through its capacity to receive *all* meanings at the level of secondary signification or the connotative. About music, said Barthes,

> no discourse can be sustained but that of difference – of evaluation. As soon as someone speaks about music – or a specific music – as a value *in itself*, or on the contrary – though this is the same thing – as a value for *everyone* – i.e., as soon as we are told that we must love all music – we feel a kind of ideological cope falling over the most precious substance of evaluation, music: this is 'commentary' (1985b, p. 279)

Saussure's work remains instructive over and above establishing principles of structuralism of clear relevance to understanding *some* important characteristics of music as a signifying system. Firstly, while Saussure's stress on a 'science of semiology' presents a certain danger in suggesting, perhaps, that music might be understood 'as if it were language', his stress on the relative autonomy of semiological systems in relation to society and the individual remains suggestive in another way.

This stress replicates our position that music cannot, on the one hand, be reduced to the condition of simply reflecting social processes or, on the other, to being a consequence of individual creativity alone. The stress remains important as long as the temptation to reduce music as close as is possible to the condition of language is resisted. Secondly, while English cultural studies (and other culturalist approaches to music) have stressed the way in which music's structural meanings may lie outside it in the structural dimensions of social and cultural processes (or at least obtain coextensively within music's structures in relation to these external dimensions), Saussure's work opens up the possibility that music might in some way 'produce meaning'. This possibility in turn makes feasible a consideration of how music might determine or influence individual consciousness and how it might therefore exercise power over individuals. In order to consider these possibilities, it is now necessary to consider the ways in which traditions of French-language structuralism and semiology have approached the question of individual consciousness or 'subjectivity'.

The Introduction of the Subject

Two further developments awaited this dual tradition of structuralism and semiology in addition to that of its application beyond language to entire mythical systems. These developments provided for an understanding of the construction of meaning through language and other symbolic forms *in relation to the exigencies of wider social processes*, and for an understanding of the creation of the individual person's or subject's consciousness through these linguistic and social processes. Neither of these topics are ones that Saussure, as such, addressed. A review of these developments is therefore important for understanding the involvement of music in the processes through which the internal worlds of individual people are socially constructed and made symbolically manifest.

The first development was the encounter of semiology and structuralism with the tradition of Marxism. The radical potential of semiology synthesized with the radicalism of Marxism in a general and largely untheorized way through the work of

Barthes (1973), untheorized, that is, because Barthes was more interested in reading cultural significance at the level of connotation than he was in understanding the precise mechanisms of its social and therefore material constitution at the level of primary signification. The tradition of structuralism – by contrast conservative and reproductive of the *status quo* through its stress on the transformational and self-regulating features of linguistic, cultural and social systems – met with the theories of Marx through the work of Althusser (1969 and 1971b; Althusser and Balibar, 1970). Here, by contrast, the assimilation of the principles of French-language structuralism within the traditions of Marxist criticism gave rise to a body of work theoretically rich in its notions of structures in dominance, overdetermination (a concept derived from the work of Freud), the relative autonomy of ideological and cultural processes, and structural causality.

Althusser argued that an injustice had been done to Marx in thinking of him as an economic determinist. Althusser's reading of Marx led him to argue that the social formation was comprised of sets of relatively autonomous social relations such as the economic, the political and the ideological. These levels of the social formation were in mutual relations of 'overdetermination', whereby contradictions within them affected each other in historically specific ways that ensured the levels' uneven development within the social formation. This network of determinations, manifesting itself therefore through mechanisms of *structural* causality (mechanisms of causality more typical of field theory than of straight-line cause-and-effect – if one thing changes, everything can change), operated within different levels and moments of the social formation, thereby guaranteeing the formation's historically specific characteristics. The economic was considered by Althusser (following Engels) to be determining only 'in the last instance', thereby rendering the social formation as a set of 'structures in dominance'. The relative autonomy of each set of structures or level within the social formation was, however, guaranteed through the notions of wholeness, transformation and self-regulation characteristic of structuralism as an intellectual tradition.

The second development was the introduction of the notion of the subject within the tradition of structuralism. Until the work of Althusser (1971a), it seemed to be assumed by the traditions of structuralism that if languages and other symbolic and cultural systems reproduced knowledge and reality for individuals, then there was no need to discuss the place or the role of the individual in the reproduction of ideological and cultural systems. Althusser changed this in drawing on the work of the French psychoanalyst Jacques Lacan in his famous essay on 'Ideology and Ideological State Apparatuses' (Althusser, 1971a). Althusser argued that ideological state apparatuses (religion, education, the family, the legal system, the political system, trade unions, and media – all social institutions that could be labelled loosely as 'cultural') operated in a manner relatively autonomous from dominant social and economic relations in preparing and socialising individuals to act and behave in accordance with the exigencies of those same relations.

Until the work of Althusser, various trajectories of Marxism had thought of ideology as essentially a false version of objective social reality, of the real conditions of existence, the real social relations that people had to enter into and endure in order to work and earn enough money to live. 'In ideology', said Althusser in quoting Marx, '"men represent their real conditions of existence to themselves in an imaginary form"' (1971a, p. 163). 'Unfortunately', he continued, 'this interpretation leaves one small problem unsettled: why do men "need" this imaginary transposition of their real conditions of existence in order to "represent to themselves" their real conditions of existence?' (1971a, p. 163).

Althusser begins to answer this question by arguing for a different understanding of ideology:

> it is not their real conditions of existence, their real world, that "men" "represent to themselves" in ideology, but above all it is their relation to those conditions of existence which is *represented* to them there. It is this relation which is at the centre of every ideological, i.e. imaginary, representation of the real world. It is this relation that contains the "cause" which has to explain the imaginary distortion of the ideological representation of the real world. Or rather, to leave aside the language of causality it is necessary to advance the thesis that it is the *imaginary nature of this relation* which underlies all the imaginary distortion we can observe (if we do not live in its truth) in all ideology. (1971a, p. 164, first set of italics ours)

What is represented in ideology, therefore, is 'not the system of the real relations which govern the existence of individuals, but the imaginary relation of those individuals to the real relations in which they live' (1971a, p. 165). It is at this point – if we can put it this way – that a marriage of Marxism and structuralism occurs (although it has to be pointed out that much that Marx argued – for example, in relation to the structured character of relations of production – itself bore the imprint of a structural mode of thinking). It is not that ideology, through the actions of individuals, 'names' 'real conditions of existence' in an imaginary form. Rather, ideology itself constructs those conditions in an imaginary form for individuals through the 'imaginary' that arises within its own structure of relations. It is not, therefore, the material quality of the 'real conditions of existence' and the purely imaginary character of ideology that guarantees their distinctiveness. It is their different functions, and consequently their distinct levels of ontology as different structures of relations. In being constituted through its own set of relations (which it was not in earlier Marxist understandings of ideology), ideology thus has a material existence matching that of relations of production. It is this – together with its own structural character – that guarantees ideology a relative autonomy in its function of reproducing relations of production.

In his 'ISA' essay, Althusser concentrates on the role of actual individuals or single subjects as agents of this relatively autonomous ideology: 'where only a single subject (such and such an individual) is concerned, the existence of the ideas of his belief is material in that *his ideas are his material actions inserted into material practices governed by material rituals which are themselves defined by the material ideological apparatus from which derive the ideas of that subject'* (1971a, p. 169). Ideas, actions according to ideas, and the role of the free subject in so acting all begin to disappear. Subjects do not act in misrepresenting *to themselves* ideologically 'their real conditions of existence'. They are 'acted' in being constituted by the very ideology which, as a set of imaginary yet materially constituted relations to the relations of production, transposes the 'real conditions of existence'. The traditional, liberal-humanist notion of individuals as the free authors of their actions (and their utterances) is thus no more than an effect of ideology. Individuals are not the authors or the 'subjects of their actions', in other words, any more than 'language is spoken by the world.' In Althusser's terminology, individuals are therefore 'hailed' or 'interpellated' into the processes of ideological state apparatuses as a crucial moment in the

production of subjects and the reproduction of dominant relations of production:

> *all ideology hails or interpellates concrete individuals as concrete subjects*,
> by the functioning of the category of the subject ... ideology 'acts' or
> 'functions' in such a way that it 'recruits' subjects among the individ-
> uals (it recruits them all), or 'transforms' the individuals into subjects
> (it transforms them all) by that very precise operation which I have
> called *interpellation* or hailing, and which can be imagined along the
> lines of the most commonplace everyday police (or other) hailing:
> 'Hey, you there!' (1971a, pp. 173–5)

However, this notion of 'the subject' does carry with it the
implication of authorship, that is, the implication of being the
'subject' of an act, as well as the implication of subjection. A crucial element in the operation of ideology is the belief that individuals are acting freely in the very articulation of their
subjection: 'the individual *is interpellated as a (free) subject in order
that he shall submit freely to the commandments of the Subject, i.e. in
order that he shall (freely) accept his subjection*, i.e. in order that he
shall make the gestures and actions of his subjection "all by himself" ' (1971a, p. 182). It is this feature of 'willing subjection'
which provides Althusser with an answer to his original question of 'why men "need" [the] imaginary transposition of their
real conditions of existence'. It is a feature in which subjects misrecognize in themselves the Subject (the defining characteristic
of the social relations of production dominant in the social form
of industrial capitalism) as the real author of their actions and
beliefs. This belief in individual autonomy does not occur naturally (that is, 'outside the ideological intervention'), says
Althusser. It occurs because 'it *has* to be so *if* things are to be
what they must be'

> *if* the reproduction of the relations of production is to be assured,
> even in the processes of production and circulation, every day, in the
> 'consciousness', i.e. in the attitudes of the individual-subjects occu-
> pying the posts which the socio-technical division of labour assigns
> to them in production, exploitation, repression, ideologization, scien-
> tific practice, etc. Indeed, what is really in question in this mecha-
> nism of the mirror recognition of the Subject and of the individuals
> interpellated as subjects ... ? The reality in question in this mecha-
> nism ... is ... the reproduction of the relations of production and of
> the relations deriving from them. (1971a, pp. 182–3, our italics)

Althusser never discussed music. His work nonetheless remains suggestive for its analysis. There seems little doubt that if music were to be situated in Althusser's theoretical scheme, it would have to be located within one or more ideological state apparatuses, either as an element of 'the media', or as part of art as a social institution (if art is practised within sets of social relations – if the practice of art, in effect, constitutes recognizable sets of social relations – and can therefore be said to evidence the characteristics of a social institution, there seems little reason why, in principle, Althusser's list of ideological state apparatuses could not be extended to include it). Being located within the realm of ideological state apparatuses, music could then be taken to constitute an element of the relative autonomy of ideological processes as evidenced through their material character. Althusser's work is suggestive, therefore, in the sense that music's relative autonomy in relation to social processes could be taken to be constituted as an element of *ideological* processes through its material characteristics, its sounds.

As grounded in the materiality of its sounds, music may thus be taken to constitute one aspect of the material world. The intimate association that is frequently presumed between music and the world of emotion and affect seems, in this context, to take on a special significance, a significance rendered additionally suggestive in the light of Saussure's desire to preserve the integrity and relative autonomy of semiological systems, and Althusser's desire to retain the relative autonomy of the ideological through the materiality of its relations. The possibility in other words arises of a material connection of a specific and possibly unique character between the sounds of music and the individual subjects they affect.

This possibility is hinted at by Pratt in his application of Gestalt psychology to an understanding of music as a symbolic form. Music, says Pratt, 'presents to the ear an array of auditory patterns which at a purely formal level are very similar to, if not identical with, the bodily patterns which are the basis of real emotion. The two kinds of pattern are with respect to their form practically the same, but the auditory pattern make[s] music, whereas the organic and visceral pattern make[s] emotion' (Pratt, 1952, p. 17). As Pratt concludes, 'music sounds the way emotions feel' (1952, p. 24). This way of thinking about music is echoed by Lévi-Strauss in his discussion of music and myth.

'Just as music makes the individual conscious of his physiological rootedness', says Lévi-Strauss, 'mythology makes him aware of his roots in society. The former hits us in the guts; the latter, we might say, appeals to our group instinct' (Lévi-Strauss, 1969a, p. 28). To the extent that music acts as myth in addition to being comparable to myth at its 'purely linguistic level' (the level of primary signification), it would seem to constitute a particularly direct and concrete manner of mediating between the subject as socially constituted and wider social processes. However, the possibility of a material, relative autonomy for music as a social form in its relations to subjects as materially (and discursively, if not socially) constituted raises the question of the more general character of the relations between signifying systems and subjects, a question we address in the succeeding chapter.

While Althusser made generalizations about the material character of ideological processes, it has to be recognized that he did not discuss their specific material qualities either collectively or individually. The material qualities of ideological processes remained for Althusser nothing more than a theoretical concept. They did not for Althusser give rise to a set of empirical realities whose precise and varied characteristics required examination in order for the *function* of ideological processes to be adequately understood. In this sense, Althusser did not go as far as Saussure in demonstrating a desire to identify semiological systems as distinct from the ideological processes within which they were operating in the same way that Saussure demonstrated a desire to distinguish semiological systems from the social processes and individuals with whom they were nonetheless involved. Because of this, Althusser demonstrates no desire either to grasp the role of the material grounds and pathways of semiological systems (in Saussure's case, language) in articulating meanings which, presumably, would 'move' from ideology to the subject in constituting the subject. It was simply enough for Althusser that ideological processes were material rather than spiritual in character.

This omission is unfortunate, because of Althusser's insistence that, rather than ideas in their spiritual quality giving rise to the materiality of actions, it is the materiality of actions – prescribed by an ideology 'existing in a material ideological apparatus' – which leads to the constitution of the subject. If the individual is 'hailed' into subjectivity by the material processes of ideology, therefore, it would seem that the subject is interpellated into ideology through mechanisms which are essentially material. It would seem, in addition, that the specific material characteristics of signifying or semiological systems might play a role in these processes of interpellation. This, however, is territory that Althusser did not enter.

Althusser's work is nonetheless important in that it is rare for a scholar in the French tradition we are examining to consider the social as somehow extending *beyond* the realm of signifying systems, subjectivity and misrecognition by the subject of their 'true' character (which, in the special case of Althusser, could be nothing other than the ideological). Althusser in other words succeeds in theorizing, at least in outline, the *social* production of the subject. In this sense – and to the extent that music may be assumed within Althusser's scheme to be ideological in character – Althusser contributes to our developing protocol for thinking of the subject as being produced socially *through* music in adding a social dimension and a dimension of subjective existence to the possibility suggested through an examination of Saussure's work that music might produce meaning. We could thus begin to conceive of a protocol broader than that derived from the work of Saussure in which, in a very general and as yet untheorized manner, society gives rise to ideology, ideology spawns signifying systems (one of which is music), music produces meaning, and this specifically musical meaning contributes to the constitution of the subject. However, the protocol remains untheorized in that it is not yet clear what the material mechanisms of production are which at the same time guarantee a relative autonomy to each level of the protocol. More specifically, it remains untheorized because it is not yet clear what the precise material mechanisms are through which signifying practices constitute subjects.

3

Music and Psychoanalysis

The problem of the precise character of the relations possible between signifying practices such as those of music and processes of subjectivity therefore remains to be addressed. While Althusser introduced the notion of the subject into the tradition of structuralism, it is, as we have seen, a notion of subjectivity that is passive, empty and cipher-like. In contrast to this, we need to keep open the possibility of a full and rich dialectic between the individual and the signifying practices such as those of music with which they interact. This, in turn, necessitates a turn to the work of Freud. It is the work of Freud which has laid the ground and terms for the discussions and analyses of subjectivity within the French tradition that we are examining.

There are, however, two additional reasons why the work of Freud is important. In the preceding chapter, we placed significant stress on the role of the material in Althusser's understanding of ideological processes. Extrapolating from this, we identified sound as the material ground of music. In other words, we identified sound in music as the material medium that would ultimately guarantee music an integrity and relative autonomy as a specific signifying system in relation to social processes on the one hand and processes of subjectivity on the other. In considering the order of relationships possible between sound as the material medium of music and processes of subjectivity to which music could be assumed to speak in its material and ideological constitution, it would seem perverse (and especially so in the light of Althusser's work) to locate music's relative autonomy within its material processes on the one hand and yet, on the other, to assume that music's connection to processes of subjectivity occurred in a manner of only spiritual and cerebral relevance for subjects. We are in other words suggesting that if music's material medium is somehow important to the integrity and relative autonomy of music, then this stress on the material should carry through into our consideration of processes of subjectivity. Only by positing a link between signifying practices on the one hand and processes of subjectivity on the other which is fully material in all its dimensions can we begin to grasp the effectivity of the ideological in constituting subjects. Freud's work is exemplary in this respect. Freud put great stress on the materiality of the human body as the site for the development and investment of individual subjectivity and identity (in this context subjectivity may be thought of as the order of processes through which identity is achieved). This is a stress of which we clearly do not wish to lose sight as we develop our ideas. The second, more specific reason why Freud's work is important lies in the potential it in itself contains for understanding music. Despite the fact that Freud himself had virtually nothing to say on the subject of music, a number of psychoanalysts who followed him did. In the same way as Freud saw certain forms of language – jokes, slips of the tongue and reports of dreams, for example – as a route to the unconscious, so the post-Freudians who wrote on music saw it as a rather more direct route of access to this area of 'primary process'.

Post-Freudian Analyses of Music

The particular characteristic of music that makes a special relationship with the unconscious seem possible, and on which much of the psychoanalytic literature as a consequence concentrates, is its ability to circumvent the external world of objects. Racker has described music as, 'a world devoid of reference to real objects, and where one does not necessarily direct oneself to other objects' (1951, p. 148). Kohut and Levarie link this particular characteristic to music's ability to circumvent the world of language when they say that, 'he [the musician] is capable of comprehending the world of sounds without the aid of our usual major form of thinking, i.e., without the aid of words and concepts' (1956, p. 18). Music is thus seen as being quite distinct from language, a characteristic which is in some cases prized. Pfeifer, for example, notes that music can move in the direction of expressing objects, but hopes that it will never be able to attain this goal: 'for if it did so, it would be in danger of turning into a kind of language and of ceasing to be an art' (1923, p. 381).

It is this combined characteristic of circumventing the world of objects and language which allows music 'direct access' to the unconscious. As Coriat observes, 'music is the purest expression of art and musical fantasy is practically untrammelled or distracted by associations rooted in reality. It reaches the unconscious with a minimum of extraneous resistance' (1945, p. 410). Thus, 'all music represents the deeper sources of unconscious thinking because it is untrammelled by the limitations of language, as in poetry, or by visual imagery, as in painting' (p. 408). Given the manner in which Freud and the psychoanalysts who followed him theorized the constitution of the unconscious (and even his detractors on grounds of gender bias still theorized the constitution of the unconscious in terms of psycho-sexual processes), music comes to have a special relationship to sexuality as a consequence of its special association with the unconscious. Coriat argues that 'music has arisen in the same way as the development of the libido from narcissistic to object sexuality'. However, 'it never obtains object-investment' (1945, p. 408). If the unconscious as constituted by psycho-sexual processes becomes the source for the energy drives of emotional and affective states, then, precisely because of its circumvention of the external world of objects, music comes to have a special relationship as well with the world of emotions. A basic intuition of many aestheticians and musicologists – as well as a basic assumption of commonsense realities regarding music – is in this sense confirmed. As Coriat argues, 'music reproduces emotional situations in a more direct way than can be done by any other form of art or any intellectual processes. It creates not only a highly emotional reality but also the highest degree of unreality because it is marked by the absence of objective contents to which emotions can be linked' (1945, p. 409).

There are, however, a range of different emphases on the question of how it is that music connects in a special way with the unconscious, primary sexuality, and the world of emotions as thus constituted. For many writers, the *origins* of music are to be located in the early vocalizations of the child. Racker, for example, refers to 'the scream born of anxiety and despair, aggression and simultaneously a cry for help and the erotic call for the object' (1951, p. 144). He goes on to observe: 'in their physical aspect it is already evident that scream and song are intimately related ... tone is a transformed scream' (p. 142). As well as developing *from* the infantile scream, however, music can also be conceptualized as developing *against* it. As Masserman observes, sound is the one sensory phenomenon against which the body has provided few defences: 'the appreciation of rhythm, timbre and volume is among the few experiences for which the body has provided no means of total exclusion. One cannot escape vibration in any way, or exclude sound even by closing the ears literally, one then feels both in one's very bones' (1955, p. 617). Since children, in the very early stages of development, have not yet successfully distinguished between self and others (whether humans or objects), they are likely to experience their own vocalizations coming as much from without as within. In this situation vocalizations may well be experienced as frightening and threatening phenomena. Music in this circumstance is presumed to result from attempts to master this kind of unpleasant experience. As Noy concludes, 'the infant cannot escape the stimulus by closing his ears. Since he *must* absorb acoustic stimulation in whatever state he is in, and however frightening the stimuli are, the infant has to develop defences against such perceptions and to integrate them' (1967a, pp. 18–19).

Both these trends (music 'developing from' and music 'developing against' infantile vocalizations) can be distinguished from a later one evident among post-Lacanian psychoanalysts, in which the origins of music are taken to be located within the body and voice of the mother rather than those of the child (although here the similar phenomenon may also arise of how the child locates the sounds: within or without). The fact however remains that, as Margolis observes, 'most authors feel that music is related to the very early narcissistic periods of psychological organisation, when the ego cannot as yet distinctly delineate the boundaries between self and reality' (1954, p. 17). This line of thinking is therefore consistent with the view that music is 'pre-linguistic' or 'sub-linguistic', as Noy observes: 'since music is a language lacking in objects and conceptualized content, it may be assumed that its origin antecedes that of spoken language; it may therefore originate from pre-verbal stages, i.e., periods in which primary thought processes were still prevailing while the clear separation of the self from objects had not yet been achieved' (1967a, p. 17).

As well as *originating* within unconscious and pre-verbal processes in a manner akin to dreams, music has also been taken to act as a *stimulus* in accessing the unconscious and occasioning experiences which behave like dreams. As Noy reports, music is taken to cause ' "the censor to weaken", opening the road to unconscious contents which may thus rise more easily' (1967c, p. 81). Music, then, can take us back to a world in which the barriers between self and objects are dissolved. This ability on the part of music is once again linked to its 'abstract' character. Tailor and Paperte, for example, argue that 'because of its abstract nature [music] detours the ego and intellectual controls and, contacting the lower centers directly, stirs up latent conflicts and emotions which may then be expressed and reenactivated through music. Music produces in us a state that operates somewhat like a dream in the psychoanalytic sense' (1958, p. 252). However, this parallel between music and dream breaks down. Since, as Noy says, 'music is experienced not in sleep, but in a state of wakefulness, it follows that in its final structure it should differ from the dream pattern' (1967b, p. 47). A number of explanations have been given for this difference, among them the operation of rules of play or of principles of repetition and variation: there is a significant emphasis within the literature on the role of repetition and variation in music in 'liberating' libidinal energy and erotic desire at the level of primary process – energy and desire which then become a source for the operation of secondary processes within which repetition and variation can give them form as the manifest content of music.

The most developed explanation for the difference between dreams and music was, however, put forward by Ehrenzweig. In noting that, 'unlike the dream, which is formed while our surface functions are paralyzed during sleep, art is created during the waking state' (1953, p. 5), he concluded that if 'a dream memory is easily forgotten ... in a work of art the unconscious symbolism stands permanently embodied ... we cannot forget it or destroy it thus' (p. 51). Ehrenzweig drew on the principles of Gestalt psychology to argue that 'during artistic perception the surface mind (which is subject to the Gestalt tendency) ... function[s] ... to cover up the inarticulate ... forms by a "good" gestalt' (p. 5). Art and music for Ehrenzweig therefore act as a defence against the intrusion of primary processes in their 'latent' form: 'the secondary elaboration process helps the surface mind to win back the lost energy charge, and the energy charge is now used in aesthetic pleasure' (1953, p. 91). The energy charge, in the words of Noy, is thus 'severed from its sources and confined to the surface level', preventing the possibility that 'the energy may be redirected from the surface to the deeper cathectic meaning implicit in the artistic creation'. With the dream, however, 'there is no danger that ... the energy invested in it' will be 'claimed back' (in contradistinction to language, which may only be 'claimed') since 'a shift of energy from depth to surface processes ... occurs spontaneously with the awakening from sleep' (1967b, p. 49).

The problem with these explanations is that it is unclear at what level in mental processes music arises. Does music occur literally 'within' primary processes, or do primary processes give rise to energies, affective states or gestures which are then 'translated' by processes of sublimation or secondary processes into the surface structures of music? And if music acts as a stimulus to occasion experiences originating in the unconscious, does this stimulus occur *only* because music has already been created? As Noy asks, 'how are latent ideas represented in sound? On what level of the psychical apparatus is the transformation performed?' (1967b, p. 50). If music *does* occur within primary processes, the question remains as to 'how ... the unconscious wish[es] or need[s] [to] achieve tonal representations'. If music *is* the result of sublimation, another question remains: 'what is the nature of the motives or wishes to find expression and gratification in music?' (p. 50). If, in other words, it is assumed that a special relation exists between music on the one hand and the unconscious, primary sexuality and the world of emotions on the other, then the questions remain as to what it is within the unconscious or primary processes that 'requires' and 'generates' music, and – on the assumption that this question can be answered – what the precise character of the relationship between primary processes and music is.

A somewhat different approach to the question of music was taken by a group of psychoanalysts drawing on ego psychology. Within this tradition, art was not viewed as transforming primary, sexual energy, but as resulting from a desexualized and neutral energy obtaining at the level of the ego. Ego psychology replicates the emphasis placed by Masserman and Ehrenzweig on containment, control and mastery, but in a slightly different way. Common to all these ego psychology theories, says Noy, is 'the conception of music as more than a mere indirect expression of basic energy and latent wishes. They all view music as an activity which is initiated by the ego' (1967c, p. 84). Music is initiated by the ego in order to serve 'as a defense against various forces', as an aid, therefore, 'in the struggle of the ego for mastering' (p. 86). Art and music are assumed to be a civilizing influence in lending a sense of the aesthetic, of order, design, structure, wholeness and unity to otherwise disparate and dangerous experiences.

According to some writers working in the tradition of ego psychology (for example, Kohut and Levarie, 1957), the more complex the music, the greater the degree of desexualized and neutral energy that needs to be invested in the act of mastery. In the opinion of Kohut and Levarie, says Noy, 'it is obvious that more intricately structured music will be preferred by persons who are inclined and able to employ their intellectual capacities in the analysis of percepts.' This somewhat elitist line of thinking links easily with Meyer's (1959) work in the stress he placed on the syntactic in music (the abstract relations that occur melodically, harmonically and rhythmically between individual notes or discrete sonic events in music), the way he developed notions of value and greatness in music according to criteria of complexity derived from the syntactic, and the way he prioritized different musics in terms of the degree of maturity they require from individuals, and the level of civilizing effects they can as a consequence be taken to achieve. However, it is unclear where these principles of formal complexity come from. As we have seen, Meyer conceived of a parallelism of structure between processes of syntax in music and the processes of the human mind, governed as they are by 'general laws' (Meyer, 1956). In a later publication, Meyer made an argument for 'a

general law of some sort', such as 'the Gestalt law of completeness, which asserts that the human mind, searching for stable
shapes, wants patterns to be as complete as possible' (1973, p. 8).
Principles of form therefore seem to derive from 'general laws'
and 'stable shapes'. Yet we are left unclear as to why the human
mind obeys 'general laws' or 'searches for stable shapes'
(assuming, that is, that it does), and how, exactly, these laws or
shapes conform to principles of syntax in music as laid out by
Meyer (this latter problem is evident also, albeit in a slightly different way, with the concept of the structural homology). As
Noy concludes, all these theories (including Meyer's), which
derive from ego and Gestalt psychology, 'affirm as the central
property of art its intrinsic tendency to conform to rules,
designs, gestalt-forms, but none explains the origin and the significance of these rules' (1967c, p. 87).

Notwithstanding their different emphases, all the theories we
have referred to (including those of ego psychologists) seem to
subscribe to a view that there are three possible functions for
music: 'emotional catharsis for repressed wishes (Id), ... mastering of the threats of trauma (Ego), and enjoyable submission to
rules (Super-ego)' (Kohut and Levarie, 1957, p. 406). These functions are nothing if not complementary in terms of the different
emphases they place on primary and secondary processes and on
the different character and purposes of these processes. All the
theories, in one way or another, stress a role for music in mediating between the unconscious and the conscious. This role is
accorded a special character and status in terms of the differences
that are taken to obtain between music and language: music's
ability to circumvent the world of objects allows it a characteristic
access to the unconscious that is not open to language. However,
while this distinctive role is suggestive for further developing an
understanding of music, it does not of itself, as Noy has made
clear, answer more basic questions to do with the origins of
music. The precise character of the relations of music to subjects
as a consequence remains unclear, as do the specific mechanisms
through which music generates meanings of such special relevance to subjects. We are, in other words, no nearer understanding the precise order of relations between music as a socially
constituted signifying system and subjects as likewise socially
constituted. These questions – and the issue of music's difference
to language – are ones that we continue to pursue.

Lacan and the Linguistic Production of the Subject

At the beginning of this chapter, we argued that a turn to the work of Freud was necessary to keep open the possibility of a full and rich dialectic between individual subjects and processes of signification such as those of music with which they interact. Freud's work, indeed, provides a conceptualization of individual subjects which does not accept subjectivity as something given, which to the contrary sees subjectivity as something continually striven for, and which sees processes of identity formation as materially grounded and mediated. It is a conceptualization which assumes language to be the route through which different moments in mental processes are revealed and can thus be accessed. It is a conceptualization which in addition has allowed for the development of theories concerning music in which music, in circumventing the world of objects and language, is seen as standing in a special relation to processes of the unconscious, psycho-sexual processes, and the world of emotions.

However, rich though it is, Freud's work conceals two problems. The first is that it produces its own omissions in relation to the principle of dialecticism. While language is seen as mediating importantly between different moments of mental processes, it is nonetheless seen as a product of these moments and their mediation, and not as contributing to them in any real sense. In the case of music, the emphasis is placed on the role of music *either* in accessing the unconscious *or* in revealing it. Again, music is not seen in any real sense as *contributing* to the formation of identity. In all cases, therefore, the relations between processes of signification and processes of subjectivity are posited in terms which render them undialectical, and in a direction opposite to that which characterizes the lack of dialecticism in the work of Althusser. This lack of dialecticism relates to the second problem evident in Freud's work. Neither in the case of Freud's discussions of language nor, for that matter, in the case of post-Freudian discussions of music is there any theorization of the precise character of the connectedness of the signifying system in question to processes of subjectivity. It is the transparent (or, to put it another way, the opaque) character of this connection that makes possible an undialectical approach to signification in which mental processes are taken to be revealed and thus accessed through processes of signification in ways which are assumed to be self-evident and thus unproblematic.

It is this omission that the work of Lacan addresses. The work of Lacan in relation to Freud reasserts the emphasis placed by the French tradition on the *production of meaning* (Saussure) and the *production of subjectivity* (Althusser). Lacan links this dual emphasis by arguing that processes of signification in the service of, and as constituting, social institutions produce subjects *through* the production of meaning. Lacan's work thus provides another dimension to the general protocol developed at the end of the previous chapter. In identifying processes of signification through language with the processes through which subjects are constituted, Lacan opens up territory appropriate to understanding the processes through which subjects might be thought of as likewise constituted through music.

The point of departure for both Freud and Lacan was an abstract concept of human wholeness in terms of which desire could be theorized in terms of the need to compensate for biological 'incompleteness' at the moment of birth. If bisexuality for Freud constituted a ground in terms of which to conceptualize the complexities of repression leading to the formation of the unconscious, then the possibility of an androgynous and biological completeness became for Lacan a concept in terms of which to theorize the inevitable biological lack that became evident at the moment of birth. The mother for children of both sexes becomes the object of the fulfilment of desires created through the fact of biological differentiation. The mother at this stage is not experienced in terms of an 'object-other', but rather as an undifferentiated extension of the child's corporeal and somatic being.

A number of objects in addition to the mother and her breast (for example, faeces and the gaze and voice of others: objects collectively referred to by Lacan as (a) objects) are identified by the child as symptomatic of both presence and absence, as points, says Silverman, 'through which the child attempts to introject itself into those things which give it pleasure, and which it does not yet distinguish from itself' (1983, p. 156). It is the 'imaginary' which becomes the location for these objects. It is within the imaginary that both identification and duality in relation to objects are registered. It is this ambivalence in relationship to objects that comes to be initially resolved through the mirror phase. In the mirror phase – and it seems certain that Lacan was here arguing metaphorically – the child recognizes in others an image of itself as the ideal of who he or she wishes to become. In a literal sense – where the child actually sees an image of itself – the image becomes ideal in the sense that the child does not recognize, for example, its own motor deficiencies. The child is led into the illusion that it is in control of its own movements as it perceives them in the mirror. In a more metaphorical sense, the ability of the child to act in such a way as to obtain the mother's breast leads to an assumption that the breast is part of the self. In the mirror phase, this principle is extended so that the child assumes itself to be the image of the mother as presented, an image in which the mother (and thus the self) appears to be in control of her (its) actions. Nursling dependency is misrecognized as control of the breast. The biological unity of the bodies of the child and the mother is thus transformed into a putative separation through which the identity of the self as distinct from others begins to take place. The developing subject begins to assign to itself a coherence which is misplaced, as Lacan explains:

> This jubilant assumption of his specular image by the child at the *infans* stage, still sunk in his motor incapacity and nursling dependence, would seem to exhibit in an exemplary situation the symbolic matrix in which the *I* is precipitated in a primordial form, before it is objectified in the dialectic of identification with the other, and before language restores to it, in the universal, its function as subject. (1977, p. 2)

It is clearly an advantage for the growing child if – in acting to satisfy its desires – it can map symbolically its universe through language. In order to understand the power exercised by language on subjects, it is necessary to understand Lacan's concept of language. Lacan's concept of language was derived from that of Saussure, but with one major difference. Whereas it seems reasonable to conclude that Saussure understood language to retain a relationship with the external world – albeit indirect and determined in its character by the functioning of language as a structure – Lacan understood language to occasion a complete break with material reality, whether as manifest in the body or in external reality. This move was made possible and, indeed, necessary, because, according to Lacan, only absence requires signification, not presence. In other words, language becomes necessary and useful as the mechanism through which the child attempts to satisfy the need for something that it presently does not have. It can thus be reasonably concluded that language *itself* provides the presence or 'substance' made necessary through the absence of the material objects of the external world. Interaction between the material realities of bodies (something that remains central to Freud's theories of the developing subject) is in this way replaced in Lacan by interactions that are centrally linguistic in character. Material realities can therefore only be experienced through language.

While not all signifiers have to be linguistic in character, all signifiers nonetheless abandon all relation to the real and, in this sense, have to be mediated through language. This means that language and signifying processes become crucial to the way in which emerging subjects relate to others and to themselves. Without the capacity to signify, it becomes impossible for emerging subjects to distance themselves from the objects of their desire and to enter into the illusion that they can 'manipulate' and 'command' them for their own ends in sophisticated ways. Finally, without the ability to say 'I', to recognize through language the distinction between others and self, there can be no subjectivity. Processes of signification thus become synonymous if not identical with processes of subjectivity.

A major consequence for Lacan was that it was not subjects who spoke language, but language which spoke subjects. This position was not only a radical departure from that of Freud. It was also a significant departure from that of Saussure, who clearly did not go so far as to say that language was *uniquely* productive of meaning (and, by implication, subjects). For Lacan, therefore, the signifier 'becomes a new dimension of the human condition' (1982, p. 78). This primacy of language in the constitution of the subject results in a situation where the source of a signifier representing a subject can never be another subject. Subjects are produced by processes of signification whose source must as a consequence be 'other' to the world of subjects:

> If the subject is what I say it is, namely, the subject determined by language and speech, it follows that the subject, *in initio*, begins in the locus of the Other, in so far as it is there that the first signifier

emerges. Now, what is a signifier? . . . A signifier is that which represents a subject. But for whom? – not for another subject, but for
another signifier. (1979, p. 198)

It is the misrecognition of the self in the [m]other – presaged
in the mirror phase – which creates the conditions leading to the
development of the unconscious. Because of misrecognition, the
subject becomes incapable of knowing in consciousness the
actual conditions giving rise to speech and awareness. They
'misrecognize' themselves as the authors of their own utterances. The problem for Lacan was then to understand the way
in which the 'unconscious is *constituted* by the effects of speech
on the subject'. The unconscious, continued Lacan, 'is the
dimension in which the subject is determined in the development of the effects of speech'. Consequently, concluded Lacan,
'the unconscious is structured like a language' (1979, p. 149, our
italics). The question for Lacan was thus one 'of rediscovering in
the laws governing that other scene . . . which Freud designated,
in relation to dreams, as that of the unconscious, the effects discovered at the level of the materially unstable elements which
constitute the chain of language: effects determined by the
double play of combination and substitution in the signifier . . .
effects which are determinant in the institution of the subject'
(1982, p. 79).

Subjects thus enter a linguistically constituted world that is
not of their own making. This world is constituted through language as a series of ordered subject positions such as those of
'father' and 'mother'. The totality of these subject positions in
turn constitutes what Lacan refers to as the 'symbolic order'. In
making this connection between language and the symbolic
order, Lacan draws on Lévi-Strauss's extended work on kinship,
in which he saw kinship as a structure of family relations
encoded and entrenched through myths and their language.
Central to all kinship systems, in Lévi-Strauss's work, is the
incest taboo. It was this taboo which Lévi-Strauss saw as the distinguishing feature separating human from animal societies.
This taboo forced families to interact with one another, to create
social units greater than the family, and so to create the basis for
human societies. In so doing, it also forced the development of
kinship structures evidencing subject positions that were in
essence separate from, while at the same time prescribing the

behaviour of, the individual subjects who occupied them. It was through these kinship structures that the incest taboo was maintained and individual subjects from one generation to another were constrained to behave in ways which did not contravene it. For Lacan as for Lévi-Strauss, familial positions were as a result structured in such a way that they were at any time of much greater consequence to the maintenance and reproduction of society than any individual who might happen to occupy them. At this stage in the development of the subject (the subject entering language and thus the symbolic order), the symbolic order is for Lacan constituted entirely through family structures.

The symbolic order, in subsuming subject positions such as those of kinship and the family which are inescapably sexed and gendered, is itself an order that is gendered. Subjects therefore enter a symbolic order whose gendered character is likewise not of their own making. It is the discourse of the family which creates gendered subjectivity by aligning subjects with the symbolic positions of 'father' and 'mother'. Sexual difference, manifest in the work of Lévi-Strauss as basic to the incest taboo and the maintenance of kinship and family structures, comes in the work of Lacan to be transformed into the symbolic. Lacan is thus forced into the position of establishing a purely symbolic marker for the structural difference between the subject positions of the 'father' and the 'mother' (in much the same way, it should be noted, as Kristeva was later forced into the creation of the 'chora'). This marker is termed by Lacan the 'phallus'. The 'phallus' stands for the binary opposition towards all those lacks, first biological, then somatic and then linguistically constituted, which motivate the child into processes of identity formation and subject development. It becomes the *all-pervasive* marker of difference signifying presence and substance in the face of absence.

The spotlight Lacan places on the intersection between processes of signification through language and processes of subjectivity opens up precisely the territory we need to enter to move forward with our project. In Lacan's thinking, language becomes both possible and necessary because of the absence of objects. It is absence which gives rise to signification, not presence. As we have seen, it is almost as if language itself provides the presence or 'substance' made necessary through the absence of the material objects of the external world. This, presumably, is what leads to the prominence of signifiers in Lacan's thinking. It is the material base of signifiers, their sounds, which 'stand in' for the materiality of the objects of the external world. However, *before* the child enters fully into the linguistic universe and develops a clear sense of the distinction between others and self, it can be assumed that the sounds of words constitute a significant aspect of the imaginary. The gaze and *voice* of others, Lacan tells us, partially constitute (a) objects. It can therefore be concluded that the sounds of words as uttered by others are experienced initially as an extension of the child's corporeal and somatic being, and only slowly, through their location in the imaginary and as a consequence of the mirror phase, come to be recognized as 'belonging' to others in contradistinction to the sounds of the words which the child itself begins to utter. Lacan's thinking can in this way contribute an additional step to the conclusion drawn from Freud's work, namely, that the possibility exists of a tight connection between music and subjects as materially constituted. If the sounds of language can be experienced as 'part of us', then 'not part of us', and then again as 'part of us', then so can the sounds of music. It is in this way that the sounds of music can be thought of as mediating effectively between the external and internal worlds in their appeal to the unconscious, sexuality, emotion and affect, in much the same way as language is conceived by Lacan as a phenomenon external to the subject which then constitutes the subject's internal world through the unconscious.

However, the promise of this line of thought for understanding music is at the same time effectively dashed as a consequence of Lacan's arguments. Music, by definition, cannot aspire to the condition of the symbolic order, at least insofar as it remains unmediated by language in its position of privilege. At the outset, therefore, the denial of a socially effective role for music can be traced to Lacan's insistence on the privileged position enjoyed by language in mediating the signification of *all* signifiers. It is to be presumed that music does not escape this mediation and thus, once again, is understood to be a consequence of language in its manner of signification. However, this consequence can be traced also to an apparent elision in Lacan's thinking where the role and function of the phallus is concerned. On the one hand, the phallus, as signifier, stands for the binary opposition towards those lacks, first biological and then somatic, which motivate the child into processes of identity formation and subject development. In this sense, it could reasonably be concluded that signifiers, as materially experienced phenomena, come to 'stand in' for the materiality of the missing objects of the external world, and thus begin to establish the difference between 'others' and 'self'. In this process, however, the child has to be introduced to the gendering of the symbolic order. This is where the phallus appears to serve a *second* function as a marker of difference between the subject positions of 'father' and 'mother'. This surely is a function of signification, even if it does extend in an 'abstract' manner as the 'essence of gendering' to encompass *all* forms of difference within the symbolic order in their relationships of power. This function thus appears to be different in kind to the function of difference in opposition to absence, which can be served by language *acting as signifier alone*. Although Lacan is far from clear on this issue, it would seem that, as the child enters language, the material base of the signifiers of language suffer the same fate as the materiality of the child's body and, indeed, the material base of signifiers other than those present in language. All these forms of materiality seem forced, in Lacan's thinking, to recede in the face of the onslaught, not of signifiers, but of the signifieds essential to signification and meaning. Only in this way could Lacan understand language to occasion a *complete* break with material reality, whether as manifest in the body *or in external reality*. The only reasonable conclusion that can be reached is that it is the *signifieds* of language, over and above the material base of the chain of signifiers which occasions their invocation, which ultimately constitute the unconscious and thus 'speak' subjects. For this reason, the materiality of sound, either in language *or* in music, can be seen to play little or no role in the constitution of subjects. It is in this way that the phallus for Lacan appears, as Silverman (1983) claims, to serve two functions, that of signifier and signified, and why in this respect its relationship to the penis as an aspect of material reality seems unclear.

It is not difficult to understand why Althusser (in drawing on the work of Lacan) would have felt little compunction to theorize the link between ideology and subjectivity in terms of the material dimensions of signifying practices. This is because – although the material dimension of sound is essential to processes of signification through language in terms of providing language with its material grounds and pathways – it is, for Lacan as for Saussure, inconsequential in terms of the actual character of language's meanings, its denotative level of primary signification. For this reason it was, indeed, simply enough for Althusser (in drawing on Lacan) that *ideological processes* were material in character. There was ultimately no need to examine the specific character of their materiality. In this sense ideology *can* move to subjectivity transparently through the actions (including, presumably, those of processes of signification) brought on by the material relations of ideology. In this sense, the position that processes of signification speak subjects could remain consistent with Althusser's position, despite the emphasis placed by Althusser on the role of material *actions* in ideology as productive of subjects. In that processes of signification constitute for Lacan a relationship of power, the question does, however, remain as to how *this* power is exercised. Can it be through a material ground and pathway that is, indeed, inconsequential to the content or significance of language? In Althusserian terms, is content or significance as symptomatic of the exercise of power thereby rendered contradictorily non-material or spiritual in the character of its transmission? To put it more bluntly, if the signifier of 'the phallus' is partially masquerading as a signified – as the lack of clarity of its relation to the penis would seem to suggest – then how is the phallus's signifying effectivity in terms of power to be theorized? It is within the context of these questions that issues involving the precise order of relations between language, music, the body, the unconscious, the conscious, cognition and affect remain of relevance.

4

Theorizing Difference in Language and Music

Lacan's work offers a powerful model in terms of which to understand the connectedness of processes of signification to processes of subjectivity. However, this model is bought at a cost, because it expunges the material as manifest in the body and in signifiers. As Silverman observes, 'the definitive criterion of a signifier is that it abandon all relation to the real, and take up residence within a closed field of meaning, not that it partake of a given materiality' (1983, p. 164). The materiality of signifiers constitutes presences as opposed to absences (which motivate their use). By bringing into play the gendered world of the symbolic order, signifiers thus charge the entire semiological field as one of power in relation to control. However, the character of signifiers' materiality becomes of little consequence, because it is the presence of signifiers in relation to other signifiers (thus giving rise to signification) rather than the specific character of their materiality which signifies presence and power. The gendering of the semiological field through the invocation of the symbolic order means that it is the power of the 'father' (symbolic 'father' or 'Name-of-the-Father') *over and above its material ground* which constitutes and positions subjects through an inscription of gendered identity on and through their bodies. It is in this way that power can be exercised by material signifiers on material bodies. The point for the exercise of this power is the lifting of signification *away* from the material ground of the signifier and *onto* the material ground of the body. There cannot, in Lacan's scheme, be any point for the exercise of power on bodies *constituted through a connectedness* of the material character of the signifier to the material character of the body. The world of the material is in this way rendered neutral and inconsequential, a ground for inscription rather than a medium for construction.

This model for the constitution of subjectivities through language is as a consequence insufficient to sustain a line of argument which seeks to ground the relative autonomy of music in the specific character of its material grounds and to posit the connectedness of music as a signifying process to processes of subjectivity as one constituted through the impact of sound as a material phenomenon on the materiality of the body. In order to keep this line of thinking open without losing the benefit of Lacan's insight that processes of signification constitute subjectivities it is necessary to reclaim the body from Lacan and weaken the stranglehold of language in his theoretical scheme. It is the work of Kristeva which shows the way forward in this enterprise. Kristeva's work retains an explicit sense of the central role of language in constituting subjectivities. However, it does this within the context of a rich theoretical scheme which seeks to explain the relations between the body, sound, and the symbolic order as linguistically constituted and articulated. This work is therefore helpful in suggesting ways in which the character of the connectedness between sound and the body might be theorized within the broader context of processes underpinning the constitution of subjectivities.

Kristeva, Language and the Subject

Kristeva's work retains the emphasis placed by Lacan on the role of language in constituting subjectivities. However, her work differs from that of Lacan in two important respects. Although, as we shall see, it is 'gathered up' and 'contained' within language, and although subjectivity in this sense remains purely an *effect* of language, the body is nonetheless retained as a player in the formation and maintenance of identity. In this sense, Kristeva's work owes a direct debt to that of Freud. However, although it is differentiated and 'semiotized' before entry into language in a way in which the body in Lacan's thinking cannot be (Lacan *seems* to retain Freud's notion of an undifferentiated bisexuality in this regard), it and its semiotic *potential* can only be accessed – albeit indirectly – through language. This access can *only* be indirect because the body, as such, cannot signify. The differentiations of the semiotized body do not become semanticized until interpellation into the language of the symbolic order.

Secondly, language is not the closed-off and 'other-worldly' phenomenon it appears to be in Lacan's work. Kristeva sees the body as a source of language, although it clearly cannot be the only one. If the body were the sole source of language, then the body could be accessed *directly* through language, and subjectivity would rely significantly on biological sexual difference. For Kristeva, however, language arises as a consequence of the *semiotic* potential of the body and the interpellation of this potential within language as fully realized in society. Language, as a consequence, is not unified, *but has feminine and masculine aspects* (those of the semiotized body and the symbolic order respectively). These complexities, involving a 'two-dimensional' language, the semiotized body, the conscious, the unconscious, cognition *and* awareness, resurrect beyond Lacan the complex set of connections involving music identified in our account of Freud's work.

Kristeva therefore achieves a subtle transformation of Lacan's thinking on the relation of signifiers to presence and absence by expanding the location of the gendered charging of the semiological field as the positive site of power to include the body as semiotized in addition to the language of the symbolic order. Kristeva thus recognizes a distinction which is elided in the work of Lacan: between the source of presence (language as signifiers *emanating* from the *semiotized* body) and the source of gendering (language as signifieds acting through the *semanticized* symbolic order). It is this elision which renders the relation of the phallus to the penis problematic in the work of Lacan and raises the problem of how to theorize the phallus's signifying effectivity in terms of power in the absence of a *consequential* material ground (as now evident in the thinking of Kristeva *through* the sounds of language and *in* the body). In this way, Kristeva 'thickens' Lacan's model of signification in relation to the formation of identity by positing a second location of agency in relation to the acquisition of language and the development of identity which acts as a pole of difference and antithesis to the symbolic order as linguistically constituted and articulated. The site of semiological difference is in effect expanded beyond the symbolic order to include the body. This is achieved, it should be remembered, without in any way removing language from its central and universal role in constituting the world for subjects. Expanding the location of the gendered charging of the semiological field beyond language to include the body is critical for Kristeva's thinking if the body is to act as one source for the acquisition of language and the formation of identity. For if the body did not manifest within itself a form of difference, there would be no basis in terms of which it could exercise agency and be of consequence in processes whereby language is acquired and identity formed. This way of thinking requires the development of a much more specific notion of the body than we have hitherto entertained. The idea that the body is semiotized – containing within itself a fundamental yet unsemanticized form of difference – raises the question of the role within the body of genetic and biological processes.

There clearly arises a need in Kristeva's thinking to theorize the locus of this semiotized body, the body which is of consequence for language and the formation of identity while at the same time remaining accessible only through language. Kristeva fulfils this need through the development of the notion of the *chora*. Kristeva introduces the concept of the *chora*, says Payne, 'in order to account for the dynamic interrelations between the semiotic and the symbolic'. The *chora*, he continues, 'comes to function both as an image opportunistically employed to fill a conceptual need in Kristeva's theory and as a precise technical term (chorion) from embryology that specifically defines the bodily site of the first signifying processes of the fetus' (1993, p. 167).

In language reminiscent of Freud's distinction between the 'nothingness' of undifferentiated sexuality and the 'being' of achieved identity, and of Lacan's distinction between the 'nothingness' of absence and the 'being' of symbolic positioning, the *chora*, says Kristeva, 'is on the path of destruction, aggressivity and death ... this is to say that the semiotic *chora* is no more than the place where the subject is both generated and negated' (Moi, 1986, p. 95). The *chora* is neither sign nor signifier, although it exists to attain these positions. As such, and prior to the fixity of these positions as neither a model for them nor a copy of them, the *chora* displays the mobility of vocal and kinetic rhythms. The *chora* 'is not yet a position that represents for someone (i.e., it is not a sign); nor is it a *position* that represents someone for another position (i.e., it is not yet a signifier either); it is, however, generated in order to attain this signifying position. Neither model nor copy, the *chora* precedes and underlies figuration and thus specularization, and is analogous only to vocal or kinetic rhythm' (Moi, 1986, p. 94). The *chora* is a modality of significance in being regulated or ordered according to the dictates, not of the symbolic order, but of the objective constraints (including the biological as well as the social) 'preceding' the symbolic order. This regulation and ordering thus remains of a mobile character. The *chora*, in being gathered up and contained within the symbolic order, nonetheless remains mediated by it. It does not, however, recognize the distinctions and relations between the subject and the object, the symbolic and the 'real' which are crucial to the symbolic order.

Kristeva's thinking on the question of the *chora* is suggestive for an understanding of music as a form of human expression and communication which *in certain ways* lies outside the world of language. The functions of the semiotic open up to the subject a pre-symbolic world of the kinetic and rhythmic. The subject is not therefore reduced solely to the function of 'understanding'. This distinction between the symbolic and the semiotic is made clear by White when he says that:

> The symbolic is ... that major part of language which names and relates things, it is that unity of semantic and syntactic competence which allows communication and rationality to appear. Kristeva has thus divided language into two vast realms, the *semiotic* – sound, rhythm and movement anterior to sense and linked closely to impulses [that is, drives] ... – and the *symbolic* – the semantico-syntactic function of language necessary to all rational communication about the world. The latter, the *symbolic*, usually 'takes charge of' the semiotic and binds it into syntax and phonemes, but it can only do so on the basis of the sounds and movements presented to it by the semiotic. The dialectic of the two parts of language form the *mise en scène* of Kristeva's description of poetics, subjectivity and revolution. (White, 1977, quoted in Hebdige, 1979, p. 164)

It is the mother's body which is understood to be the site of the ordering principle of the semiotic. Human drives involve investments of energy that in Kristeva's thinking connect the child's body to that of the mother. These drives, oral and anal, are for Kristeva already differentiated and, as such, are what guarantee the differentiated character of the body and thus its semiotic quality. However, since the body of the mother is already situated in the symbolic order, it is the mother's body, itself already 'semiotized', that provides for the mediation of both symbolic law and *chora*. In being oriented and structured around the body, the semiotic *chora*, it should be remembered, 'is on the path of destruction, aggressivity and death'. It is 'the place where the subject is both generated and negated'. The body and the kinetic, the body and vocal and kinetic rhythms thus appear to have a close relation, and to be closely related to the generation and negation of the subject. This bodily and kinetic world of the subject is accessible only through the language for which it is a precondition, which contains, conditions, shapes and structures it, and through which it finds life. That is to say, this world is accessible only through signifying practices and texts. Kristeva explains these relations by observing first of all that the genetic is implicit in the mobility of the semiotic and in this way functions as an innate precondition for language: 'genetic programmings are necessarily semiotic: they include the primary processes such as displacement and condensation, absorption and repulsion, rejection and stasis, all of which function as innate preconditions, "memorizable" by the species, for language acquisition' (Moi, 1986, p. 97). The processes and relations of the genetic and the semiotic can only receive expression, continues Kristeva, through language as articulated diachronically (through speech or *parole*). However, inasmuch as these processes and relations do not constitute, but can only aspire to, the condition of signifiers and signs, they reside in and constitute the unconscious, and, for Kristeva as for Freud, can thus only be accessed through the analysis of signifying practices such as dreams. Consequently 'theory can "situate" such processes and relations diachronically within the process of the constitution of the subject because *they function synchronically within the signifying process of the subject himself*, i.e., the subject of *cogitatio*. Only in *dream* logic, however, have they attracted attention, and only in certain signifying practices, such as the *text*, do they dominate the signifying process' (Moi, 1986, p. 96).

Kristeva's position on language and subjectivity thus retains much of Freud's thinking, and in two respects: in relation to the body as a player in the development and maintenance of identity; and in the potential of the unconscious to disrupt through language the presumed coherence of the symbolic order. However, this position nonetheless remains consistent with theories of the linguistic constitution of the subject as developed by Lacan. For Kristeva as for Lacan, language is crucial for the distinction between self and other, between subject and object, and thus for the constitution of identity. It is the symbolic order entered through language which imprints difference onto that of the semiological which is already biologically within the body of the mother. This principle of semiological difference is then transferred biologically and genetically to the body of the unborn child in an asemanticized form – asemantic because the unborn child has yet to encounter language and the symbolic order. This principle of semiological difference provides the fundamental signifying logic that impels the child into language and which, at the same time, provides the basis in the form of its vocal and kinetic rhythms for the disruptions of the fixities of the symbolic order. In this way, Kristeva develops a most subtle theoretical model for the development of identity through the acquisition of language in which the symbolic order acts as a partial source for its own disruption and challenges.

The body and the *chora* symbolize femininity for Kristeva in distinction to the masculinity of the symbolic order. It is in this way that Kristeva politicizes the unquestioned power of the phallus, and as a consequence suggests that the dominant, masculine, symbolic order constitutes a site for political struggle through the potential for its disruption by the effects of the feminine *chora*. The unconscious plays a critical role in this disruption, an unconscious that, as in the work of Freud and Lacan, can only be accessed through the textuality of language. In the work of Kristeva, however, the concern with the textual is not a by-product of psychoanalytic practice. It is the consequence of a concern with linguistic theory and literary criticism, and is therefore central to the development of her theoretical scheme. Texts thus remain a critical site for Kristeva in the politics of gender and subjectivity. While the masculine and feminine aspects of language throw light on the contemporary politics of gender, they do not, however, mechanically reproduce them. Both aspects of language are available to women and men alike.

While 'Kristeva links symbolic language to masculinity and semiotic language to femininity', says Weedon, she 'argues that both aspects of language, the feminine and the masculine, are open to all individuals irrespective of their biological sex'. The effect of this theoretical move, concludes Weedon, 'is to break with the biological *basis* of subjectivity' (Weedon, 1987, p. 89, our italics). For this reason, the influence of the semiotic can be seen at work in women *and* men writers. For Kristeva, explains Weedon, 'the feminine is a mode of language, open to male and female writers.' As Kristeva argues, continues Weedon, 'the return of the repressed feminine is manifest, for example, in the "marginal" discourse of the literary avant-garde, such as the poetry of Lautréamont and Mallarmé and the prose of James Joyce. These texts are seen as exceeding phallocentric, logocentric discourse', Weedon concludes, 'putting the subjectivity which supports it into question and showing subjectivity *in process*' (1987, pp. 69–70). The feminine in language also appears to be close or related to the 'condition of music'. The feminine in language, says Weedon, is 'manifest in symbolic discourse in such aspects of language as *rhythm and intonation*'. As such it 'is at its strongest in non-rational discourses which threaten the organisation of the symbolic order and the stability of its meanings, such as art, poetry and religion' (p. 89, our italics).

Difference in Language

If the work of Lacan allows a glimpse into the manner in which sounds, and as a consequence sounds in music, might be thought of as mediating between the external and internal worlds in their appeal to the unconscious, then Kristeva's work goes a step further in positing an integral and fundamental relationship between sounds and the human body. As the site for the generation and negotiation of the subject, the *chora* provides a site within which *sounds as sounds speak to the very basis and core of subjectivity*. Sounds, together with rhythms, gestures and colours, form for Kristeva one of the means through which the energy drives linking the bodies of the mother and child in *one* sensate universe are channelled and directed. Further, these sounds, in their kinetic impulses of rhythm and intonation, can be taken to be imprinted with a fundamental semiological difference that goes beyond the 'essence of gendering' as manifest in the work of Lacan. In Kristeva's work, sounds are thus bound into an 'ordered' world evidencing the potential for forms of awareness *beyond* those of the purely cognitive. Kristeva's work thus provides the 'concrete connection' lacking in post-Freudian accounts of the relations between music and the unconscious, as well as a sense of fundamental ordering in sound which lies *unambiguously* outside the realm of the semantic. These advances move beyond the promises for understanding music evident in the work of Lévi-Strauss and Althusser respectively in pointing to the possibility of a music structured *according to asemantic principles* whose sounds are capable of affecting directly the materiality of the human body.

Unfortunately, Kristeva's work is unable to develop further in this direction. The reason for this is that her work is insufficiently distanced from that of Lacan to be able to underwrite a theoretical scheme capable of sustaining an understanding of music which would actually *fulfil* the promises evident in the work of Lévi-Strauss and Althusser, as well as in that of Saussure and Freud. The problem is that there is little sense in which the semiotic *chora* is theorized beyond its pre-symbolic and pre-Oedipal location as a source for disruption. Kristeva extends the traditional categories of semiology to account theoretically for the *manner* of disruption by introducing the concept of *signifiance*. This concept accounts for the transformation of the signified through the signifier, and the consequent 'loss' or 'disappearance' of the subject (since subjects are spoken by language: signifier and signified acting together in the arbitrary yet temporarily fixed relationship that gives rise to the sign) as they attempt to 'master' a discourse, a signifying practice that is constantly mobile, constantly on the move. A good illustration of *signifiance* 'in action' is provided through Hebdige's analysis of British punk culture of the late 1970s.

This analysis was carried out within the context of the emphasis placed on processes of stylization and the concept of the structural homology by English subcultural theory of the 1970s. However, in doing this, the analysis also draws on the notion of *bricolage* as developed by Lévi-Strauss (1966 and 1969b). This notion of *bricolage* is clearly implicit in the concept of stylization as developed within English subcultural analysis.

It is the notion of *bricolage* which allows for the changes in significance which occur when symbols with previously existing and customary meanings are relocated and recontextualized through processes of stylization. The additional step that Hebdige takes in developing his reading of punk culture, however, is that of rethinking the notion of *bricolage* through that of *signifiance*. Rather than conceptualizing the replacement of one substantive meaning with another, equally substantive meaning that results from a change, however slight, in the original meaning brought on by the activities of relocation and recontextualization, Hebdige conceptualizes the disappearance of the original, substantive meaning through a loss of the signified in the signifier, and so a parallel loss of the subject in the processes of *signifying practice* as opposed to those of *signification* (which would result in the maintenance of substantive or transparent meanings and thus of the subject).

In 'feeding' the concept of *bricolage* through that of *signifiance*, Hebdige accounts for cheeks pierced with safety pins, green hair, and electric kettles worn as purses (the electric cord tucked into a belt around the waist) in the following way:

> There was a homological relation between the trashy cut-up clothes and spiky hair, the pogo and amphetamines, the spitting, the vomiting, the format of the fanzines, the insurrectionary poses and the 'soulless', frantically driven music. The punks wore clothes which were the sartorial equivalent of swear words, and they swore as they dressed – with calculated effect, lacing obscenities into record notes and publicity releases, interviews and love songs. Clothed in chaos, they produced Noise in the calmy orchestrated Crisis of everyday life in the late 1970s – a noise which made (no)sense in exactly the same way and to exactly the same extent as a piece of *avant-garde* music. If we were to write an epitaph for the punk subculture, we could do no better than repeat Poly Styrene's famous dictum: 'Oh Bondage, Up Yours!', or somewhat more concisely: the forbidden is permitted, but by the same token, nothing, not even these signifiers (bondage, safety pins, chains, hair-dye, etc.) is sacred and fixed. (1979, pp. 114–15)

The radical potential of the arbitrary yet *customarily* conventional relationship between signifier and signified was utilized to undermine conventional meaning. As intimated, this undermining did not consist simply of the replacing of one conventional meaning with another, unconventional one, which could then be grasped and understood. There was instead a steadfast refusal to assign meaning, to allow processes of signification to take their 'usual' course. Hebdige elaborates on this process by analysing the use of the swastika as a symbol relocated within punk subculture. 'Conventionally, as far as the British were concerned', says Hebdige, 'the swastika signified "enemy".' In punk usage, however, 'the symbol lost its "natural" meaning – fascism. The punks were not generally sympathetic to the parties of the extreme right.' As a consequence, Hebdige was forced to resort, in his analysis of the swastika's significance, 'to the most obvious of explanations – that the swastika was worn because it was guaranteed to shock' (1979, p. 116). This, concludes Hebdige:

> represented more than a simple inversion or inflection of the ordinary meanings attached to an object. The signifier (swastika) had been wilfully detached from the concept (Nazism) it conventionally signified, and although it had been re-positioned ... within an alternative subcultural context, its primary value and appeal derived precisely from its lack of meaning: from its potential for deceit. It was exploited as an empty effect. We are forced to the conclusion that the central value 'held and reflected' in the swastika was the communicated absence of any such identifiable values. Ultimately, the symbol was as 'dumb' as the rage it provoked. The key to punk style remains elusive. Instead of arriving at the point where we can begin to make sense of the style, we have reached the very place where meaning itself evaporates. (p. 117)

As Hebdige notes, 'this absence of permanently sacred signifiers (icons) creates problems for the semiotician. How can we discern any positive values reflected in objects which were chosen only to be discarded?' (p. 115). One thing is certain, however, and that is the triumph of the signifier over the signified. In terms of Kristeva's thinking, this is strong evidence of the operation of the semiotic outside or beyond the rationality of the symbolic order. In being placed outside or beyond the symbolic order, the subject, whether instigator or audience, is deconstructed, lost, 'disappeared', as Heath explains in introducing the work of Barthes:

> Significance is a *process* in the course of which the 'subject' of the text, escaping (conventional logic) and engaging in other logics (of the signifier, of contradiction) struggles with meaning and is deconstructed ('lost'); significance – and this is what immediately distinguishes it from signification – is thus precisely a work; not the work by which

the (intact and exterior) subject might try to master the language ...
but that radical work (leaving nothing intact) through which the subject explores – entering, not observing – how the language works and
undoes him or her ... Contrary to signification, signifiance cannot be
reduced, therefore, to communication, representation, expression: it
places the subject (of writer, reader) in text not as a projection ... but
as a loss. (Heath, 1977, p. 10)

While Kristeva theorizes the *effect* of the semiotic *chora* on the
symbolic order and the subject, therefore, she does not theorize
the manner in which the semiotic and the 'semiotized body'
could be thought of as being responsible for the development of
further, asemantic forms of organization, ordering, regulation
and structuring beyond the mere presence within them of fundamental difference. Such a theorization would, indeed, have
required the positing from within the *chora* of *more formal* yet
asemantic structures developed well beyond the mere presence
within the *chora* of basic difference. However, Kristeva's purpose in developing the concept of the *chora* – that of engaging in
certain forms of literary analysis and criticism – did not require
such an extensive theorization. It in any case seems unlikely that
the influence of Lacan would have permitted it. This more
extended theorization of the mobility of kinetic and vocal
rhythms would nonetheless have been helpful in pointing to
possible theorizations of music as a process of signification, and
thus to the possibility of a 'second semiology' capable of
analysing music. However, Kristeva does not develop a fully-
fledged, second semiology in terms of which possible alternatives to the seeming integrity of the linguistic symbolic order
can be theorized. Kristeva's theorization of the potential for disruption and resistance constitutes a *re-working* of established
semiological concepts, not a re-conceptualization *ab novo*. Those
'other' linguistic discourses that can receive life and be accessed
as a consequence of the disruption of the processes through
which the symbolic order is constituted and articulated therefore seem to have little coherent source of their own other than
the genetic, the biological and, through language, the imprinting
of the symbolic order. They come to be understood in terms of
their *difference* from the dominant symbolic order, a difference
that resides in their unconsummated aspirations to signify and
their containment within the symbolic order. The *chora* seems to
display little or no autonomy in its relationship to the symbolic.

Difference in Music

We argued earlier that a return to the more positive scenario for understanding music elaborated from the work of Saussure, Lévi-Strauss, Althusser and Freud would require a 'reclamation of the body from Lacan' and a weakening of the stranglehold of language in his theoretical scheme. It is now possible to understand how Kristeva's work moves in this direction through her reaffirmation of Freud's emphasis on the body as a player in the development and maintenance of identity and through her theorization of the semiotic *chora* as other to and disruptive of the symbolic order as constituted and articulated linguistically. Kristeva's descriptions of the characteristics of the *chora* and the effects of the *chora* in language are in this way suggestive for understanding music. However, as we have seen, Kristeva does not fully reclaim the body or weaken the stranglehold of language to a degree that is sufficient for the creation of a conceptual space adequate for understanding music.

However, this lack of an adequate conceptual space for understanding music has not prevented a number of poststructuralist writers following in the footsteps of Lacan and Kristeva from commenting on music and its relationship to sound in the earliest stages of life. To the possibility discernible in Lacan's work that sounds and therefore the sounds of music can mediate between the external and internal worlds is added Kristeva's emphasis on the integral and fundamental relatedness of sounds and the human body, the implication of this relatedness in the generation and negation of the subject, and the primacy of the mother's body in the transmission of the semiotic. In the view of most of these poststructuralist writers, music is seen to originate within the primacy of the mother's voice for the newborn infant. As Brett notes, 'post-Lacanian psychoanalysts ... have ... [developed] the idea of the mother's voice as a "sonorous envelope" surrounding the newborn infant – a blanket of sound alternatively regarded as "the first model of auditory pleasure" or an "umbilical net" ' (Brett, 1994, p. 12). Claudia Gorbman reports Guy Rosolato (1974) and Didier Anzieu (1976) as arguing that 'auditory space ... is the first psychic space' (Gorbman, 1987, p. 62). This space, continues Gorbman in her account of Rosolato's work, 'does not know the limits to be imposed later by the realities of psychomotor development; it can project its voice into space, it can hear and be heard in the dark, through walls and around corners' (p. 62). Rosolato himself comments that 'music finds its roots and its nostalgia in [this] original atmosphere, which might be called a sonorous womb, a murmuring house, or *music of the spheres*' (1974, p. 81). Sound and music thus stand for union with the mother. 'The imaginary longing for bodily fusion with the mother is never erased', says Gorbman, 'the terms of the original illusion of fusion are largely defined by the voice' (1987, p. 62). Brett reports Rosolato as outlining 'the image of the child attempting to "harmonize" with the mother once its voice has been differentiated, and this differentiation is what ultimately stimulates the "dream of recovery" of a "lost object" ' (1994, p. 12). Gorbman concludes that 'the mother's voice is central in constituting the auditory imaginary, before and also after the child's entry into the symbolic. From this – and from even earlier auditory perceptions and hallucinations – musical pleasure may be explained' (1987, p. 63).

However, as Brett hints, post-Lacanian interpretations of the centrality of the mother's voice to the newborn infant imply trauma as well as pleasure, thus replicating earlier views on the ambivalence of sound in the early life of the child developed by Freudian psychoanalysts. Chion, for example, in a passage notable for its ironic reference to the famous opening of the fourth Gospel ('In the beginning was the word'), creates an image of the mother's voice which is distinctly nightmarish:

> In the beginning, in the uterine night, was the voice, that of the Mother. For the child after birth, the Mother is more an olfactory and vocal continuum than an image. One can imagine the voice of the Mother, which is woven around the child, and which originates from all points in space as her form enters and leaves the visual field, as a matrix of places to which we are tempted to give the name 'umbilical net'. A horrifying expression, since it evokes a cobweb – and in fact, this original vocal tie will remain ambivalent. (1982, p. 57)

Silverman, expanding on the psychoanalytic dimensions of this theory in a manner reminiscent of Kristeva's *gendered* theorization of the *chora* in relation to the symbolic order, observes that the mother's voice: 'is either cherished ... as what can make good all lacks ... or despised and jettisoned as what is most abject, most culturally intolerable – as the forced representative of everything within male subjectivity which is incompatible with the phallic function, and which threatens to expose discursive mastery as an ideal' (Silverman, 1988, p. 86). As Silverman concludes, the image of the mother's voice is as a consequence

> always charged with either intensely positive or intensely negative affect ... pleasure for one psychic system almost invariably means unpleasure for another system ... the maternal-voice-as-sonorous-envelope takes on a different meaning depending upon the psychic 'lookout point'; viewed from the site of the unconscious, the image of the infant held within the environment or sphere of the mother's voice is an emblem of plenitude and bliss. Viewed from the site of the preconscious/conscious system, it is an emblem of impotence and entrapment. (pp. 72–3)

The problem with this manner of thinking is that music, even in its relevance to the preconscious and conscious, is reduced ultimately to the condition of the pre-symbolic, the pre-linguistic, the pre-discursive and the unconscious. The possibilities we noted as implicit in the work of Freud for the analysis of music are not therefore developed by post-Lacanian thinking, and they are certainly not developed any further by post-Lacanian thinking in a manner consistent with the more forward-looking directions elaborated from the work of Saussure, Lévi-Strauss and Althusser. Music's materiality does not seem capable of guaranteeing it a relative autonomy as a signifying practice distinct both from society and the individual, in this case, the pre-linguistic and pre-symbolic subject. To the extent that music retains its materiality, it is the material base of the signifier devoid of a signified – it is *signifiance* run rampant, signifiance in its purest form, a form, as Kristeva argued, that can never exist in reality. Music can thus contribute little to the formation and maintenance of identity and is concomitantly incapable of achieving a level of signification to match that of language. This connection is made clear by Francis Hofstein:

> At the same time that she nurtures, the mother speaks, a speech charged with rhythm, pitch, timbre, tempo, and intensity, an imprint; word/sounds anchored to her body like the mouth to the breast ... Thus the amazement, the incomprehension coloured with anxiety, then the still doubting integration by a 15–month-old who discovers, in the morning, the word for a fly [*mouche*], and who in the evening hears mother say 'Come let mommy wipe your nose [*viens*

que maman te mouche]'. Speech from which, if you take away the signified, you get *music* – which holds there the acoustical image, before
'language restores in the universal [the child's] function of subject'.
(1972, pp. 111–15)

The problem here lies not in positing a special relationship
between sound and the body, and hence music and the body. As
we shall see, the equations drawn between the vocal and kinetic
rhythms of the *chora*, the body, the voice, sound and music do
remain suggestive and helpful for an understanding of music.
The problem lies in the character of the relationship which in so
much post-Lacanian thinking is in one way or another taken to
exist between the body and language. The body is correctly
theorized as constituting the material grounds and pathways for
the development, investment and experiencing of emotional
energy and affective states. However, the thinking of Lacan and
Kristeva in one way or another assumes that the body, in constituting the material grounds and pathways for emotional energy
and affective states, displays no logics or potentials for signification which can stand independently (although relatedly) alongside those of language. It is assumed that the body can only take
on significance in relation to the development and maintenance
of identity by being interpellated in the universe of language.
However, language is a mode of signification whose material
grounds and pathways, in being essentially inconsequential to
the meanings which are taken to constitute subjectivities, *can be
taken to have little or no direct consequence for the body in terms of
signification as distinct from simple, brute awareness.* In this sense
the body remains both 'pre-linguistic' and 'sub-linguistic'. *Its*
materiality can only be constituted linguistically and *indirectly*
through consciousness in its role of providing the grounds and
pathways for subjectivity *as felt affectively and emotionally.* This
presumed superior power of language in comparison to music is
difficult to reconcile with the lack of a clear material pathway
through which the power of language can be exercised.

In observing that the pleasures of music can be explained by
reference to the centrality of the mother's voice in the constitution of the auditory imaginary (and, in this context, it is worth
recalling Althusser's claim that the relative autonomy of the
ideological imaginary is guaranteed through its material character), Gorbman observes also that 'of course, music is subsequently a highly coded and organized discourse' (1987, p. 63).

This reminder is reminiscent of Noy's observation that music is unlike dreams in being experienced in a state of wakefulness, in a state of full consciousness. The arguments of post-Lacanians do not however help in accessing the 'highly coded and organized' character of this discourse in any other than a linguistically embodied manner (the power and influence of linguistically conceived and embodied explanations for music is a point to which we will return in another, non-Lacanian context, in chapter 6). It is this inability to access the discourse on its own, musical terms which has proved problematic for those musicologists interested in the relationship between music and subjects. For example, some twenty years after his initial work on the relationship between music and mind, Meyer developed a position on the apprehension of music more inclusive of the whole human being and thus the human body. The language in which this position is couched is reminiscent of Kristeva's reference to the connectedness of the body and the kinetic in the *chora*, the connectedness of the body and vocal and kinetic rhythms which appears to have such a close relation to the generation and negation of the subject. A competent listener, says Meyer: 'perceives and responds to music with his total being . . . Through such empathetic identification, music is quite literally *felt*, and it can be felt without the mediation of extramusical concepts or images. Such kinesthetic sensing of the ethos or character of a music event is what the term *ethetic* refers to' (1973, p. 242). However, this ethetic relationship, which stands at the heart of musical apprehension for Meyer, poses considerable difficulties for analysis: 'ethetic relationships are unquestionably important . . . [but] are hard to analyze with rigour and precision . . . [There is an] absence of an adequate theory of ethetic change and transformation' (pp. 245–6). Again: 'the analysis must end here . . . [because] the rigorous analysis of ethetic relationships is beyond my knowledge and skill' (p. 267).

Accessing a musical discourse that is 'highly coded and organized' would seem to require not only a 'reclaiming of the body from Lacan'. It would seem to require also a more general reclaiming of the body from language. Two confusions need to be unravelled here. The first has to do with the relationship between the body and signification. While the body provides the material grounds through sexuality for the reproduction of human beings as material and biological organisms, and while processes of identity formation and maintenance would not be possible without the material grounds and pathways provided by the body, it follows neither that the material and biological processes of the body give rise to identity and the revelation of its characteristics through signification, nor that such processes, in being gathered up and contained within processes of the formation and maintenance of identity, can somehow be reduced to the condition of these latter processes and their presumed constitution through signification. Although the body is always implicated in processes of signification, in other words, it neither 'causes' them nor is it reducible to their conditions.

The second confusion has to do with the relationship between language and other modes of signification. While language is implicated in a fundamental fashion in the creation of the constitutive characteristics of human societies, and while individuals in society cannot exist outside language (any more, indeed, than they can exist outside any other form of signifying processes), it does not follow either that knowledge and experience can be accessed *only* through language, or that, because of this, language stands as *the* model for all signification (in the sense that other modes of signification cannot be 'in contradiction' of those of language). Knowledge and experience can, in other words, be accessed *directly* through modes of signification other than that of language, and these modes of signification cannot necessarily be reduced to or 'contained' within the condition of language. It is the persistence of these two confusions in Freudian and Lacanian thinking which has made it difficult to make much progress in understanding music as a mode of signification on its own terms. The conflation of these confusions (in which language comes to 'stand' for all signification, and the body is either reflected or constituted in its 'pre-linguistic' state through language) makes such an understanding virtually impossible. If music has a special relationship to the body in the order of its directness and power, and if the body, in one way or another, has to remain 'pre-linguistic' or 'sub-linguistic' rather than, perhaps, simply 'non-linguistic', then there is little hope for an adequate understanding of music. It is the work of Lacan which has proved the greatest obstacle in this regard.

Post-Lacanian work does not therefore represent any advance in theorizing music as a form of signification with its own specific characteristics and its own specific form of sociality. It is thus not difficult to understand the general character of statements made by poststructuralists on the subject of music. If music is traditionally and conventionally conceived as an 'extra-linguistic' and therefore 'non-linguistic' cultural form, then it cannot, as a matter of definition, approach to the condition of language, and so to the condition of the symbolic order. As Kristeva herself has observed, 'while music is a system of differences [presumably because the mother's body is already differentiated, "semiotized"], it is not a system of signs. Its constitutive elements do not have a signified' (1989, p. 309). Because, presumably, music has not advanced in any significant way beyond the condition of the *chora*, it remains close to the condition of a signifier in processes of *signifiance*. As Kristeva says, music 'takes us to the limit of the system of signs' (p. 309). Music, she continues, 'is a system of differences that is not a system that means something, as is the case with most of the structures of verbal language' (p. 309). Music therefore has a 'trans-linguistic status' (p. 309). As a consequence – as little more than a signifier *per se* – it is an ' "empty" sign' (p. 309).

As we intimated in chapter 2, Barthes's thinking on music was informed to an appreciable extent through the influence that Kristeva's theorization of language exerted on his notion of the text. The omission of music in Barthes's earlier work on myth and narrative is noticeable. Both are defined in universal terms which at the same time exclude music (or, at the very least, fail to mention it). Not only written discourse, said Barthes, 'but also photography, cinema, reporting, sports, shows, publicity, all these can serve as a support to mythical speech. Myth can be defined neither by its object nor by its material, for any material can be arbitrarily endowed with meaning' (1973, p. 110). Narrative, said Barthes,

is first and foremost a prodigious variety of genres, themselves distributed amongst different substances – as though any material were fit to receive man's stories. Able to be carried by articulated language, spoken or written, fixed or moving images, gestures ... narrative is present in myth, legend, fable, tale, novella, epic, history, tragedy, drama, comedy, mime, painting ... stained glass windows, cinema, comics, news item[s], conversation ... Narrative is international, transhistorical, transcultural; it is simply there, like life itself. (1977, p. 79)

During this period, Barthes perceived a tension between the actuality of meaning and the requirements of demystification. We constantly drift, said Barthes, 'between the object and its demystification, powerless to render its wholeness. For if we penetrate the object, we liberate it but we destroy it; and if we acknowledge its full weight, we respect it, but we restore it to a state which is still mystified' (1973, p. 159). The choice for Barthes at this time was clear. The requirement to demystify processes of ideology as implicit in the creation of cultural arte-facts was greater than the need the mythologist has to maintain a meaningful aesthetic relationship with those artefacts' sub-stantive meanings. The mythologist must as a consequence endure the pain that results from being 'condemned to metalan-guage' (p. 159).

The resolution of this tension and pain lay for Barthes in the notion of the text that he later developed under the influence of Kristeva. We must, he said, 'immerse ourselves in the signifier, plunging far away from the signified into the matter of the text' (1985a, p. 125). The struggle, he said: '... must be taken further now, it is not signs that must be cracked wide open – signifiers on one side, signifieds on the other – but the very idea of the sign ... It is Western discourse as such, in its foundations and elementary forms, that we must now try to break apart ... In the West ... we must wage a deadly serious and historic battle with the signified' (p. 85). Barthes's emphasis on the signifier in the battle against Western discourse was not, however, intended to result in a permanent state of 'non-meaning', the 'non-mean-ing' that Hebdige argues to be characteristic of punk culture. As Engh observes, 'the move to the field of the signifier is not to be understood ... as a valorization of nonmeaning against mean-ing'. Rather, she concludes, Barthes 'wants to loosen the fixity of meaning, to pluralize it' (Engh, 1993, p. 71). As a consequence, the text is a field 'where neither the subject nor the object of knowledge can remain untransformed' (p. 70). As Engh com-ments, Barthes 'appears to withdraw from his earlier commit-ment to ideology critique and to immerse himself in an individual *jouissance*' (p. 71).

It is within this context that music became crucially important for Barthes. 'Again and again', says Engh, 'Barthes, who seemed to observe a sort of taboo on music in his early, semiological work, turns to it as the unrepresentable figure par excellence of

the text' (1993, p. 73). By music, said Barthes, 'we better understand the Text as signifying . . . ' (1985c, p. 312). Barthes is not,
however, concerned with the music of musicology: 'let the first
semiology manage, if it can, with the system of notes, scales,
tones, chords, and rhythms; what we want to perceive and follow is the effervescence of the beats' (p. 312). He is concerned
with a realm of signifying practice which lies outside the world
of signs, meaning and signification, a world in which music,
interestingly enough, is taken to appeal directly to the body.
Music, said Barthes, is 'a field of *signifying* and not a system of
signs, the referent . . . is the body. The body passes into music
without any relay but the signifier' (p. 308). Understanding this
realm of signifying practice requires, said Barthes, 'a second
semiology, that of the body in a state of music' (p. 312).

Language for Barthes therefore retained its privileged position in the world of signs, meaning and signification. If language
(and a certain form of language at that) is privileged in this way,
then it is inevitable that music will be rendered as inferior by
such trends. In Barthes's opinion, music appeals to the body in a
manner which renders it non-linguistic. In thus eluding the
rational, music says nothing. Music, says Barthes, 'speaks, it
declaims, it redoubles its voice: *it speaks but says nothing*: because
as soon as it is musical, speech – or its instrumental substitute –
is no longer linguistic, but corporeal; it only says, and nothing
else: *my body is put into a state of speech: quasi parlando*' (p. 304).
Such statements do little but reproduce a hegemony of language, and of particular forms of language at that. There seem
to have been few ways within poststructuralist thought of prob-
lematizing and politicizing dominant linguistic discourses to the
point where the integrity either of alternative linguistic discourses or of 'non-linguistic' discourses can emerge in their own
terms *and in independence from biology*. Indeed, a symptomatic
reading of some of the dominant lines of thought within poststructuralism reveals how poststructuralist views of language
are exclusionary and unsympathetic to discourses and processes
of social mediation which do not fall easily within their preferred categories. As we have suggested, this tendency affects
even the work of those scholars who have sought to 'ground'
discourse in extralinguistic forces and dispositions, as
Middleton observes in the context of Barthes's writings on
music. 'Like other French poststructuralists who wanted to

ground discourse on extralinguistic forces and dispositions', argues Middleton, 'the later Barthes is open to the suspicion that "anything goes": that along with meaning, the category of critique is abandoned, leaving the field open to political quietism, untheorized spontaneity, or apolitical hedonism' (1990, pp. 266–7). Either we have language, discourse and reality, in other words, or we have the spontaneously unstructured world of ruptured, ecstatic *jouissance*, replete with luscious, Dionysian pleasures.

5

Music as a Medium in Sound

One purpose of this book is to understand the processes through which music affects people. In undertaking this task we have assumed that music is not an object, a 'thing' but, indeed, a set of processes, and a set of processes that inevitably involves people. As such, we have assumed also that music is an *inherently* social process. However, we have not conceptualized music's social condition in terms of extrinsic forces which 'determine' music and thus render it as little more than an expression of 'the social'. In dereifying 'the social', we have assumed that music's social condition is intrinsically musical and thus not reducible to other forms of sociality. If, therefore, the motor rhythms of the bass guitar riff in the Rolling Stones' song 'Satisfaction' are accepted as evidencing a particular form of sexuality as socially and culturally constituted, then we are *not* arguing that this form of sexuality is *first* constituted socially and culturally and *then* in some way imparted to a set of sounds whose formal, structural characteristics are suited to its acceptance or articulation. The question, then, is not that of understanding the relationship between 'music' and 'society'. It is rather that of understanding the constitutive features of music as a social process in relationship to other, equally non-reducible realms of social process. In terms of this position, the motor rhythms of 'Satisfaction' are themselves taken to constitute socially and culturally the form of sexuality in question through their very articulation. They are taken at the time of their articulation to occasion in individual subjects as socially and culturally constituted the structure of the feeling of this form of sexuality in a manner specific to themselves, a manner which cannot be reduced to the manner in which other, similar and comparable forms of sexuality are constituted socially and culturally through media other than music.

The notion of the structural homology seemed to show the way forward in understanding the character of this relationship while respecting music's specifically structural and abstract (which is to say, non-denotative) qualities. However, a critical omission in the application of this notion was a failure to lay a ground of connectedness between music and other social processes and, relatedly, to theorize the role of the individual (as socially constituted) in these processes (both musical and non-musical) *and* in the grounds and relations obtaining between them. In assuming that both music and individuals are socially constituted, our task consequently became that of understanding how, as different and relatively autonomous, yet complementary aspects of wider social processes, musical processes and processes of subjectivity relate to one another.

Considerable progress on this front has been made through our interrogation of French-language structuralism, semiology and psychoanalytic theory. The idea that music signifies through processes that are inherently structural in character has been lent credibility and strengthened through our consideration of the work of Saussure and especially that of Lévi-Strauss. As we saw, the notion of the structure as developed through the French-language tradition influenced considerably the notion of stylization as evidenced in the work of English subcultural theory. Indeed, by the late 1970s, English cultural studies had benefited in one way or another from the work of Lévi-Strauss, Barthes, Althusser, Lacan and Kristeva. However, in being interpellated within broad frameworks for social and cultural analysis drawn from the work of the Italian cultural theorist Antonio Gramsci (1971), the focus of attention in English cultural studies was placed more on theorizing the relative autonomy of different levels or moments of social and cultural formations in relation to one another than on thinking through processes of signification and subjectivity *within* this new and different context with the order of precision evidenced by French-language scholars. It was for this reason that the notion of the structural homology as it emerged from notions of stylization (and from the early work of Raymond Williams) manifested the ambiguities and ambivalences that we noted in chapter 2. The more precise notion of the structure to emerge from the French-language tradition together with the quite clear problematic indicated by Lévi-Strauss for understanding music goes a considerable way towards reducing those ambiguities and ambivalences.

Considerable progress has also been made on the question of how music, as a structural mode of signification, can impart its meanings to subjects. A direct material link between the sounds of music and the somatic pathways of the body has been posited in which the manner of connection circumvents the world of objects and the world of language. The positing of such a link is made possible through the work of Kristeva, building as it does on the work of Lacan and Freud, and, relatedly, through the later work of Barthes. In theorizing a world of sound 'outside' that of language, the work of Kristeva and Barthes goes to the limits of a semiology of language and to the brink of a semiology of music. That it cannot cross that boundary is a consequence of the tyranny of language. In their different ways, Lacan, Kristeva and Barthes attempted to understand and confront that tyranny. However, because they could not escape its influence in their own work, they ended up reproducing it, again in their different ways. In the case of Kristeva and Barthes, this resulted in the production of an ideal 'Other' to the world of the symbolic order of Western discourse.

This tendency to the production of an ideal 'Other' appears to have been understood by Barthes shortly before his death. 'In what was probably the last text he wrote', says Engh, 'Barthes seems to be moving toward a critique of the shared status of music, women, and the foreign in his work, all of which seem to offer access to a domain in which one can be exempted from the "social military service" of meaning' (Engh, 1993, p. 76). In the love of a foreign country, said Barthes, 'there is a kind of reverse racism: one is delighted by difference, one is tired of the Same, one exalts the Other' (Barthes, 1989, p. 297). As Engh points out, 'this racist love of a foreign country is linked ... to women and to music':

> Music has a privileged place because it can replace everything else: it is the degree zero of this system: according to the needs of enthusiasm, it replaces and signifies journeys, Women, the other arts, and in

a general manner any sensation. Its signifying status, precious above all others, is to produce effects without our having to inquire as to their causes, since their causes are inaccessible. Music constitutes a kind of *primal state* of pleasure: it produces a pleasure one always tries to recapture but never to explain; hence, it is the site of a pure effect ... an effect severed from and somehow purified of any explicative reason, i.e., ultimately, of any *responsible* reason. (Barthes, 1989, p. 299)

As Engh indicates, this seeming awareness of the production of 'Otherness' through music connects back to Barthes's earlier concern with the semiological analysis of the production of ideology through cultural artefacts. Both a 'first semiology' and a 'second semiology' seem required to understand music, therefore. As Engh concludes, both forms of semiology are relatively undeveloped in musicology (although, as we shall see, the work of Tagg has made *some* progress where a first semiology is concerned):

Immanent, at least, in this last work are the elements of a critique: the dawning recognition of a certain privileged irresponsibility enjoyed in the realm of the Other, and of the zero-degree status of music when it goes uninterrogated by ideology critique, by that 'first semiology' which Barthes had earlier dismissed. These final words in his opus implicitly return us to the early writings. Without dismissing or renouncing the insights and critical lessons of the second semiology, the necessity of the first semiology is invoked. Musicology is only beginning to elaborate that first semiology, to understand the ways that music's systems operate in relation to power and the social, and to analyze musics in their specific historical and discursive conditions. Neither will these analyses suffice without the second semiology, which understands, in a way that the generalizing discourses of ideology and history cannot, what is at the heart of the matter when we repeat 'I love it'. (Engh, 1993, pp. 77–8)

The development of both a first and second semiology in respect of music thus seems critical. This is a point to which we will return in chapters 7, 8 and 9. However, it is the development of a second semiology – or, to be more precise, a semiology distinct from the semiology which developed from the work of Saussure – which is fundamental to grasping the processes through which music affects people. As Middleton notes, 'semiotic theory emphasizes that connotation is built on a prior system of denotation, it is *secondary*' (1990, p. 220). While, with respect to language and images, a first semiology can serve to analyse meanings at the level of both the denotative (primary signification) and the connotative (secondary signification) – with a second semiology indicating simply the state of 'Otherness' to which literary and artistic work grounded in such media can aspire – with *music* a second semiology is fundamental to grasping the processes through which music articulates significance and affect in a purely structural and abstract (which is to say, non-denotative) manner. With music, a first semiology can, as we shall see, only function at the level of the connotative or of secondary signification, and then only with limited success if not grounded appropriately in a second semiology.

The development of this second semiology is thus critical to our project. However, this semiology cannot be developed independently of an understanding of how music functions as a structure, any more than Saussure's semiology can be understood independently of *his* notion of structure in language. In the same way that the arbitrary functioning of the signifier as the point for the invocation of meaning can only be understood in terms of the principle of difference according to which sounds are ordered within the structure of a language, so the particular functioning of sounds in music in the order of their material connectedness to the body will only be able to be understood in terms of the principle according to which sounds are ordered within the structure of music.

If we are to take the direction seemingly indicated by Barthes towards the end of his life, and the direction indicated by Lévi-Strauss – if, in other words, we are to cross the boundary which separates the limits of a semiology of language from the beginnings of a semiology of music – then music will have to be conceived of as moving beyond the state of fundamental, asemantic difference as evidenced in the *chora* and, as Gorbman and Noy remind us, as developing a full set of formal yet asemantic characteristics in the world of waking consciousness. Affect and the asemantic would thus take their place equally alongside the linguistic and the cognitive in the world of the conscious. It is this that requires the development of a second semiology beyond the state of pure 'Otherness' envisaged by Barthes. In this context, it is interesting to observe that even poststructuralists are forced to admit that music signifies in a manner different from language, even if that manner rests ultimately upon the manner of linguistic signification. As Kristeva observes, 'verbal language and music are both realized by utilizing the same material (sound) and by acting on the same receptive organs' (1989, p. 309). The manner in which Kristeva casts music in an inferior mould to language rests, however – and necessarily so – on an understanding that sounds in music do *not* signify in the same way as they do in language. 'While the two signifying systems are organized according to the principle of the *difference* of their components', she says, 'this difference is not of the same order in verbal language as it is in music' (p. 309). This is a curious yet suggestive statement given Kristeva's other observations that 'while music is a system of differences, it is not a system of signs' and that, as a consequence, it 'is a system of differences that is not a system that means something'.

This latter conclusion can only be reached if the notion of difference is equated unexceptionally with that of opposition in terms of which the notion of difference in language is customarily operationalized (it is because difference in language – that is, the difference between language's sounds – is based on opposition that units of meaning such as phonemes can be reliably and consistently identified). This is an equation to which Kristeva appears to subscribe, and it is for this reason that her notion of a different order of differences in music has to remain undeveloped. However, it is possible to conceive of a 'different order of differences' for music. The necessity of undertaking this task is, indeed, confirmed by problems encountered in identifying meaningful units of sound in music. As Middleton has observed, this project of establishing clear and consistent units of difference in music is fraught with difficulties. 'The lack of an agreed formal method of segmentation', he says, 'does leave many obscurities unquestioned':

> For example, spectrographic analysis shows that the concept of a 'note' is actually an imposition on the dynamic, processual quality of all sound; and even if we accept the widespread existence of what has been called *abstraction notale* ... – that is, a culturally acquired scalar model into which listeners fit all sounds, even when they are pitch-mobile or slightly divergent from recognized pitch steps – this does not of itself mean that 'notes' are of phonemic status and independence, always and in all music, nor does it rule out the possibility of dialectical interplay, of phonemic significance, between abstracted notes and subsegmental and suprasegmental features. (1990, p. 178)

The need for another method of analysis in relationship to music becomes clear. This method does not need to replace those based on difference, as we shall see. It does, however, need to add to them in some crucial and *fundamental* ways if music is to be analysed on its own terms. The way forward in this enterprise was indicated in the 1960s when Ruwet, as Middleton notes, 'developed an analytical method based on the concept of "equivalence" ' (p. 183). Ruwet's method drew on Roman Jakobson's description of poetry, in which similar sonic items are seen to be combined into a syntagmatic string rather than forming a basis for the paradigmatic selection of just one item, as in 'language'. It is this notion of a syntagmatic string of similar terms which is well suited to analysing repetition and variation or transformation in music. In this way, comments Middleton, 'relationships of equivalence *across* segments seem to be at least as important as distinctions marking segment boundaries.' This approach to the semiological analysis of music also 'helps to account for the difficulties of segmentation in music ... as well as the difficulty of associating distinct contributions to meaning with minimal units' (Middleton, 1990, p. 183).

The question of 'relationships of equivalence *across* segments' is one to which we will return. However, as Middleton notes, there are some problems with this method of analysis: 'which parameters are to be regarded as pertinent and on what grounds? What are the criteria for a judgement that two entities are sufficiently similar to be considered equivalent?' (1990, p. 183). Such questions, says Middleton, 'must be referred to *listeners*, for the answers depend on what is heard and how it is heard' (p. 188). In this sense, concludes Middleton, 'the method's "objectivity" is not only limited (for initial assumptions *are* made, as Ruwet himself recognizes) but limiting' (p. 188). It is, of course, listeners who likewise decide which units and configurations of sound are meaningful in language. However, the principle of difference in opposition, together with the seeming consistency with which similar sounds are associated with similar meanings, has resulted in the possibility of semiological analyses of language being able to decontextualize language from the social and cultural contexts in which it is used without harm to the explanatory power of the analyses. Analyses of language carried out in this fashion seem to retain a high degree of 'objectivity'. This is a point to which we will return.

Difficulties of method notwithstanding, Ruwet's emphasis on the notion of equivalence in analysing music – his emphasis on 'relationships of equivalence *across* segments' – keeps alive Lévi-Strauss's intuition of music as 'pure structure'. This 'pure structure' does not, however, emanate from structures grounded in systems of linguistic difference as demarcated through opposition. It aspires to the condition of differences and similarities *as articulated structurally between sonic phenomena* recognized and identified by people as being of *asemantic* musical significance. Our task therefore becomes that of understanding how music can be considered to be both structured and structuring as a signifying process distinct from language. Yet our task is more than that. For once we have understood how music functions as a structure there remains the question – also kept alive through Ruwet's work – of how, precisely, these structures interact with people.

However, this route of understanding is not just one-way. As we saw in discussing Saussure's work, the semiological and the structural are bound up with one another in a manner which militates against a hierarchy of understanding. As a consequence, it is as necessary to understand music's 'semiological moment' to understand musical structures as it is to understand musical structures to understand what it is that is conveyed *through* this semiological moment. If we are to understand the character of the sounds of music acting as a structure, in other words, then *our* point of entry, *our* point of interrogation cannot be anything other than the sounds of music as they impact on us and *reveal* musical structures to us. A first step in grasping the specific characteristics of musical structures is as a consequence to concentrate on this semiological moment. Further, if we are in this way to access the manner in which musical structures are constituted, then we need to distinguish clearly between the conditions of primary and secondary signification. That is, we need to distinguish clearly between those elements in music which can be analysed with a degree of legitimacy using a first semiology at the level of connotation, and those which 'act asemantically'. It is in establishing a distinction between these elements and exploring the manner in which they relate to one another that we can establish more clearly the need for the second semiology that is yet to be developed. It is understanding the characteristic mode of operation of these 'asemantic' elements as they act through music's own semiological moment that in turn will lead us to an understanding of how sounds in music act as structures.

Primary Signification and Secondary Signification

The distinction we are drawing here between two levels of signification in music has been discussed extensively by Middleton in *Studying Popular Music* (1990). Middleton draws a distinction, on the one hand, between syntactical and semantic analysis, and, on the other, between primary and secondary signification. As we have noted, the syntactic in music has to do with the manner in which individual notes relate to one another melodically, harmonically and rhythmically. The semantic has to do with connotative impressions. An example of such an impression might be that of the qualities of 'oceanness' as customarily experienced in hearing Debussy's *La Mer*. While these distinctions between the structural and the semantic on the one hand, and primary and secondary signification on the other, are not identical, they are closely related. As Middleton observes, 'all . . . conceptions of primary signification . . . have a common thread: content is defined through its *structure*, which is closely tied to the syntactic form' (1990, p. 222). Because of the compelling desire to interpret social and cultural meanings in popular music, the level of primary signification and, more locally, syntactical analysis has largely been ignored in popular music studies, so that 'much popular music analysis, commentary and criticism is marked by a "rush to interpretation", centring usually on the area of *connotation*: the feelings, associations, evocations and ideas aroused in listeners by songs' (Middleton, 1990, p. 220). This is in contrast to more conventional music theory and music analysis, where the focus has been on 'primary signification' and syntactical analysis to the exclusion of virtually all else, including the analysis of social and cultural meanings.

An example of popular music analysis which concentrates on secondary signification, the semantic and the connotative at the expense of primary signification is to be found in the work of

Tagg. Tagg's method is drawn from the field of linguistics, which he sees as fertile ground for musical analysis. The field of linguistics has identified the phoneme as the smallest unit of sound which allows one utterance to be distinguished from another, and the morpheme as the smallest unit of sound having meaning. Tagg has developed parallel concepts for the analysis of music. Drawing on Seeger (1977, p. 76), he developed the concept of the museme. This he equates to the morpheme in language. In the same way that the morpheme in language depends on phonemes, the museme depends on 'musical phonemes' or 'basic *elements* (*not units*) of musical expression' (Tagg, 1979, p. 71). Tagg identifies musemes through a process he terms 'interobjective comparison'. This process involves the identification and isolation of an element of musical expression in one piece of music and its comparison to other, highly similar elements in 'other music in a relevant style and with similar functions'. This process reveals a 'consistency of sound events between two or more pieces of music' and is achieved by 'describing music by means of other music' (1982, p. 49). Tagg then creates a hypothesis of meaning – 'affectual meaning in associative verbal form' (p. 50) – for a museme. This hypothesis is subsequently tested through a process of hypothetical substitution. This process of hypothetical substitution or commutation involves the alteration of one element of musical expression within a museme in order to corroborate or falsify 'the affectual meaning in associative verbal form'. Tagg goes on to explain how musemes can form the basis of a complete 'sound':

> Having established extramusical 'meaning' at the micro level, one should proceed to the explanation of the ways musemes are combined, simultaneously and successively. Unlike verbal language, where complexities of affective association can generally only be expressed through a combination of denotation and connotation, music can express such complexities through simultaneously heard sets of musemes. Several separately analysable musemes are combined to form what the listener experiences as an integral sound entity. Such 'museme stacks' can be seen as a vertical cross-section through an imaginary score ... In popular music, museme stacks can often be found to correspond to the concept of 'sound'. (1982, p. 53)

There can be little doubt that Tagg's analyses have provided important insights into meaning in different kinds of music (see, for example, Tagg, 1979, 1987 and 1991). Tagg's analyses of the theme from the television show *Kojak* (1979) and the ABBA hit song 'Fernando the Flute' (1991) are extensive and sophisticated, and it is not possible to do them justice by giving brief examples of the kinds of conclusions he reaches. It is nevertheless possible to *illustrate* the character of Tagg's method by referring to his conclusions concerning the *Kojak* theme. Tagg argues that the theme's 'basic compositional technique is melody/accompaniment (figure/ground, individual/environment)'. The melody, 'played on heroic French horns *à* 4', consists of musemes expressing 'calls to attention and action upwards, onwards and outwards, virile and energetic [and] strong, swaying, confident motion which propels the action into the broad, bold confidence of virile, heroic, martial action'. The accompaniment consists of musemes expressing 'the atmosphere of a large American city, its subculture and aspects of unrest, unquiet, threat, danger and jerky, jabbing unpredictability, [and] general, constant, bustling activity, agitated and insistent but positive, shimmering and luminous (bright)' (1979, p. 230). The *Kojak* theme, then:

> consists basically of the development of a relationship between figure and ground. The male individual starts off as an ambiguous heroic and villainous figure on an unclear footing with an affectively equally ambiguous environment. He is soon to become a clearly heroic figure who dominates his positive/negative and consistently exciting, bustling environment for some time before it in turn dominates him, increasing the threatening side of this bustling excitement. After this, the male individual then dominates his ambiguous environment. He re-emerges from his situation as 'underdog' to conquer the environmental threat and to be hailed by his environment as its master. In the last three seconds of the piece the intensity of the hostile aspects of the environment increases once again. (Tagg, 1979, p. 231)

Tagg's conclusions regarding 'Fernando the Flute' evidence a similar approach to analysing affect in music. They are also reminiscent of Lévi-Strauss's structural method of analysing myths (Lévi-Strauss, 1972) in that 'Fernando' is seen as attempting to resolve magically two opposed and ultimately irreconcilable tendencies. In this way, Tagg's analysis of 'Fernando' is seen to provide an example of how music can, in Lévi-Strauss's words, substitute 'for experience and [produce] the pleasurable illusion that contradictions can be overcome'. One can see 'Fernando', says Tagg:

as a natural and sincere attempt to correlate two conflicting types of affective experience facing the citizen of Western Europe. On the one hand are all the feelings of disgust, distress and anger caused by viewing, reading or hearing second hand about all the injustice, terror, misery, starvation and oppression in the world. Most people here see themselves, correctly or incorrectly, living in a state of material security in that no widespread starvation or totally overt legalised terror seems to afflict us for the time being. The gap between the perception of these two worlds, symbolised in *Fernando* by the quena flutes versus soft disco backing, by the irregular versus regular periodicity, by the 'there-and-then' versus the 'here-and-now', by the 'difficult' versus 'easy' listening, by the verbal description of fear, guns, fighting, etc. versus the reminiscing of the chorus, by the 'sincere involvement' versus the 'relaxation' etc. is a real problem of conscience and a great cause of anxiety to many. How can this conflict of experiences be treated, expressed? It is possible that Abba, by the very act of actually trying to express something which brings 'there' and 'here' in one song, have actually contributed towards a development in people's sensitivity towards the individual and global aspects of the problem. (Tagg, 1991, p. 138)

However, despite the insights that this kind of analysis provides, it would be fair to comment that Tagg chooses to analyse musical works which favour his mode of analysis. Firstly, the television, film and popular music analysed can be situated within the affective parameters established in European 'art' music of the nineteenth and twentieth centuries, affective parameters subsequently fixed and codified by Hollywood. Because of its tendency to locate the meanings of twentieth-century popular music in an earlier and significantly different tradition, Tagg's method needs to be interrogated from a somewhat wider perspective. Secondly, the music Tagg analyses is influenced strongly by verbal and visual denotation. Not only is the repertory of nineteenth- and twentieth-century European 'art' music 'particularly rich in deliberately intended extramusical meanings and accompanying verbal and visual signals' (Middleton, 1990, p. 234). The method of analysis itself is 'heavily dependent on orientations provided by accompanying extramusical aspects of the message – on "reconstitutions" of intentions discovered in lyrics, programmatic elements (such as titles) and visual images' (Middleton, 1990, p. 233). As Middleton concludes,

It would be nonsensical to suggest that this is illegitimate: clearly, words and images are part of the total message in these cases; nevertheless, complete correlation is *purely speculative*. Moreover, a great many popular songs do not possess associated visual images and have lyrics with much less specific, less concrete content ... Tagg has not yet applied his analytic technique to a pop recording with relatively bland, unimportant or 'musicalized' lyrics. The less precise and the less suggestive the words, the harder it becomes to tie particular connotations to the music. (1990, pp. 233–4, our italics)

There are, moreover, two problems of a theoretical as opposed to a methodological character with Tagg's approach. They both relate, in one way or another, to the question of the embeddedness of processes of secondary signification in those of primary signification, and the way in which the syntactical and the structural may give rise to the semantic and connotative in music. Firstly, as we have seen, it is not possible to isolate musemes and the basic elements of musical expression which contribute to them in the same, consistent manner in which it is possible to isolate phonemes and morphemes in language. It is for these reasons that Tagg uses the concept of the museme in a flexible way. Secondly, Tagg appears to understand TV themes and mainstream popular music as continuing to have meaning within the ambit of late nineteenth- and early twentieth-century 'classical' music. This understanding remains arguably more valid for TV themes than it does for popular music. This notwithstanding, the process of isolation is in itself potentially distortive, involving as it does the replacement of the original, syntactical and structural context of primary signification in an actual piece of music with that of the rather more arbitrarily derived context of semantic analysis. As we shall see, it is more than likely that a piece of music (or even a sequence of pieces, as with popular songs played on the radio) not only provides an important, *actual* context for all levels of signification occurring within it that makes the isolation of individual constellations of sonic events of questionable legitimacy, but also in itself is implicated in a *virtual* fashion in all levels and moments of signification simultaneously. It is therefore questionable how valid it is to interpret musemes in isolation. Such interpretation tends to assume a consistency of effects for 'musemes' which varying contexts for the articulation of meaning and affect in music may not support (Middleton, 1990).

The problem with Tagg's analytic method, then, lies not so much in what it can say (although, as Middleton rightly notes, problems of distortion remain), as in what it *cannot* and therefore *does not* say. As Middleton concludes, 'While Tagg is admittedly strong on the importance of syntactic *process*, it remains true that his method is built, first and foremost, on the interpretation of segmented elements and units and that in the assessment of how these elements and units then cohere a significant role is played by processes of aggregation' (1990, p. 234). The silences not only privilege associative verbal and visual forms in analysing musical meaning, therefore, but, in arising from a privileging of methods derived from linguistic analysis, once again reproduce the hegemony of language and render music – as *music* – a second-class citizen. It therefore becomes necessary to confront the issue of primary signification *in music*.

Music as a Structured and Structuring Medium

In confronting this issue, it is helpful to recall two principles established earlier. The first is that our primary task has become that of understanding how, as different and relatively autonomous, yet complementary aspects of wider social processes, musical processes and processes of subjectivity relate to one another. The second is that we have refused to accede to the argument that sounds in music function in the same manner as sounds in language, that is, through a connection of a purely arbitrary character between the signifier (the 'evidence' of language acting as a structure) and the signified (the 'contribution' of the subject as constituted socially). The only insight that up to this point we retain in terms of understanding how sounds and subjects might interact in a manner other than the arbitrary is that drawn from the notion of the structural homology. We would as a consequence agree with Middleton that it is worth retaining 'the notion of the homology in a qualified form' (1990, p. 10), a form which in our case will benefit from previous discussions of the French-language tradition of structuralism, semiology and psychoanalytic theory, and the advantages and disadvantages that can be discerned therein for an understanding of music. A first step in developing this qualified form of the homology is thus to consider how its basic premise, that of a parallelism of structures between two sets of processes, can usefully be applied to the relationship obtaining between musical processes on the one hand and processes of subjectivity on the other.

For the sounds of music to engage in primary signification (and, through that, secondary or connotative signification) it can be argued that there must exist some relationship of inherent organization between the sounds of music and individual yet socially constituted states of awareness as elements of signification. It is to be noted that these states of awareness must *in any case* take on a certain character that derives from the particular and necessary relation they have to the material world if they are to act successfully as elements of signification in music. Elements of signification as articulated through music cannot be grounded *directly* in, or generalized *directly* from, the objects, events, qualities and processes of the material world. If they were, they would act as signifieds in relation to signifiers, and music would be no different from language, which it clearly is. Elements of signification must therefore stand in an *indirect* relationship to these objects, events, qualities and processes if they *are* to be capable of encapsulating the qualities of the *structures* and *states* of the human world: structures and states for which the objects, events, qualities and processes presented by the material world can act only as demarcators and agents of articulation.

The work of Bierwisch explores the possibility of the existence of an homology or form of inherent organization between the sounds of music and forms of individual awareness. Bierwisch argues that music engages in a quite specific mode of articulation based on the concept of analogous encoding. In order to develop this concept further, Bierwisch draws an important distinction between the logical form as the meaning of linguistic signs and the gesticulatory form as the meaning of musical signs. For Bierwisch, 'the central category of the logical form is the proposition' (1979, p. 50). A proposition is 'the conceptual representation of a (real or fictitious) fact' (p. 50). Logical forms, continues Bierwisch, 'have in common with identified facts only a logical structure'. As a consequence, 'logical forms ... are without dimensions' (p. 51). On the other hand, 'the structure for which I suggest the term "gesticulatory form" is related to the entirety of emotional, affective and motivational states and processes' (p. 53). Bierwisch's thinking on the gesticulatory form has something in common with the notions of impulses (energies and drives) and gestures (vocal and kinetic) typical respectively of post-Freudian and post-Lacanian pronouncements on music. The *gesture* for Bierwisch becomes to the gesticulatory form what the proposition is to the logical form. It is, so to speak, 'the emotional sense of a complex of physiological states or processes' (p. 55). However, the basis of the relationship between the proposition and the cognitive structures and processes it evokes on the one hand, and the basis of the relationship between the gesture and the emotional, affective and motivational states it evokes on the other, are quite different, as Bierwisch makes clear:

> While a proposition has, so to speak, an extensionless logical structure whose projection onto the temporally organized forms of linguistic signs remains more or less external in nature, a gesture is as such of a temporal nature. *It is the structure of a state or process and does not just replace it.* A proposition can represent facts with any temporal structure and temporal classification you like, but in an indirect and abstract manner. A gesture, on the other hand, is directly and in and of itself a temporally structured pattern. (1979, p. 55, our italics).

Unlike propositions, which are connected in a logical and therefore linear manner, gestures must be capable of articulating emotional, affective and motivational states and processes that are simultaneously multidimensional. Bierwisch's description of gestures is in this sense reminiscent of Ruwet's emphasis on 'relationships of equivalence *across* segments' in music, and of Middleton's identification of the possibility of relations between subsegmental, segmental and suprasegmental features. It is this difference to language which explains the problems (identified by Feld) many people experience in expressing through language their musical experiences. A gesture, therefore: 'can be subdivided in itself'. Further 'a basic gesture might be overlapped by modifying gestures or might be superseded temporarily'. To put it simply, concludes Bierwisch, 'propositions are logically connected, gestures are temporally connected' (1979, p. 56). As a consequence, 'the basic principle which turns gesticulatory forms into the meanings of musical signs is clearly that of analogous encoding.' Movement of pitch thus 'represents movement in emotions through something like an abstract "space in motion" which can be grasped through its synaesthetic relatedness to the physical field of movement, to its characteristics of gravitational force, distance and height' (p. 56).

It will not do, therefore, to characterize music in a negative sense in terms of what it is not. Music for Bierwisch is neither a secondary symptom or manifestation of language in its 'difference' from language. Nor, in its difference, is it an ontological or historical precursor awaiting interpellation in language to be given meaning and sense. The 'tightness' in the relations between music and individual awareness for which Bierwisch is arguing has indeed led some writers to think of music as more fundamental to human development, prefiguring language in the same way that Piaget claims metaphor to precede signs (1971, pp. 106–19). Middleton, for example, has argued that analogy

> may be just as deep a mental principle as binarism – or deeper. As part of the human search for similarity and mutuality, it may go back ontogenetically before the childhood stages of learning the manipulation of difference to an infantile and even foetal involvement in unity with the maternal and metamaternal environment. Piaget ... proposes a system of developmental *levels* in the evolution of our mental representational processes, with *metaphor* (ruled by analogy and an iconic relationship between signifier and signified) preceding sign (ruled by difference and a conventionalised relationship between signifier and signified). He insists on a 'pre-logical' level, prior to explicit logical systems and governed by 'participation', that is, by analogical fusion of the individual in the generic. So the importance of analogy and equivalence in music – especially striking in popular music – may have deep roots. (1990, p. 216)

However, analogy and music for Bierwisch cannot in this way be 'pre-logical' and therefore 'pre-linguistic'. Bierwisch argues that language and music developed *simultaneously* from pre-human communication in such a way as to make possible the representation of cognitive structures on the part of language and the representation or evocation of emotional and affective structures on the part of music. It is for this reason that 'it is not sufficient to say what musical meanings are not'. Positive characterizations of music must begin by considering, says Bierwisch, 'that music and language became differentiated out of pre-human communication (although, to be sure, through complex and complicated intermediary stages)' (1979, p. 30).

The German musicologist Georg Knepler develops further

this argument that language and music developed from pre-human communication, and in so doing provides another account of the manner in which musical processes and processes of subjectivity can be considered to manifest a relationship that is based on analogy. According to Knepler, the acoustical behaviour of animals evokes, in a direct and substantially unmediated manner, particular orders of relationships existing inescapably in the here-and-now which are experienced by individuals as powerful and all-encompassing states incapable of significant symbolic distancing or control. Such behaviour, continues Knepler, spilled over into early human societies. 'It could be said', he says, 'that the acoustic systems of animals ... must have been followed by a phase in which people acquired language and music' (1977, p. 72). While we do not subscribe to the implications of continuous historical development evident in Knepler's arguments, the idea that the direct and substantially unmediated affective power evidenced and articulated through the acoustical behaviour of animals is folded into the logics of many of the world's musical systems seems instructive in understanding the ways in which the presence of sound in music might differ from its presence in animal communication and, indeed, in language. Knepler argues that music may thus be conceived as having two levels of codification. One is very old, and has to do with what Knepler terms the 'tuning elements' (*Einstimmungselemente*) of the acoustic behaviour of animals – the sonic phenomena through which animals are 'in tune' with their environment, each other and their mutual affective states. The other has to do with a development that is analogous to, but *not* identical with, the development of language:

> In music are integrated into one another *modi operandi* which emerged originally in quintessentially different circumstances. It is *one* thing if living beings are tuning into one another through acoustical utterances; it is another if they produce through acoustical utterances a framework for cognitive statements. This observation has far-reaching implications: first of all, it makes both possible and necessary the surmounting of all one-dimensional notions about the genesis and functioning of music. Music does not have one root. It did not emerge from 'the cry', neither from 'language', nor from the exigencies of 'labour' ... Music has at least two roots apart from the practical exigencies through which it was created. The origins of acoustic elements through which beings tune into one another reach

back to pre-history ... to pre-linguistic, pre-musical and pre-human times; the origins of the elements of music which are analogous to language reach back to the relatively recent times of the initial history of people. (Knepler, 1977, pp. 125–6)

Knepler's concept of 'tuning element' suggests that there exists an element of necessity between the inherent sonic qualities of particular instances of acoustic behaviour in animals and the logic of the order of the animals' relationships to each other and the material environment experienced internally and somatically as powerful and all-encompassing affective states. It will be argued that the qualities of 'non-linguistic' sounds folded by people into musical utterances display an element of necessity in their evidencing and evocation of an order of human relationships mediated somatically and experienced as powerful and encompassing internal affective states. Such a possibility does not however require that meaning or significance in music be reduced to the level of the vocal evidencing and evocation of internal affective states experienced in a directly somatic and relatively unmediated manner, even when these states and their evocation through sound are folded into the logic of a particular musical system.

If music, as a medium of signification, evokes in a concrete, direct but *mediated* manner the structures of the human world and the states of being that flow from them and sustain them, then it does so in a manner which is capable of calling forth, in Knepler's terminology, both 'biogenic' and 'logogenic' elements. While biogenic elements are appropriate especially for 'tuning' – the function of empathetic, homologous and immediate evocation – and logogenic elements for that which Langer has referred to as 'logical expression', both can influence each other and become involved in each other's functions:

If biogenic elements are appropriate particularly for the function of tuning (and without denying the potential for the making of statements), logogenic elements make themselves available in a multiple way for the making of statements (without denying the potential for 'tuning') ... Through the thousands of years of music history, what could be referred to as two relatively closed and partial systems of music (biogenic and logogenic) become engaged in multiple sets of inter-relationships. Biogenic elements can be semanticized; logogenic elements, on the other hand, can be subsumed within *modi operandi* which are normal for biogenic elements. (Knepler, 1977, p. 125)

It would therefore appear that the sounds of music are not *merely* somatic in their functioning (as the poststructuralist arguments of scholars such as Kristeva and Barthes have heavily implied). As Langer has argued, while the subject matter of music 'is the same as that of "self-expression", and its symbols borrowed, upon occasion, from the realm of expressive symptoms ... the borrowed suggestive elements are *formalized*, and the subject-matter "distanced" in an artistic perspective' (1942, p. 222). Neither, in the opinion of Knepler, Bierwisch nor, indeed, Langer, does music represent nothing more than a special and therefore inferior case of language. The visceral realities of sounds as 'signifiers' in music are *themselves* of relevance, materially, culturally and subjectively. Since it can be argued that biological materiality itself forms a dialectically efficacious pathway of social, cultural and biographical mediation, these realities can be understood as constituting just as integral a part of the complex web of social, cultural and biographical processes as any other form of experience (Giles and Shepherd, 1988, p. 121). The biogenic elements in music are thus called forth, subsumed, embedded, implicated and articulated in the homologous *and symbolic* relations taken to obtain between music as sounds and states of awareness as elements of signification.

The position we are advancing seems to be consistent with that advanced by Volek on the semiotics of music. For Volek, the semiotics of music 'has of necessity to deal essentially with the structural iconicity of musical works' (1981, p. 246). It is this principle of structural iconicity, encompassing as it does the concept both of the rules of the *dynamic combination* of signs (that is to say, the syntactical dimensions of music) and of the *practical functioning* of signs (that is to say, the processual and textural dimensions), that becomes for Volek the defining, although not exclusive, characteristic of music. Although Volek's use of the term 'sign' seems at times to vacillate uneasily between the traditional concept of 'signifier' and what we later refer to as the sonic 'medium' in music, we would agree with his basic insight that 'musical structures are understood as "basic signs in the semiological world of music", in terms both of their syntagmatic processuality and of their paradigmatic realm of potentialities.' It seems useful, says Volek, 'to call such signs and *only* such signs musical signs' (1981, p. 248).

The position we are developing may seem problematic in that, for any sounds to provide a basis for signification as socially constructed, there must remain the possibility for the social negotiation of meaning through the medium of those sounds. There cannot, in other words, be the kind of one-to-one or essential relationship in music between sounds and states of awareness as elements of signification that might seem to be suggested through the character of the homology being claimed here as in some way fundamental to music. The conceptual space must be created for a certain looseness or slippage between sounds and states of awareness if people are to be capable of negotiating the construction of meaning *in relation* to music's sounds. In understanding the importance of looseness or slippage, it is helpful to consider two other, possible conditions of relatedness between the sounds of music and music's meanings. It might, for example, be assumed (and this assumption is close to the dominant trend in musicology) that the sounds of music somehow contain within them meanings which are then instilled or articulated in listeners in a direct and mechanical fashion. *In this sense*, the sounds would demonstrate a technology or instrumentality of articulation. This position is clearly incompatible with the one we are developing. However, it might also be assumed that – while the sounds of music do not contain meanings within them, and cannot therefore instil or articulate meanings in listeners – any particular configuration of sounds in music could only call forth from listeners or instigate in them the construction of *one* possible meaning or set of meanings. While meanings would remain socially negotiable between people in the sense that such meanings (*different* possible meanings, that is) could be articulated musically through *different* possible sounds (sounds or sets of sounds nonetheless 'retaining' only one possible set of meanings), it would remain the case that meanings were fixed in the condition of their relatedness to the sounds of music, and that the sounds of music were as a consequence produced in a direct and mechanical way by such meanings. If the social negotiation of meaning through the *medium* of music's sounds is to remain a possibility conceptually, therefore, it must remain the case that sounds do not determine meanings, and that, conversely, meanings do not determine sounds. It is for this reason that the looseness and slippage between sounds and states of awareness must, conceptually, remain a condition of the position we are developing.

The basic concept we wish to propose in terms of which sounds in music may be thought of as offering up a structured and structuring ground for a construction of meaning that nonetheless remains socially negotiable is that of the 'medium' (Wicke, 1989 and 1990b). The term 'medium' is used here in a very specific sense drawn from the world of science: to mean an agent or a material substance in which a physical or chemical process takes place, but which remains unaffected by the process. As applied to an understanding of music, the concept of the medium has two distinguishing characteristics. Firstly, it conceptualizes the use of sounds in music as being, indeed, of a structural nature, both 'internally' and 'externally'. Secondly, while the medium conceptualizes sounds in music as being in this way structured and structuring, it in no way assigns an *agency of achieved meaning* (and, *in this sense*, an agency of meaning construction) to them. It is as a consequence of this that we believe the concept of the medium to differ significantly from that of Nattiez's *niveau neutre*. We would argue that music can only be understood to display a *niveau neutre* in the sense of shaping the material grounds and potentials for meaning construction, not the processes of meaning construction themselves.

It is because of this second characteristic that the concept of the medium allows space within which the construction of meanings through music's sounds can be understood as being socially negotiated but *not* arbitrary. Just as the characteristics of the medium in a physical or chemical process determine the kind of processes possible within it without determining their character, the characteristics of the medium of music are of decisive importance for the *kind* of cultural processes that may be realized through it. However, the characteristics of the sounds as medium cannot determine the characteristics of the cultural processes they make possible. As a consequence, they cannot determine meanings. This notwithstanding, it is *equally* important to bear in mind that the specific form of music as a medium does *not* result from the music being an object of appropriation of the external world and external reality, but is itself an agent which *mediates* this process of appropriation in a culture-specific form. As a structured and structuring medium for – rather than agent of – the construction of meanings, the sounds of music both restrict and facilitate the range of meanings that in any instance can be constructed through them.

The Technology of Articulation

The inherently *structural* character of sounds as the material medium of music distinguishes (*inter alia*) the concept of the 'medium' from that of the 'signifier'. The concept of the 'signifier' is, we would argue, inappropriate in approaching questions of signification in music. Its use, together with the use of related concepts such as 'signified', 'phoneme' ('musical phonemes') and 'morpheme' ('museme') in distinguishing and segmenting sounds into individual 'units' of meaning can only give rise to the kind of problems identified in Tagg's work. Because the medium of sound in music *is* implicated through its 'internal' and 'external' *structural* characteristics in processes of meaning construction, it interpellates or extends itself into these processes in a manner in which sounds in language do not (or, to put it more accurately, do not have to in order to facilitate processes of meaning construction). This act of interpellation or extension necessarily involves the inherent material qualities of sounds, qualities that display characteristics of 'extension' or 'dimension'. Sounds in music thus have implications beyond their brute presence in music in a way that sounds in language do not, although sounds *in* language do display similar characteristics of extension or dimension. It is at this point that a distinction drawn by Bierwisch between a proposition, which has 'an extensionless logical structure whose projection onto the temporally organized forms of linguistic signs remains more or less external in nature' and a gesture, which 'is the structure of a state or process and does not just replace it' becomes relevant. The analogic coding by music of what Bierwisch calls the gesticulatory form – or logical structure of gestures – in other words requires that the sounds of music deploy themselves in a manner directly analogous to the characteristics of extension evident in the gesticulatory form.

Sounds acting as a medium thus become *materially* involved in calling forth from people elements of signification in a manner in which sounds as signifiers do not. What is involved here

is more than the level of association implicit in the arbitrary connection of signifier and signified. It is not simply the case that
there is an association, a parallelism of structures operating
between sounds as a medium and states of awareness as elements of signification. There is rather a *technology of articulation*
(which does not, however, imply an immanence of meaning in
the sounds of music or a fixed, one-to-one relationship between
sounds and meanings). To be sure, sounds recognized as signifiers cannot help, within established discourses of meaning, but
call forth a response. This response may or may not evidence a
high degree of affectivity. However, whatever that degree may
be, it is not related directly or by necessity to the characteristics
of the sounds of the signifiers. By contrast, while sounds recognized as a medium do *not* act to create meanings or states in the
sense that they determine their character, they nonetheless cannot help but call forth a response that *is* affective, and affective
to a degree and in a manner related to the characteristics of the
sounds of the medium. As Bierwisch has observed, 'a sound
pattern which is supposed to show excitement has to be excited.
On the other hand, the sentence, "He is excited" contains neither
more nor less excitement than the sentence, "He is not excited",
although it is saying the opposite' (1979, p. 62). This characteristic of signification through music is difficult to conceive independently of a technology, which is to say, an instrumentality of
articulation. We have moved, it would seem, from the realm
of homology, of Bierwisch's analogy and Knepler's combination
of the biogenic and logogenic, to Volek's iconicity.

     This realization creates a requirement, namely, that we
engage in an explanation of the role played by the characteristics of 'extension' or 'dimension' in sounds acting as a medium.
This requirement in turn creates something of a difficulty not
present in the equivalent explanation of the role of sounds acting as signifiers in language. Saussure, it will be remembered,
was quite clear in his definition of a signifier as a 'sound-image'
rather than sound itself. What he was saying, in effect, was that
it was the *experience* of a sound – involving as it customarily
does some editing and interpretation of the sound as part of
external reality as science may comprehensively describe it –
that provides the ground for the mapping or investment of the
signified. However, although the subject is in a sense locked into
the sound-image that is termed the 'signifier', it is still relatively

easy to distinguish between the experience constituted by the sound-image and the experience constituted by the mental concept or signified customarily associated with the signifier. This ease occurs because that is the way language is constructed, that is the way in which it works. Its mode of analysis is implicit in its mode of construction. Further, *because* of its mode of construction, there is no need to *analyse* the characteristics of the sound-image. It is enough, simply, that a sound-image, *any* sound-image, is present in processes of signification through language.

The situation with music, however, is more difficult. If, in processes of signification through music, there exists a technology or instrumentality of articulation, then the distinction between the medium and elements of signification as levels of analysis becomes much less easy to establish. As we shall see, the material binding that occurs in processes of signification through music means that, once realized as a sound-image, the sounds of the medium in music approach the condition of their elements of signification. This difficulty may be understood another way. In approaching the analysis of language through language, it can be argued not only that the mode of analysis is implicit in the mode of meaning construction, but that both modes are essentially cognitive in character. They do not have to engage *initially* the whole human body in order to function successfully. They have only to engage initially the electro-chemical circuits of the brain. In approaching the analysis of music through language cognitive processes of awareness are, by contrast, being applied to processes that are fundamentally corporeal and affective in character. As a consequence, the levels of analysis created cognitively through language to grasp processes of the construction of music and musical experience do not have a logical status in objective reality matching those created to grasp processes of the construction of language and linguistic experience. That is, the 'separateness' of levels of analysis for music created linguistically are *not* matched by an equivalent 'separateness' of moments of meaning construction as they occur in objective reality (sound as medium, elements of signification, states of awareness, states of being and so on) in the same way that the separateness of levels of analysis for language created linguistically *are* matched by an equivalent separateness of moments of meaning construction in objective reality (signifier, signified and so on). While the legitimately conceived discreteness of signifiers in relation to other signifiers within a linguistic structure matches the legitimately conceived discreteness of signifiers in relation to signifieds in various processes of meaning construction, in other words, the discreteness of signifiers *vis-à-vis* signifiers is not matched by a legitimate discreteness between 'different' moments in processes of meaning construction through music (this is because of the principle of 'relationships of equivalence *across* segments'). A clear disjunction can therefore be said to exist between processes which are corporeal and affective in character and the modes of analysis created mentally and cognitively to understand them.

Because the levels of analysis created cognitively through language to grasp processes of the construction of music and musical experience do not have a logical status in objective reality matching those created to grasp processes of the construction of language and linguistic experience, it is not so easy as it is with language to decontextualize processes of meaning construction in music from their necessary involvement with people. Assigning music an 'objective' status to match that customarily assigned to language can only as a consequence be achieved by reducing music to the condition of its sounds, a conceptual move customary within musicology which we have steadfastly resisted. Once meaning in music is taken to be located in processes obtaining *between* the sounds of music and people rather than *in* the sounds of music themselves, elements of signification can no more easily be disengaged from people's somatic states of awareness than they can from the sounds of music as medium. Such a move is unnecessary to establish language as 'objective', however. Signifieds are legitimately conceived as being discrete from signifiers and do not, *as integral aspects of themselves*, bring into play the entire person (the entire human body). This move with music is further necessary because – as we have seen from Middleton's work, Ruwet's work and our criticisms of Tagg's work – individual units of meaning cannot so easily or legitimately be identified and decontextualized *in music* (that is to say, decontextualized in music as distinct from their decontextualization from people) as they can in language. *In this sense*, modes of analysis which 'dispense' with people as they exist in relation to language cannot as a consequence be so easily established in relation to music. As we saw in considering Ruwet's work, the listener has constantly to be 'involved in analysis' in order to establish units of equivalence and difference.

This necessary 'involvement of people' in the analysis of musical experience means that such analysis is also more difficult to decontextualize from social and cultural considerations than is the analysis of linguistic experience. If people can be easily 'dispensed with' in linguistic analysis then so can questions of social and cultural context. While language is *always* imbricated with social and cultural meanings, therefore, the levels of cognitive activity involved in the construction through language *of social and cultural meanings* are nonetheless not difficult to identify and isolate. For the reasons we have already established, it is not difficult, for example, to identify and isolate the signifier 'bird', and to discuss it and its customary relationship to the signified 'bird' or *comparatively across languages* in its relationship, for example, to the signifier and signified *'oiseau'*. Similarly, both Lévi-Strauss and Barthes have, in their different ways, illustrated the relative ease with which structuralist and semiotic modes of analysis can be applied respectively to *secure* analysis at 'the level of language' *before* lifting it to 'the level of social meanings' implicit in myth and culture. The establishing of such levels of analysis in music is more difficult. Such difficulty is implied in the ease with which Lévi-Strauss can refer to music at the level of language as a model for myth and again as myth itself – as at the same time hitting us 'in the guts' and appealing to 'our group instinct'. As each affective moment passes in music it is not therefore easy, cognitively and conceptually, to separate sounds from the experiential moment of sound-images, or sounds and sound-images from the *same* experiential moment constituted through the calling forth of socially and culturally mediated subjective states of awareness as elements of signification. This *one* experiential moment is articulated through a material binding underwriting a technology or instrumentality of signification. It is thus not possible to access easily the role played by the characteristics of 'extension' or 'dimension' in sounds acting as a medium independently of an analysis of sonic media (mediums) acting *within* particular musical traditions *as socially and culturally constituted*.

The distinction between sounds acting as a medium in music and media acting within particular musical traditions as socially and culturally constituted is nonetheless important in recognizing the distinction that exists between *auditory* time and space and *musical* time and space. This is why it is so important to examine music as a distinctive signifying practice of which individual pieces are evidence rather than to approach the question of its affectivity through the analysis of individual pieces which might, in their totality, be thought to constitute music. It is the characteristics of 'extension' or 'dimension' in sounds acting as a medium as 'lifted' or 'interpellated' into music as socially and culturally constituted and recognized as being temporal and spatial in character that moves our discussion for the time being from its more semiological to structural aspects. We can, in other words, begin to consider how each passing *auditory* and *affective* moment reveals to us sounds in music acting as a structure.

A way forward in this undertaking is provided by the work of Victor Zuckerkandl (1956). Zuckerkandl has engaged in a thorough analysis of time and space as revealed through the experience of music. This examination is undertaken with respect to music in the tradition of functional tonality (more colloquially, 'classical' music). The examination is of particular interest given that the concepts of musical time and space derived by Zuckerkandl from his analysis of functional tonal music differ radically from and are incommensurable with those of commonsense reality as entrenched by the analyses of classical physics. It is also of interest given that the music of functional tonality has elsewhere been argued to articulate at the level of social and cultural realities these *classical* notions of time and space which have underpinned the civilizations of the modern world (Shepherd, 1991b, pp. 96–127). It is important to remember, therefore, that Zuckerkandl's analysis is neither of *auditory* nor of *musical* time and space alone. The analysis is of auditory time and space *in the service of* and as articulated through the experiences of a musical tradition possessing a range of specific social and cultural characteristics. It is the fact that a disjunction can in this way occur between the experiential qualities of sounds acting as a medium in a certain musical tradition and certain experiential qualities of the social and cultural realities as thus articulated that makes possible, cognitively and conceptually, a distinction in levels of analysis, a distinction, it should be remembered, that may *not* occur or 'be reproduced' in the actual mechanisms of meaning production in music.

Prior to a discussion of Zuckerkandl's analysis, it is possible to make some general statements about sounds acting structurally as sound-images in music. Firstly, it is possible to distinguish between relationships *between* sounds identified as discrete – the 'external' structural or syntactical character of the use of sounds in music – and the inherent, *internal* characteristics of sounds identified as discrete – the 'internal' structural character of the use of sounds in music. In more common language, this distinction is usually referred to as that between syntax and texture or, more precisely, syntax (relations between sounds) and timbre (the character of sounds themselves). Secondly, it is possible to note that, while all syntax is structural in character, not all structure is syntactical in character (this is because the character of sounds themselves is a character that flows from specific formal, 'internal' structures). Further, while there is no good reason to suppose that syntactical and wider elements of structure cannot be implicated in the creation of connotation through music, such creation can only occur because of the prior and inescapable location of structure in processes of primary signification. As Middleton observes, 'semiotic theory emphasizes that connotation is built on a prior system of denotation, it is *secondary*.' The absence of denotation in music does not of necessity imply an absence of primary signification.

This distinction between syntax and timbre allows for a slightly more detailed conceptualization of the notion of 'extension' or 'dimension' in relation to musical experience through sound-images derived from the medium in a culture-specific manner. The timbre or texture of sound relates to sound's inherent characteristics, to the dimensions of its material existence whose tactile character renders it in a certain sense similar to the existence of material bodies in time and space. This analogy can be continued. The sounds of music are revealed in time and space, *auditory* time and space. Their syntactical relatedness gives rise to a sense of time through rhythm and a sense of space through pitch. As Bierwisch observes, 'movement of pitch presents ... something like an abstract "space in motion" '. Pitch and rhythm together thus also give rise to a sense of movement, of motion. The revelation of sounds in auditory time and space seems to be motivated by a desire to articulate movement, to be in a constant state of motion. Music and stasis seem, in principle, irreconcilable.

6

Music as Structure

In order to understand how music functions as a structure, it is necessary to understand how the structures of sound in music, acting both externally and internally, relate both within themselves and to one another in the manner of their revelation through each passing auditory and affective moment. As indicated in the previous chapter, if we are to understand the character of music as a structure, then *our* point of entry, *our* point of interrogation cannot be anything other than the sounds of music as they impact on us and reveal to us music acting as a structure. An understanding of the ways in which each passing auditory and affective moment reveals music acting as a structure can be gained by exploring the character of the auditory as opposed to visual environment, the ways that this environment relates, respectively, to music and to language, and the ways in which music, in a culture-specific manner, invokes the time and space of the auditory environment in the service of social and cultural processes.

The Auditory Environment, Music and Language

If the referential base of language – its capacity for 'naming' – makes it distinctive, it does not, however, make it unique. Humanly created visual images also refer to identifiable objects and events in the material environment (whether 'natural' or people-made). The uniqueness of human language rests on a combination of what it refers to and *how* it refers to it. Human language developed as a means of communication in sound. However, what language primarily refers to (isolatable objects, events, people and concepts) are phenomena identified and manipulated fundamentally through the sense of vision. Where environmental circumstances allow (rain forests, for example, usually allow for visual identification of a prey only moments before the kill) the sense of vision reveals more quickly, more precisely and more effectively than does the sense of hearing the location of objects in visual time and space. The process of precisely defining and manipulating objects in visual time and space is one that thus depends more on the sense of vision than it does on the sense of hearing. The implications of the special, 'cross-sensory' manner in which verbal language operates can best be highlighted by comparing the *experiential* qualities of sound and vision as sensory pathways for human awareness of the world.

Sound has properties which distinguish it quite clearly from the sense of vision. Sound brings the world into people from all directions, simultaneously and dynamically. While it is frequently possible to locate the source of a sound, it is a fundamental experiential characteristic of sound that it lifts off the surface of its material source to occupy and give life to the space not only between the source and the listener, but also around the listener. While a sound may have a discrete material source, therefore, it is experienced as a phenomenon that encompasses and touches the listener in a cocoon-like fashion. Since people typically hear not one, but several sounds at once, they are encompassed and touched by a world of simultaneously structured objects and events. And since sound is evanescent, going out of existence at the very moment that it comes into existence, people are encompassed and touched by a world that is constantly in process and dynamic, a world that only exists while it is being articulated through sound.

The attributes of the material world as experienced through vision, on the other hand, do not lift off the surface of that world and come into the observer. They are experienced as inhering in that world, as being inseparable from and essentially constituting it. Experience and the location of its source become identical.

Further, vision is selective. While more than one object or event may occupy the gaze at any one time, vision does not provide an encompassing awareness of the world in the way that sound does. A gaze can be controlled more easily than can hearing, and in this sense the world of vision becomes more safe and permanent than the world of sound. Vision encourages projection into the world, occupation and control of the source of experience. Sound encourages a sense of the world as received, as being revelationary rather than incarnate.

Sound reminds people that there is a world of depth which is external to them, which surrounds them, which touches them simultaneously from all directions, and which, in its fluidity and dynamism, constantly requires a response. Unlike vision, the medium which facilitates division and control, sound serves to remind people of their tangible relationship to the material world. Images are assimilated silently within the head (at least initially). Sound, however, is the only major medium of communication that can vibrate perceptibly within the body. The sound of the human voice could not be amplified and projected were it not for chambers or resonators of air inside the human body (the lungs, the sinus passages, the mouth) that vibrate in sympathy with the frequencies of the vocal cords. Equally, the sound of the human voice could not be amplified were it not for the objects of the external world, objects whose configurations, textures and movements mould and shape the sound of the voice as it comes into people from all directions simultaneously. Consequently, the human experience of sound involves, in addition to the sympathetic vibration of the eardrums, the sympathetic vibration of the resonators of the body. Sound, shaped and resonating with the properties of the internal and external configurations, textures and movements of the objects of the external world, can thus be felt in addition to being heard. It transcends actual tactile sensations in the sense that interpersonal tactile awareness and the particular forms of sensory experience that flow from it is generally an awareness at the surface of the body which then finds internal resonance. Sound, however, enters the body and is in the body. It may thus be concluded that not only does sound reveal the internal properties of inanimate material sources and the order of their relationships to the material world around them. It reveals also the inner, physiological life of individuals in terms of the way the internal configurations, textures and movements of their bodies affect the quality of sound production. Sound is ideally suited to revealing and connecting the internal and external worlds.

Language, like music, is a means of communication in sound. However, because it is based on reference to an object-world that is mediated and defined in an ultimately visual fashion, it does not as a consequence *have* to invoke the sonic characteristics of that world in realizing its fundamentally denotative function. That it may sometimes do so in practice through devices such as onomatopoeia speaks more to the 'musical' potential of sound than it does to any basic prerequisite for successful denotative communication through sound. The use of sound in language to refer to visually identifiable and manipulable phenomena in external reality is therefore 'arbitrary'. That is, there *cannot* be a connection between the inherent characteristics of the *sounds* of language and the inherent *visual* characteristics of the phenomena the sounds refer to. The relationship between sound and meaning cannot be dictated in any other way than by convention. 'Birds' can just as effectively be referred to as *'oiseaux'*. This clean separation between sound and meaning, based as it is on an imposed sensory divorce, permits language in a certain sense to disengage itself from the world on which it operates. In Saussurean terms, it guarantees language an autonomy relative to the world, both material and social. Thought in language can as a consequence be manipulated independently of any inherent visual characteristics emanating from the external, material world. It is this ability of thought in language independently and *symbolically* to precede action on the external world which in part has made it possible for people to create and reproduce their own material worlds. And since material reproduction is impossible without social reproduction (a point made graphically by Althusser), it is language which has also made possible the creation and reproduction of the social worlds which processes of material reproduction in turn sustain.

It has become paradoxically the case, therefore, that sound in language can only *indirectly* evoke the *structures* of the human world and the states of being that flow from them and sustain them. This is because, firstly, there is no element of necessity in the relationship between the sounds of language as signifiers and the delimited objects and concepts which form the basis of signifieds as mental concepts and, secondly, because the qualities of the structures of the human world are not encapsulated within these signifieds, but only demarcated and articulated through the logical relationships in which they are placed. If music, as the 'other' process of signification articulated through sound, is, like language, in a particular kind of relationship to the structures of the human world and the states of being that flow from and sustain them, then we would argue that this relationship, and the evocation that is made possible through it, is *concrete* and *direct* in nature. If people's ears tend to be led away from the inherent qualities of sound as signifiers in linguistic practice, then it is of relevance that these same people seem to associate music in some way with sound as sound. In contradistinction to language, which refers *outside* its sonic medium to a constructed reality that is essentially non-aural in its perception and management, music seems to refer *inside* its sonic medium to another kind of constructed reality. This constructed reality is not, however, simply and *exclusively* intra-sonic and intra-musical, as has from time to time been argued within the fields of musicology and music aesthetics. Our position is that it is constituted in relation to the structures of the human world and the states of being that flow from them and sustain them.

Auditory Time-Space in the Service of Music as a Structure

Insights into the ways in which music can gather up and reveal to us the structures of the internal and external social worlds and the relations obtaining between them are provided in the work of Zuckerkandl. In examining the tradition of 'classical' music from a phenomenological and experiential, as opposed to a musical-analytical perspective, Zuckerkandl shows us why 'movement of pitch presents ... something like an abstract "space in motion",' why pitch and rhythm together thus also give rise to a sense of movement, of motion, and why music and stasis seem, in principle, irreconcilable. Although we experience motion in music we cannot be said to perceive it directly. The only way that a note may be said to be in motion is in the form of a *glissando*, and this is a comparatively rare phenomenon in

functional tonal music. Apart from this exception the notes of
the European art-music tradition are static in the sense that the
vast majority of pitch changes are relatively abrupt and discontinuous in their *stepwise* motion. But musical experience does
not result *simply* from pitch differences, which may be sufficiently described in terms of the material universe (music acting
at the 'level' of the medium). It occurs as dynamic qualities,
which are beyond the realm of classical physics. As Zuckerkandl
argues, classical physics can supply a full and accurate description of a tone that corresponds to the details of our perception of
it as an auditory event. However, this physical description –
inscribed as part of a linguistic discourse – cannot go far in
explaining our perception of the tone as a musical event:

> What we have thus described is tone as everyone hears it ... as
> every apparatus registers it: the single tone removed from any musi-
> cal context, tone as an acoustical phenomenon. It is not tone as a
> musical phenomenon. Precisely the quality that characterizes the
> tone as an element in a musical context, that makes it a musical phe-
> nomenon, its dynamic quality, was absent from our description. And
> there was reason for its absence. Among the qualities that belong to
> the tone as an acoustical phenomenon there is none that is not deter-
> mined by a particular element of the physical process and only
> changes, and always changes, if something changes in the physical
> process. This does not hold for the dynamic quality of tones. Nothing
> in the physical event corresponds to the tone as a musical event.
> (Zuckerkandl, 1956, pp. 22–3)

When Zuckerkandl says 'nothing in the physical event corresponds to the tone as a musical event', he means that nothing (or,
more accurately, very little) in the *description* of the tone as a
physical event can contribute to the description and explanation
of the tone as a musical event. However, if the tone as a physical
event changes, there *will* be corresponding changes in the tone
as a musical event, changes, however, whose precise character
cannot be determined by the changes in the physical event.
Simply put, the description of an A at 440 hertz is identical
whether the note occurs in the context of A major or E major.
The context makes all the difference to the note's dynamic quality. The note in other words 'feels' like a key-note, a note at rest
in its finality, or like a note 'incomplete', a note wanting to take
the three downward steps to the finality of the key-note. The
different role or function performed by the same note in each

instance will result in a different musical perception, a different dynamic quality. This dynamic quality displays different tendencies of motion in each case. It will have 'arrived from' and wish to 'go to'.

If there is a sense in which the dynamic quality of an 'identical' note is experienced as being different according to its harmonic context – that is, 'charged' differentially according to its tendencies of 'motion', then the same phenomenon obtains with rhythm. There is a very real sense in which notes in 'classical' music seem to gather up within themselves the condition of their relatedness to all other notes in a piece. That is how they come to have the particular dynamic quality they do. Zuckerkandl invokes the notion of field theory to explain this phenomenon: 'The remarkable fact, which we also encounter elsewhere in nature, that a part of a whole is, so to speak, aware of its being a part of its relation to the whole and its place in the whole, and also imparts this knowledge to the observer – that, consequently, the whole is in some manner present in the part – to this fact our thinking seeks to do justice by the *field concept*' (1956, p. 205). He then goes on to explain how this works in relation to rhythm (in addition to harmony and, by implication, melody) by examining how we typically experience simple duple metre (a bar or measure of 2/2):

A piece of music is played; there is no accentuation. We count with the tones one-two-one- ... Why did we say 'one' instead of 'three'? What peculiarity in our perception of the third beat makes us count thus and not otherwise? If the new beat did nothing but bring us a further fraction forward in time, the phenomenon would be incomprehensible. If we involuntarily and unconsciously count 'one' to beat number 3 this expresses the fact that it is not so much *further* as *back* that this beat carries us – and back to the starting point. To be able to come back, one must first have gone away; now we also understand why we count one-*two*, and not one-*one*. Here, 'two' does not mean simply 'beat number 2' but also 'away from'. The entire process is therefore an 'away from–back to', not a flux but a cycle, a constantly repeated cycle, for the 'one' that closes one cycle simultaneously begins another. (pp. 167–8)

Functional tonal music, however, is not the music of a society with a cyclical sense of time. Neither is it a 'single-level' music. Functional tonal music is essentially the music of direction and culmination. The notes of functional tonal music constantly point outside themselves in the desire to 'move on' and 'achieve fruition'. Furthermore, functional tonal music is an architectonic music. It displays several 'levels' which 'interact' to produce the particular experience common to all pieces of music conceived in this style. In view of these two characteristics, it is more accurate to think of the musical time revealed through functional tonal music as having a wave rather than a cyclical structure. Firstly, this structure allows for both a sense of recurrence and of continual forward motion. Secondly, whereas it is difficult to conceive of cyclical motion containing different 'levels' within itself, such a concept is relatively easy to imagine with wave motion.

As Zuckerkandl points out, we do not experience the wave motion of rhythm by way of 'conscious thought', by way of counting cognitively rather than experiencing affectively. Counting can only help us to represent to ourselves a *kinetic* impulse that is *revealed* to us and that we experience *directly*:

> Hearing music, we oscillate with its metric wave. Each tone falls on a particular phase of this wave; each phase of the wave imparts to the tone that falls on it – and through the tone, to the auditor – its particular directional impulse. Not because I count 'one' to a tone (or because the tone was emphasised by an accent – for often it is not) do I know that I am at the beginning of a measure, but because I feel that, with this tone, I have reached the wave crest and at the same time have been carried beyond it, into a new wave cycle. But because every tone . . . is characterised for my reception by a particular quality, and because in these qualities the place of the tone . . . on the metric wave is expressed, I am able to hear directly from the tone . . . in what part of the entire measure I am at the given moment. (1956, pp. 204–5)

Musical experience thus contains the listener, 'positions' the listener, as it were. Musical experience does not occur because listeners step outside the present and through the action of their consciousness bring previous and future tones into simultaneous existence with present tones. Previous and future tones are brought into simultaneous 'virtual' existence through the 'action' of the present tone itself. Past tones cannot as a consequence be thought of as 'going out of existence':

> 'Two', then, follows 'one' – in other words, if 'two' is present, 'one' is past. Is this pastness equivalent to nonexistence? Could 'two' be

what it is if 'one', because it was no longer, were really nonexistent? 'Two' is not simply the beat that follows 'one'; it is something quite different, namely, symmetrical complement, completion and fulfilment. The whole course of 'two' is in direct correspondence with 'one', it *is* this correspondence, in every instant of the existence of 'two' 'one' is also contained, as the partner in this relationship, the object of the symmetrical completion. If 'one', once past, were lost in nonexistence, extinguished – as, according to the hourglass concept, past time is extinguished – 'two' would be simply a second 'one' and nothing more. (Zuckerkandl, 1956, pp. 224–5)

This is not a viable possibility if a sense of metre is to be maintained. A similar conclusion may be reached concerning the 'non-existence' of tones not yet realized:

'Two' follows 'one' – this too means if 'one' is present, 'two' is future. Is this all we know about 'two' – that it is not yet if 'one' is? Yet 'one' is something quite different from the beat upon which 'two' will follow; it is the beat which *proceeds towards* 'two', with which we ourselves move towards 'two' ... Through its entire course we experience 'one' as something to be completed, its existence is a need for symmetrical completion. 'One' could not be what it is if 'two', because it was not yet, were really nonexistent, if the future 'two' were not already part of the existence of the present 'one'. (1956, p. 225)

Such considerations lead Zuckerkandl to summarize his understanding of musical time in the following way:

The present of musical meter ... contains within it a past that is not remembered and a future that is not foreknown – and *not as something to be supplied by thought but as a thing directly given in experience itself* ... What becomes of the point (or the saddle) 'now' between the two abysses of 'no more' and 'not yet', in the face of a present in which 'now', 'not yet' and 'no more' are given together, in the most intimate interpenetration and with equal immediacy? This is a present from which not I, thanks to my particular powers, look backward into the past and forward into the future, but which *itself* thus looks backward and forward. These particular powers of remembering and foreknowing, then, are not required in order that future things and past things shall *not be nothing*. The past is not extinguished, but not because a memory stores it; it is not extinguished because *time itself stores it*, or, better put, the being of time is a storing of itself; the future is not an impenetrable wall, but not because a foreknowledge or forefeeling anticipates time; it is not impenetrable because time always anticipates itself ... the present of musical experience is not the dividing point that eternally separates past and future; it is the stage upon which, for every ear, the drama of the being of time is played – that ceaseless storing of itself and anticipating itself which is never repeated, which is every instant new. (1956, pp. 227–8, first set of italics ours)

It is at this point that Lévi-Strauss's discussions of the relative characteristics of music and myth begin to take on additional significance. One of the characteristics which distinguished myth from language for Lévi-Strauss, it will be remembered, was 'a time referent of a new nature'. This is the time referent through which individual relations in myth as deployed *in* time resonate with other, similar relations. This new time referent was 'simultaneously diachronic and synchronic', integrating 'the characteristics of *langue* on the one hand, and those of *parole* on the other'. It is Zuckerkandl who provides the justification for the parallels that Lévi-Strauss draws between myth and music when he claims that while the elements of music are deployed in a time which is 'irreversible and therefore irredeemably diachronic', music nonetheless 'transmutes the segment devoted to listening to it into a synchronic totality, enclosed within itself'. *At the level of language*, music therefore displays the third time referent evident in myth that is 'simultaneously diachronic and synchronic'. That is why the structural principles according to which music functions are fundamentally different from those according to which language functions, why, according to Lévi-Strauss, 'it must be possible to discover in musical discourse some special function that has a particular affinity with myth', and why, in displaying a characteristic that is specific to myth, music, through its very operations at the level of language, must also be regarded as 'myth coded in sounds instead of words'. It is for these reasons that Lévi-Strauss is correct in concluding that 'mythology occupies an intermediary position between two diametrically opposed types of sign systems – musical languages on the one hand and articulate speech on the other.'

It is this principle of 'the virtual in the actual' which explains the emphasis placed by Ruwet and Middleton on the role of repetition, variants, varied repetition and transformation in music. Such procedures are evident in the ways in which melodies, themes, motifs and melodic, harmonic and rhythmic gestures either repeat 'unchanged' in a piece, or repeat in a form which is varied, but not varied to the point where it is not recognizably a variant of the original. Such sameness (actually a 'difference', because the same auditory event occurring at two places in a piece will generate different dynamic qualities) and difference explain the way in which equivalence rather than 'difference' is fundamental to the way in which music functions as a structure. This is a point to which we return later in the chapter.

Zuckerkandl's arguments can thus be summarized as follows. Each auditory event perceived as meaningful in music of the functional tonal tradition has a dynamic quality emanating from its spatial and temporal location in relation to other like events. This dynamic quality is akin to the directional charging of a force field *at any particular moment*. Zuckerkandl's work distinguishes between the actual charging of a force field *in the passing present* and virtual chargings that constitute the remainder of the force field. Actual chargings are articulated concretely and directly. They are experienced as the dynamic quality of each passing auditory event (or 'note'). Virtual chargings are what are inescapably articulated through each actual charging as it passes: the collectivity of all other actual chargings that constitute a piece of music as they are gathered up and their complex relatedness from the unique perspective of each musical moment released as the actual charging of the passing present. The point is that the character of the relatedness of auditory events in music can no more be thought of as a consequence of the 'placing' of notes *in* musical time and musical space (that is, notes placed in the pre-existing, empty hopper of musical time and musical space which then lends definition to their relatedness) than can individual auditory events in material reality be thought of as being 'placed' and 'related' in *auditory* time and space. Auditory events may be deployed in mechanical, which is to say, visual time and space, but they cannot be thus deployed in auditory time and space. Auditory time and space (which is really a unified auditory time-space field) does *not* constitute a pre-existing, empty hopper in the same way that visual time and space is frequently conceived of doing. Auditory events *are* auditory time and space. Auditory time and space (time-space) can only be articulated and is thus articulated (as a unified field) *inalienably* through the articulation of auditory events in relation to one another. Similarly, the *virtual* force field of musical time and space – the social phenomenon made possible by the materially grounded phenomenon of auditory time-space – can only be articulated and is thus articulated *inalienably* through the articulation of the actual chargings (phasings) of the musical present in relation to one another. In this sense, it is easy to see why Bierwisch would claim that a gesture (which, after all, is a phenomenon inalienably in movement in exactly the same way in which a dynamic quality is inalienably in movement as the cusp or 'saddle' of the unfolding musical present) 'is as such of a temporal nature' and '*is* the structure or state of a process and does not just replace it' (our italics). Zuckerkandl, it would seem, has successfully identified and isolated the active characteristics or dimensions of sounds acting syntactically in a particular musical tradition which provide such an appropriate ground for the mapping or, more precisely, the iconic articulation of Bierwisch's 'gesticulatory forms'.

Music as Structure

It is now possible to gain an insight into how music functions as a structure distinct from language. In the case of both music and language, the structural principles of their modes of articulation are grounded in the phenomenon of the relatedness of entities. In the case of language, this principle of relatedness is grounded in the phenomenon of exclusion which guarantees that the significance of an entity is, indeed, associated *exclusively* with it. A sound recognized as meaningful within a language is recognized as such because of its *difference* from all other sounds, a difference based in *opposition*. This condition of relatedness between sounds recognized as meaningful in language is thus one of *repulsion*, not attraction. The basis of the identification of a sound in language as meaningful is therefore that it 'has nothing to do with other sounds', *apart* from establishing its difference from them. That is why *sounds* as signifiers in language (as opposed to meanings or signifieds) can be deployed in the commonsense spatio-temporal framework of the everyday world without affecting it or *being affected by it*. In not pulling the inherent qualities of other sounds into this realm of articulation and signification, sounds in language do not, as it were, 'pull the strings' of the spatio-temporal framework in which they are deployed. Sounds and framework are quite distinct from one another. This means that the spatio-temporal characteristics of the phenomena evoked by language (which of necessity articulate the spatio-temporal framework of which they are evidence) can have nothing to do with the character of the deployment of the *sounds* of language in *visual* time or space. While the logical form of a proposition maintains a logical structure in relation to the phenomena represented, therefore, this structure can only be abstract, *as opposed to material*, in character. It can have no necessary connection to the spatial-temporal characteristics of the phenomena represented, *or* to the character of the sounds of language as deployed in visual time and space. To use Bierwisch's words, the proposition as a consequence has 'an extensionless logical structure whose projection onto the temporally organized forms of linguistic signs remains more or less external in nature'.

Things must be this way if language is, in a certain sense, to disengage itself from the world on which it operates and thereby to possess the capacity independently and symbolically to precede action on the external world in facilitating the ability of people to create and reproduce their own material and social worlds. That is why there is a disjunction between the material conditions of the world and the material conditions of the language evoking it, and why Lacan is so correct in his implication that the point for the exercise of power through language is the lifting of signification *away* from the material ground of the signifier and *onto* the material ground of the body. The abstract as opposed to material character of the logical structure of linguistic propositions arises, therefore, *not* because the structure has no material grounds of its own (which it does with the sounds of language and within the electro-chemical circuits of the brain), but because it has no material *connectedness* of a logical or necessary character, *either* to the material conditions of the world *or* to the material conditions of language. *This, surely, is the defining condition of the cognitive as opposed to the affective.* The character of material connectedness is that of a 'jump' rather than a 'grab'. Signifier and signified must remain quite distinct from one another, a distinctiveness both guaranteed and required, it will be remembered, by the cross-sensory basis of verbal language.

Language thus serves to structure the world through relations of difference, but a difference based on opposition if not repulsion. Music, in contrast, serves to structure the world through relations of difference based on attraction. Each phase or charging is distinct and different from every other phase or charging, but *only* by virtue of the collectivity of all other actual chargings that constitute a musical event *as* they are gathered up and their complex relatedness *from the unique perspective of each musical moment* released as the actual charging of the passing present. It is for this reason that, in being deployed in the commonsense spatio-temporal framework of the everyday world (as that framework and world have been *in part* produced through language by the acting *together* of both signifier *and* signified), *the sounds of music move to supplant that framework in creating their own*. Sounds and their framework become synonymous, *and synonymous in a manner of consequence to the world in which we live* (which is why the commonsense spatio-temporal framework of the everyday world is produced *only* in part by language).

As we have argued, music is capable of *evoking*, in a concrete and direct, yet *mediated* and *symbolic* fashion, the structures of the world and the states of being that flow from them and sustain them. In operating on people through a technology of articulation, we can now argue that the sounds of music serve as well to *create* those structures, and to create them in a dialectic of perception and action *consistent* with the quintessentially symbolic character of human worlds. Musical time-space is in other words of consequence for the spatio-temporal framework of the everyday world in a manner similar to, but importantly different from, that of the logical structures of propositions. The distinctness and autonomy of both language *and* music relative to people and the world is an essential condition of the symbolic character of human worlds. Language's distinctness and autonomy are guaranteed through the arbitrary character of the relatedness of sounds in language to mental concepts and so to the particulars of the world. The sounds of language point outside themselves, but not to a world with which they have any *necessary* connection. Music's distinctness and autonomy are guaranteed through its intra-sonic and self-referring character. The sounds of music, through their technology of articulation, have a *necessary* connectedness both to people and thus to the world. In *symbolically* creating and structuring the world, music 'pulls it in' rather than keeping it at a distance. Whereas language deploys the world, music encompasses it. Like myth, music 'provides its own context' (Lévi-Strauss, 1972, p. 215). It is in this sense that, in Lévi-Strauss's words, 'cosmology is true' (p. 216).

Addendum 1   The Hegemony of Language in Understanding Music

It is only at this point that the extreme hegemonic influence exerted by language in understanding the characteristics of music as a relatively autonomous structure becomes clear. Indeed, it is this influence which has actively prevented such an understanding. That this is so can be illustrated by explaining why it is that music theory and music analysis, the subdisciplines of musicology concerned with 'how the notes work', have been able to contribute little to a discussion of the issues raised in this book. They have been able to contribute little, in other words, to the question of how music signifies, and how, exactly, musical experience is constituted. This is because music theory and music analysis have taken as their starting point not musical experience, but the production of music. They have in other words been more concerned with how the notes are 'placed' than with their effect once placed.

As we have seen, the procedures for analysing processes of articulation and meaning construction through language are suggested by the manner of operation of such processes. Processes of analysis and processes of articulation and meaning construction are both cognitive in character. The cognitive analysis of music as an affective phenomenon is, as we have observed, a rather more difficult undertaking. Moments of articulation and meaning construction do not 'sit up' quite so easily for observation and discussion as they seem to in language, quite possibly because the 'moments' as we identify and discuss them here may not have an autonomous or even relatively autonomous existence *as they occur in actual instances of meaning construction through music*. The sound-image experienced as a musical sound cannot easily be distinguished from the affective experience that *has* to occur if the sound-image is, indeed, recognized as musical. On the other hand, because of the sensory divorce between (visual) image and (aural) sound that seems to underlie the use of sounds as the basis for language, there is always the potential for an awareness, however dim, that a linguistic utterance is in some way distinct from that which the utterance signifies. The conclusion that can be drawn from these differences between music and language as signifying practices is that there occurs a certain difficulty, a certain psychic tension in moving from affective experience to cognitive analysis and back again.

Cognitively speaking, it is easier to distinguish between the material sounds which make the medium of music possible on the one hand and affective states of awareness on the other than it is between the *sound-image* which flows from the medium and such affective states. Having made this distinction, it is then easier to remain with this world of material sounds – which can be handled in an almost exclusively cognitive manner – than it is to return to the messy, affective world of sound-images and states of awareness. This is not the place to reflect on the ideological reasons which have led many music analysts (including historical musicologists) to stay away from discussion of the relatedness of music's sounds to the affective awareness they instigate. Ideological forces have, nonetheless, resulted in an overwhelming tendency for music theorists and music analysts to take the cognitively easy path and to reduce music – conceptually – to the condition of its sounds, a tendency which as we have noted is replicated also within historical musicology. Having eliminated people – conceptually – from their understanding of 'music', it has then not been difficult for musicologists as a whole (but with the notable exception of ethnomusicologists) to accede to another set of related ideological forces in assuming music – or at least music thought of as 'good' – to be asocial in character (Shepherd, 1991b, pp. 9–74).

This criticism of music theory and music analysis as disciplines is not intended as a criticism of the *work* they have achieved. It is, however, to note that the work is more directly related to the production of music than it is to an understanding of musical experience. This is not to say, either, that the production of music is unrelated to the experiences it instigates, which it clearly is. It is, however, to observe that work conceived within an analytic framework which is almost completely cognitive in orientation is likely to be thin on protocols for *connecting* the sounds of music to music as an affective experience. As we have seen, there is every good reason why the cognitive and linguistic *analysis* of music will probably encourage the illusion that moments in the construction of musical meaning display an autonomy that they do not in reality possess. It is then but a short journey from the unjustified separation of these moments to the selective repression of some. With this repression comes the impossibility of analysing musical experience.

Zuckerkandl's work demonstrates that this experience is one which is lived *within*. Musical space and musical time *reveal* their qualities to the listener. This point became crucially clear in Zuckerkandl's discussion of tonal time, when he explained that an awareness of this time depended not at all upon a process of conscious recalling and anticipation. Tonal time does not lend itself to physical description, it will be remembered. It is not constituted *through* the placement itself of notes. It is constituted as a *consequence* of such placement. However, music theory and music analysis as disciplines reflect consciously on notes as sounds in the order of their relationships. In this sense, the signifiers of language, conceived legitimately as distinct in the order of their relatedness, can relate easily *and legitimately* to individual components of sound *as sound* in the order of the relatedness of their placement. Music theory and music analysis can in this fashion stand *outside* the notes and reflect on their placement. Their categories of pitch, melody, harmony, pulse, metre, rhythm and so on as a consequence have more in common with the categories of those who produce music – with the categories of those who have to think consciously about the placement of notes in space and time – than with the understanding of those who experience the fruits of such placement. As Kerman has pointed out (1985, pp. 60–112), the growth of music theory as a discipline has to be understood more in terms of its relationship to the craft of composition than it does in terms of its relationship to the more humanistic concerns of understanding musical experience. In this context it is instructive to recall Palisca's words that 'musical aesthetics is not musical scholarship; it is musical experience and musical theory converging on a philosophical problem', as well as to note Mendel's observation that while most historical musicologists are motivated in their professional activities by a love of the music they study, historical musicology as a discipline will 'for some time ... continue to be busy establishing what are called *individual facts'* (Mendel, 1962, pp. 13–14, our italics).

It would, of course, be wrong to make a too easy equation between composition, performance and cognitive processes on the one hand, and the experience of music and affective processes on the other. Judgements as to the effectiveness of notes placed depends, ultimately, on judgements of an experiential and affective order. Again, musical experience and musical affect rarely occur independently of processes of cognition. However, it would seem that processes of composition in music of the established Western canon do depend significantly on cognitive modes of awareness, a dependence further facilitated by the role of notation in this tradition. There is a sense, perhaps, in which music created with the aid of notation can be 'built' as well as tried out and 'rethought' in real time. This dependence on cognition and notation seems to extend also to various performance practices within this tradition as well as to certain other Western music, most notably various genres in the tradition of popular music. Here, however, the practice of improvisation raises an interesting case. It seems not unlikely that successful improvisation in popular music involves a complex interplay in real time of affective and cognitive processes.

What is probably true for improvisation in various genres of popular music is probably true also for the creation of music in most of the world's traditions. That is, musical creativity involves the interplay, in various and complex ways, of processes that we would recognize and describe as cognitive and affective in character. Those who create music, in other words, have to manage a certain deftness in moving between these two worlds. If certain musics as practised in the West over the last few centuries witness a certain emphasis on cognition in creative processes, then this is probably linked to certain predominant trends in thought and understanding (Shepherd, 1991b, pp. 11–48, 96–127, and 160–3), trends which in turn have made possible academic, intellectual thought, the development of music theory and music analysis as modern disciplines, and *their* discursive effect upon musical creativity. The point, however, is that the deftness displayed by musicians in managing the psychic tension involved in moving from the affective to the cognitive and back again seems not to be displayed in music theory and music analysis as academic disciplines. They are thus hardly well placed to assist in understanding processes of signification and meaning construction through music.

It is this which explains the somewhat anomalous position occupied by Meyer in the field of music theory. To Meyer must be credited the 'humanization' of theory and analysis. He offers a bridge from music theory to historical musicology in the pursuit of criticism by putting people in theory's thinking. Yet, like most music theorists, Meyer's point of departure is not the dynamics of musical experience itself, but the categories and procedures involved in music's creation and construction. Because the production of music is not unrelated to the experiences it instigates, Meyer is able, convincingly and perceptively, to draw striking *parallels* between musical processes and 'mental' processes. However, because such work is highly cognitive in character and likely as a consequence to be thin on protocols for connecting the sounds of music to music as an affective experience, Meyer is unable to make *connections* between the sounds of music and people sufficient to *explain* rather than describe musical experience. Meyer cannot get at music's technology of articulation. That is why Meyer experiences problems with the analysis of ethetic relationships. The problem, ultimately, lies in the fact that the ability to place notes is frequently tied to the ability to describe sound's material properties *in language*. We have been at some pains to argue that while music occurs in a world of language that it cannot escape, musical experience is not constituted linguistically and cannot, as a consequence, be reduced to the condition of language. The problem, ultimately, is that music theory and music analysis are based on the description of sounds as physical events occurring *in* time and space and *are constituted as linguistic discourses*. As linguistic discourses, music theory and music analysis are quite different and distinct in the character of their *thinking* from the character of musical *experience*. They cannot 'reach out' to musical experience in any convincing or useful manner. The tyranny of language thus prevents Meyer from reaching out from the analysis of the formal organization of music's sounds to establish a viable connection with human awareness in a similar but opposite manner to that in which it prevents Kristeva from reaching out from 'acognitive' modes of human awareness to encompass the sounds of music in all their formal yet asemantic glory. It is this gap which this book aims to close. 'Ethetic relations', 'vocal and kinetic rhythms', music's 'synaesthetic relatedness to the physical field of movement' can thus *only* be explained by leaving behind the analysis of musical production and concentrating instead on the analysis of musical experience *as it is grounded in sound as a sonic medium*. This is why this book seeks to concentrate on an analysis of music as a distinctive signifying practice of which individual pieces are evidence, rather than to seek to explain and understand music as a signifying practice through the analysis of individual works.

An example of the problems in analysis that can arise through a failure to close this gap can be provided through an examination of the work of Robert Walser on Heavy Metal rock. A concept central to Walser's work is that of musical discourse. This concept reiterates Gorbman's assertion that 'music ... is a highly coded and organized discourse'. It has to be said at the outset that Walser's understanding of the concept of discourse is ambiguous and uncertain. Noting that 'traditionally, only language has been thought to be discursive', he then proceeds to observe that 'recent usage has opened up the concept of discourse to refer to any socially produced way of thinking or communicating' (Walser, 1993, pp. 28–9). This interpretation of the term 'discourse' gives rise to a tension between its more established understanding, in which, in the tradition of poststructuralism, discourses produce meanings and subjects, and an understanding which sees discourses as in some way produced by individuals and societies. This sense of uncertainty is reinforced in Walser's further statement that 'discourses are formed, maintained, and transformed through dialogue; speakers learn from and respond to others' (p. 29). This reduction of discourse to the condition of ordinary communication is, to say the least, curious and marks a significant departure from the work of Foucault, among others. It becomes apparent that Walser is using the term to refer to the conventionalized character of meaning in general, whatever the material means and mode of articulation.

Notwithstanding this, the notion of the possibility of *musical* discourse as advanced in Walser's work seems to accept a principle underlying our main line of argument, namely, that music, while existing in a world mediated through language in a manner of fundamental importance to human societies, is nonetheless a form of human expression retaining its own distinctive processes of articulation and its own distinctive locations of meaning. As Walser observes,

> Musical meanings are always grounded socially and historically, and they operate on an ideological field of conflicting interests, institutions and memories. If this makes them extremely difficult to analyze, it does so by forcing analysis to confront the complexity and antagonism of culture. This is a poststructural view of music in that it sees all signification as provisional, and seeks for no essential truths inherent in structures, regarding all meanings as produced through the interaction of texts and readers. It goes further in suggesting that subjectivity is constituted not only through language, as Lacan and others have argued, but through musical discourses as well. (1993, pp. 29–30)

Although Walser's work marks out the territory necessary to consider the possibility of a specifically musical discourse, there *does* remain a lack of precision in relation to the notion which renders it as little more than a general term covering the entire range of complexities involved in signification through music as we describe them in this book. Unfortunately, this lack of precision extends also to Walser's understanding and elaboration of these complexities. Walser claims to 'have specified meanings' in 'musical texts' as 'discursively produced' (1993, p. 55). Yet, on closer examination, it is clear that his analyses of 'musical' discourses amount to little more than analyses of linguistic discourses as these are applied to musical experience. Reference is made to 'interviews with heavy metal fans and musicians', for example, and the claim is made that: 'their conversations with each other – at concerts, through magazine letter columns, and among friends – as well as their consumption choices themselves, constitute a dialogue with the shifting structures and meanings of the genre' (p. 55). Meanings as thus accessed in relation to the structures of music then become the basis for an analysis of the meaning of the music itself. Musical meanings are understood to be *negotiable* in character. This negotiation, however, is carried out through language. For example,

> the Christian heavy metal band Stryper demonstrates that the specific musical gestures of heavy metal operate within a code to communicate experiences of power and transcendental freedom because their attempt to appropriate the codes of metal is posited on the suitability of precisely such experiences for evangelism. The power is

God's, the transcendent freedom represents the rewards of Christianity; the intensity is that of religious experience. Stryper appropriates and reinterprets the codes of heavy metal, using metal's means to produce different meanings. Metal's noisiness might seem incompatible with a Christian agenda, but Stryper exploits just that subversive aura to make more appealing what would otherwise seem a wholly institutional message. Stryper presents Christianity as an exciting, youth-oriented alternative; they offer their fans a chance to enjoy the pleasures of heavy metal and feel virtuous at the same time. (Walser, 1993, p. 55)

We wish to be clear on what we are claiming here. We are *not* claiming that the analysis of linguistic discourses as applied to music is in some way inappropriate or invalid. We have always accepted that the constitution of music as a form of expression is affected – although *not* determined – by such discourses. What we *are* claiming is that Walser is not being precise enough in his identification of various discursive levels and the order of relations between them. Such precision would result, *not* in a denial of the relevance of the analysis of linguistic discourses to the negotiation and constitution of meaning at the connotative level of secondary signification through music, but in a clear idea of the differences between musical and linguistic discourses and of the character of the manner in which the former are manifest.

How is the question of *musical* meaning – a level of meaning necessary if we are to talk meaningfully and legitimately about *musical* discourses – related to structures and codes in music, if at all? Revealingly – in the light of Walser's claims on various categories of cultural theory to account for the complexities of signification through music – his understanding of structures and codes in music is that of a musician, not a cultural theorist with an intimate knowledge of music's sonic, technical features. The discussions of music undertaken in Walser's work draw on standard categories of musical production such as 'timbre', 'volume', 'mode', 'harmony', 'rhythm' and 'melody'. The assumption that goes unexamined here is that because such concepts are used – either explicitly and consciously, or implicitly and intuitively – by practising musicians in the production of music, the categories they represent are actually to be found in music's sonic events as identifiable technical characteristics. The point here is *not* that some musics – constructed *according* to these categories – do not display sonic characteristics which can be legitimately represented, described and analysed in terms of them. It is that these concepts and their accompanying categories and terminologies are constructs: linguistic constructs which constitute discourses essentially extrinsic to the sonic events of the music they describe. Since the categories are *not* intrinsic to the sounds of music, they can *of themselves* be of little assistance in specifying the cultural character of those sounds in music. We are not, however, implying that there is anything inherently misleading or wrong about using these categories in analyses of the sonic characteristics of music undertaken from a cultural theoretical perspective. We are saying, simply, that they themselves cannot lead to analyses which are socially and culturally sensitive. As a consequence, when analyses of these characteristics use *only* these categories – and others derived from them, as in descriptions of harmonic sequences using standard shorthand such as I, IV and V – it is difficult in the extreme to see how the analyses can be connected in any significant way to categories of cultural theoretical analysis.

The difficulties that Walser's work – and, indeed, that of others such as McClary (1991) – encounters can be made clear by acknowledging the distinctions that exist between sound as a material phenomenon, the experience of sound (Saussure's 'sound-image'), and the use of language to mediate awareness of this experience in ways specific to language which then makes talk about music possible. While it is not possible to experience the sounds of music in a manner unmediated through the effects of language, it does *not* follow from this that the experience is reducible to the conditions of experience instigated through language. As we will argue, the experience of sound in music is based upon a dialectical interaction between sound's material characteristics and the human body as itself a material site for the mediation of cultural and subjective processes. The experience of sound in language is likewise based upon the material characteristics of sound as invoked in language, but without these characteristics having any links of a *technological or instrumental character* with the characteristics of the corporeal processes through which awareness of the denotative and conceptual is made possible. That linkage is and must remain arbitrary in character if language is to retain the characteristics which allow it to act instrumentally and open-endedly on both the external *and* internal social worlds.

The problem with Walser's work – and that of some other

scholars – is that these distinctions are not made, let alone maintained. The confusion that inevitably results can lead only too
easily to a collapsing of the experience of sound *as sound* within
music to the condition of the language used to mediate awareness of it and to make talk about it possible. This language –
constructed, it should be remembered, from *outside* the experiences central and essential to processes of music to make discussion of them possible – gives rise to categories of understanding
and analysis which are then applied to the music in question. It
is *essential* to remember that such categories – while they may be
relevant, and importantly so, to manipulating and further developing the music in question – are *not* inherent to the sounds of
music as material phenomena *or*, therefore, to their experience.
While, therefore, there is *always* and *unavoidably* a dialectic
between musical experience and its management through language which of necessity inflects the experience in one way
rather than in any other, the dialectic could not exist were it not
for the relative autonomy in principle of the musical experience
in relation to its linguistic mediation.

The linkages between sound in music as a material phenomenon, the socially and culturally constituted experience of this
sound, and the processes – including those of linguistic discourse – implicated in social and cultural constitution cannot be
teased out because the necessary conceptual space in Walser's
work does not exist – or, if it exists, it is cloudy and murky to the
point that makes meaningful elaboration impossible. Musical
discourses for Walser thus translate into an awareness of the
heuristic principles constituting *langue* in music, and according
to which musical sounds are actually made. As he says,

> As a musician, I cannot help but think that individual texts, and the
> social experiences they represent, are important. My apprenticeships
> as a performer – conservatory student and orchestral musician, eth-
> nic outsider learning to play Polish polkas, jazz trumpeter, pop
> singer, and heavy metal guitarist – were periods spent learning
> musical discourses. That is, I had to acquire the ability to recognize,
> distinguish, and deploy the musical possibilities organized in styles
> or genres by various communities. Each song marshals the options
> available in a different way, and each musical occasion inflects a
> song's social meanings. Becoming a musician in any of the styles I
> have mentioned is a process of learning to understand and manipu-
> late the differences intrinsic to style, which are manifested differently
> in each text and performance. (1993, p. xii)

Unfortunately, the heuristic principles in terms of which sounds are rendered into actual music within any particular style or genre themselves lie *outside* the sounds of music and therefore musical experience. As we have seen, they are immanent in the logic of gestures or 'gesticulatory forms' that mediate between wider cultural and subjective processes and the articulation of sounds into music. To the extent that musical *langue* or deep structures receive actual, concrete expression, therefore, they frequently do so through language or linguistic discourses constructed to make the management and operation of principles of musical expression possible. It is the conflation of these processes which underpins Walser's notion of musical discourse. When links between the 'musical' and the 'cultural' are posited, therefore, there is no solid theoretical ground on which they rest. What results is an arbitrary aggregation or mechanical mix which represents no advance over the use of standard linguistic metaphors in traditional, liberal humanist musicology to describe musical experience. The arbitrary character of the links between 'music' and 'culture' results in textual readings which seem distinctly privileged in tone:

> Heavy metal revolves around identification with power, intensity of experience, freedom, and community. Musically, a dialectic is often set up between the potentially oppressive power of bass, drums, and rhythm guitar, and the liberating, empowering vehicle of the guitar solo or the resistance of the voice. The feeling of freedom created by the freedom of motion of the guitar solos and fills can be at various times supported, defended, or threatened by the physical power of the bass and the violence of the drums. The latter rigidly organize and control time; the guitar escapes with flashy runs and other arhythmic gestures. The solo positions the listener: he or she can identify with the controlling power without feeling threatened because the solo can transcend anything. (Walser, 1993, p. 54)

We are back here in the realm of determined, immanent meaning. However, as Walser reminds us, negotiation of this meaning can *only* occur because 'discourses ... have the power to organize the exchange of meanings' (1993, p. 55).

Addendum 2   The Generalizability of
Zuckerkandl's Arguments

The question inevitably arises as to the generalizability of
Zuckerkandl's arguments to musical traditions other than that
of functional tonality. There is a certain sense in which the arguments cannot help but remain specific to this tradition. The
greatest wave, the greatest phase in any piece of functional tonal
music (if we can put it this way) has to do with a final resolution
of tension, the culmination of movement at a final point of
arrival. Lesser phases within the piece tend to replicate this
greater logic as part of the overall drive towards satisfaction.
Local instances of tension unresolved and direction unfulfilled
act to defer ultimate gratification, as do local instances of resolution and culmination which act as generators of tension and
direction at higher levels of phasing (Meyer, 1959). It is in this
way that functional tonal music articulates a sense of teleology,
a sense of a final resting place in whose service all other musical
moments act. At the level of social and cultural realities functional tonal music articulates a Newtonian-Laplacian view of the
universe, a visual-mechanical sense of time and space that is
'flat', homogeneous, unified and governed by one point of
focus, the 'vanishing point' or, to move back into music, the key-
note (Shepherd, 1991b, pp. 96–127). In this sense, and in this
sense *only* (that of the socio-cultural articulation of time-space),
the notes of functional tonality *do* emphasize their difference 'in
opposition'. In gathering themselves into each other at the
'level' of musical articulation, they constantly point outside
themselves to each other at the 'level' of socio-cultural articulation, always wanting to 'move on' to the 'next step' in the teleological discourse. In thus detracting as far as is possible from
their inherent auditory qualities, notes in the functional tonal
tradition ape the condition of language in attempting to obscure
the condition of music, an attempt rendered more successful by
the creation of music theory and music analysis as discourses
grounded in language. The sense of time and space articulated
at the level of social and cultural reality by functional tonal
music thus runs counter, and paradoxically so, to the sense of
time and space that is inevitably invoked in the articulation of
the culture-specific time-space sense through the use of sound at

the level of auditory time-space, that is, the use of sound acting from its basis as a *medium* in music.

It was as a consequence observed that the disjunction perceptible between the experiential qualities of sounds acting from their basis as a medium in this particular musical tradition and the experiential qualities of the social and cultural realities thus articulated made possible, cognitively and conceptually, a distinction in levels of analysis. In noting that this disjunction may *not* occur or 'be reproduced' in the actual mechanics of meaning production through music, it has, on the one hand, to be accepted that the character of the mechanics of a particular medium in music acting out its role as a technology of articulation may well be 'influenced' by the form of the social and cultural realities thus articulated. The character of the mechanics of a particular medium can never be value-free since, in all cases of musical articulation, a technology of articulation has to exist: a technology *resulting* from auditory time-space acting in the service of a particular musical tradition. However, in the same way that music's significance, its states of awareness, its social and cultural realities can never be determined by the medium's technology of articulation, so the medium's technical characteristics can never be determined by the elements of signification of the musical processes in which it is embedded. While the medium may never be distinct as a moment of *meaning* through music, therefore, it must retain a certain, relative autonomy as a moment in the *analysis* of meaning through music. It can thus be accepted that the medium displays a *certain* autonomy of operation that is *not*, however, value-free.

In realizing that a medium is constituted as a consequence of acoustic time-space acting in the service of a particular musical tradition (and accepting also that a medium can *never* exist independently of actual instances of musical articulation), it is possible to argue that Zuckerkandl's work points to a more general understanding of syntax across musical traditions. While the particular *way* in which the individual sounds flowing from media (mediums) in functional tonal music gather up, contain within themselves and reveal virtually to individuals their contexts of spatial and temporal 'extension' may be specific to this musical tradition, the fact that they *do* gather up, contain within themselves and reveal virtually to individuals their contexts of spatial and temporal 'extension' may not. Zuckerkandl's capacity to concentrate on the phenomenology of musical experience in a particular tradition rather than upon an analysis of its stylistic characteristics using the traditional tools and approaches of music theory and music analysis therefore allows for an invaluable insight into the workings of music as a distinctive signifying practice which, unlike those of language, draws attention to the necessary involvement in them of individual subjects as socially and culturally constituted. It is in other words difficult to conceive of syntax in musical traditions as a whole not behaving in a manner which runs counter to the discreteness of the 'signifier' in language, and, in running counter to the idea of one denotative and connotative field in relation to one sound (in this case, the morpheme) at a time, running counter to notions of visual, mechanical space and its associated, spatialized sense of time. It seems not unlikely, in other words, that the syntaxes of all musical systems function in a revelationary rather than the discrete linear manner which seems more appropriate to an understanding of syntax in language.

7

Music's Semiological Moment

Having examined the manner in which syntax functions
structurally within music and discussed the issues which arise
from this examination, it now remains to discuss the workings
of music's 'internal' structures, those of its 'matter' or timbre.
Syntax, it should be remembered, is not synonymous with structure in music. Neither is structure in music reducible to syntax.
The syntactical time and space with which we have been dealing is, of course, of a very different order from the mechanical or
visual time and space of the classical understanding of the material universe. It is similar conceptually to the intrinsically relational or relative time and space of gravitational force fields, a
time and space that are continually in motion *as* the immaterial
substance of such force (Capek, 1961). No phenomena capable
of experiential or analytic isolation within such fields of force
can take on significance in an isolated fashion. This is precisely
why it is inappropriate to conceptualize individual auditory
events in their musically syntactical potential as 'signifiers'.
While the sound 'birds' uttered in isolation will retain the core
of the meaning it traditionally carries, for example, a musical
pitch will not. The concept of the 'medium' thus *allows* for the
complexly interpenetrative character of auditory events perceived as 'discrete' units of syntax in a manner in which the concept of the 'signifier' does not. The concept of the 'signifier' is
thus of little use as a basis for analysing the relationship
between sounds and the syntactical meanings with which they

are involved. This is because, in living through their musically syntactical function, individual sounds *in and of themselves* carry no meaning. However, it remains entirely possible that individual sounds in music can carry meaning, not acting in their function as 'modes of syntax', but acting in their function as 'musical matter'. If auditory time-space can act in the service of a particular musical tradition then, so it would seem, can auditory matter, or the tactile dimensions (the textures or timbres) of sounds themselves.

Zuckerkandl does not deal with this aspect of sound or tones. This is hardly surprising, given that music in the functional tonal tradition has always played down the role of timbre in sounds, and so the material presence of sounds themselves. Timbres in functional tonal music have tended to become standardized as 'pure' and therefore to be conceived as 'neutral' or 'transparent' in their articulative role (Shepherd, 1991b, pp. 152–73). Given the sense of time and space articulated at the level of social and cultural realities through music in this tradition, this is again hardly surprising. Although each individual phase in this tradition is constituted through processes of a multidimensional and multifaceted character, the character of the phases thus articulated gives rise to a sense of 'one moment at a time', 'one step at a time' in the philosophical march towards teleological completion. To allow timbre to play a role in overlapping – or, more accurately, influencing or inflecting – the syntactical moment would be to muddy the waters in deflecting the experience of the moment from its appointed purpose. Functional tonal music thus aspires to the condition of language not only in attempting to articulate one sense at a time, but in downplaying as far as is possible the role of sound itself in processes of meaning. For this reason, the somewhat idiosyncratic tradition of functional tonal music *may* be the one best suited for revealing the analytic disjunction that can be discerned as existing between the medium of music as a technology of articulation and music itself.

Sounds in other musical traditions are not thus constrained. Their timbrel dimensions call forth meanings in a direct and concrete yet symbolic manner. However, in their timbrel dimensions, sounds act not so much in the manner of linguistic signs in *referring* to actual phenomena in the external world, but as matrices of internally structured sounds to evoke states of awareness. These states of awareness may, however, be associated with phenomena in the external world. It is because 'sounds' themselves *are* in fact constituted by complex bundles of sounds that, among other reasons, it becomes extremely difficult in many cases to identify the 'museme' – in a manner parallel to that in which the morpheme is identified – as the smallest unit of sound having meaning. In the same way that people in oral-aural cultures quite legitimately have difficulty distinguishing between 'words', 'phrases', 'sentences' and complete poems and songs (Lord, 1964, p. 25), it seems likely that in music one person's discrete sonic event may be implicated in the 'bundle of sounds' that constitutes another person's discrete sonic event. This is another reason why sounds in music functioning in this manner cannot be legitimately thought of as 'signifiers'.

Sounds at this level (the level of timbre) may work in one of two ways (homologously, but in relation either to other sounds or to non-sonic phenomena). First, they may refer to actual sounds in the external world. This reference may be a direct copy, as in the use of drums to signal the mental concept of 'militariness', or a symbolic evocation, as in the case of the 'cuckoo calls' in Beethoven's Sixth Symphony or the 'sounds of the sea' in Debussy's *La Mer*. This use of sound in music is the one that may appear to come closest to the use of sounds in language. Such sounds are not, however, capable of denoting actual phenomena in the external world: they refer only to the characteristic sounds of phenomena and not the phenomena themselves. This form of reference may be thought of as 'denotative' in character, but mimetically and thus homologously so. Second, there are those sounds which evoke symbolically various internal states. This, in fact, is the core of musical articulation, a point to which we will return. An example of this manner of signification is provided by arguments to do with the relationship between various voice timbres and gender identities (Shepherd, 1991b, pp. 152–73). Another example is provided through the use of a distant and hollow quena flute sound to evoke the feeling of a distant and unobtainable love (Tagg, 1991).

Musical sounds of this type, which have been analysed extensively by Tagg (1979, 1982, 1987 and 1991), may *seem* to approach to the condition of signifiers (the term used by Tagg is, it will be remembered, the 'museme'). Their ability to evoke meaning is not context-bound in a musical sense. When a black gospel singer begins her performance, for example, the effect upon the congregation, whether positive or not so positive, is instantaneous. There is no need for a continually unfolding context of sounds for the congregation to discern meaning in the timbrel characteristics of a particular sound. The broader context of the music may well confirm and augment the original impression, but the voice quality, which the congregation recognizes as coming from 'within the person', signifies in and of itself.

But although these sounds may be thought of as approaching the condition of signifiers, they do not function arbitrarily. First, they can in every case be argued to have a structural relationship with their 'associated' states of awareness. Thus, in the case of the drum sounds, the state of awareness is the mental concept of drum sounds in actual military situations, not the mental concept of 'militariness' evoked by actual military drum sounds. The relationship between sound and state of awareness is structurally tight because the sound is presumably a direct copy, or a nearly direct copy, of drum sounds in actual military situations. The structural relationship of 'cuckoo calls' and the 'sounds of the sea' to these sounds as they occur in the external world is similar in character. The character of the structural relationship of the internal characteristics of voice timbres to the logics and structures of gender identities has been discussed elsewhere (Shepherd, 1991b, pp. 152–73).

Second, although it cannot be established incontrovertibly, it seems likely that the relationship between sounds in the external world – whose invocation can be thought of as constituting third-order states of awareness – and the second-order states of awareness that are evoked through their invocation in music is likewise structural (see figure 1). That is, there may well exist a structural relationship between the internal characteristics of drum sounds and the logics and structures of 'militariness', between cuckoo calls and 'pastoralness', and the sounds of the sea and 'oceanness'. Finally, it seems entirely possible that there exists a structural relationship between the internal logics and structures of these second-order states of awareness as 'conventionally' and 'customarily' evoked through music (those, for example, of 'pastoralness' and 'oceanness') and the logics and structures of the inner life (the 'first-order' states of awareness)

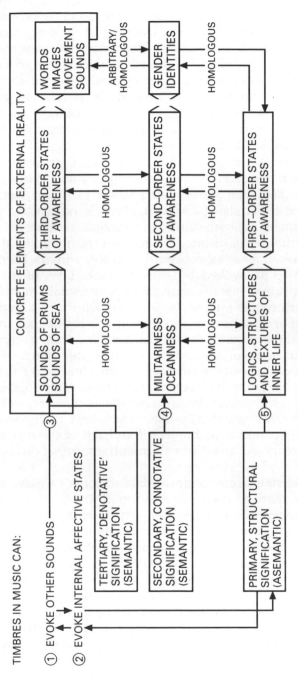

Figure 1 Matter in music

to which they in turn speak. Indeed, this has to be the case if signification is to occur since the meaning of music can never be
'in' the medium of its sounds. 'Oceanness', for example, is not
contained as a meaning 'in' the characteristic use of sound in
music which gives rise to this concept (connotation), this feeling
(*primary* signification). It is evoked in part and indirectly
through the sounds' homologous evocation of the sounds of the
sea, which in turn give rise in a homologous fashion to the
concept or feeling of 'oceanness'.

Two features of these connections are worth noting in conclusion. Since the sounds of music start out by acting in a mimetic
and so homologous fashion in relation to other sounds (for
example, the sounds of the sea), there is nothing to prevent
them acting at the same time in an iconic fashion in evoking
more directly the logics and structures of the inner life (the 'first-
order' states of awareness occurring at the primary level of signification) to be evoked by second-order states of awareness
(occurring at the level of connotation or secondary signification)
such as 'oceanness'. There is, in other words, a circuit rather
than a line of signifying connections involving sounds in music:
sounds in the external world, whose invocation constitutes
third-order states of awareness; second-order states of awareness (connotation and secondary signification); and first-order
states of awareness (primary signification). These experiential
moments in the circuit are all mutually reinforcing as the con-
cretization made possible by their structurally homologous 'fits'
moves their connections towards the realm of the conventional
and customary. All these possible relations are set out in figures
1 and 2.

It would thus seem inappropriate to think of these kinds of
sounds in music as giving rise to signification in a *purely* arbitrary or conventional fashion. Such sounds may well have
become conventionalized through constant and repeated usage
in terms of the predictable meanings to which they are *likely* to
give rise, and in this sense the work of Tagg is welcome and its
conclusions of value. However, it should not be forgotten that a
structural basis for the meanings constructed through this
dimension of sound in music has to lie behind their conventionalized aspects. The 'abstract' (visually 'non-denotative') character of the 'internal properties' of sounds in other words means
that they *have* to function in a structural manner if they are to

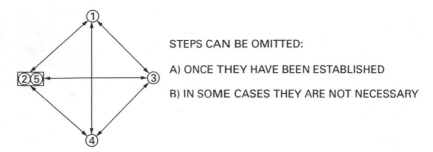

Figure 2 Circle of homology

function at all in being *implicated* in processes of meaning construction, if, in other words, a technology of articulation is to occur through the circuit of signification just described.

The Sonic Saddle

Having discussed the various dimensions and attributes of sounds acting as a structure in music, it is now possible to move our discussion back from more structural to semiological concerns in anticipating in the following chapter a formal statement of the characteristics of the second (or, as it will turn out) third semiology that we have developed. We are now in a position, in other words, to describe how each passing auditory and affective moment can reveal sounds in music acting as a structure. However sounds in the medium of music appeal to and evoke states of awareness, be it syntactically or 'directly' (and 'indirectly') through their internal structures, one thing is certain. Evocation can only occur in the continually unfolding present *through* the tactile dimensions of sound, the matter of sound as it is presented to us. It is only in this way that the sounds of music can operate through a technology of articulation. The concept of the 'saddle' of the continually unfolding present – a term coined by Zuckerkandl – is thus crucial to understanding the articulation of meaning through music. Meaning in music is articulated through the continually unfolding saddle of the medium, which is to say, the sonic saddle of the present. However, while the saddle of the medium occurs as an aspect of external reality, as the sounds of the auditory time-space of the external world, it is possible to conceive of the sonic saddle *only* as an experiential phenomenon made possible by the medium. As sound-image, the saddle occupies a position in processes of the articulation of meaning through music similar to that of the signifier in processes of the articulation of meaning through language.

The sonic saddle is nothing if not versatile. It contains within itself several 'levels' of articulation. *Its* technology of articulation – embedded within that of the medium – is multidimensional and multifaceted, not only in the mechanics of its syntactical operation, but also in the 'overlay' of its timbrel dimensions *and* the capacity of its internal structures to change in a continuous manner, to give rise to 'inflections' of pitch and timbre (a feature of articulation of particular importance to many genres of music within the tradition of popular music). This character of a phase, discontinuous in its adjacency to the next phase, may in other words change and reconfigure itself before the discontinuous advent of the character of the next phase. This gives rise to a sense of internal movement to match, complement, inflect and even 'contradict' the motion or phasing established syntactically.

The concept of the saddle requires further elaboration with respect to its syntactical implications. Zuckerkandl's analysis of syntax and motion concentrated heavily on each successive musical moment. That is why his analysis is so helpful in developing the notion of the saddle and the way in which it can gather up syntax within it. Syntax, however, can have many levels within it (and is not, as we shall see, solely dependent upon the parameters of pitch and duration). It does not occur *only* at the most general and all-encompassing level of a musical event. It can in principle occur at all levels of the event. Syntactical patterns and their components (for example, motifs and themes in the tradition of functional tonality, melodies and hooks in popular music) in other words repeat 'exactly' or nearly enough so as to be heard as variants and transformations at various syntactical levels. This feature of music has been documented extensively with respect to the functional tonal tradition by Reti (1958). The relations – which are still of a syntactical order – set up through this aspect of music form the real basis of 'equivalence' in music as opposed to 'difference' (which is in reality to say 'opposition' or 'repulsion'). What is really at stake here, then, is a 'difference in attraction' rather than a 'difference in opposition'.

This 'difference in attraction' applies as much to timbre and inflection as it does to pitch and duration. It was earlier noted that timbre in music *can* function 'out of context' with regard to the evocation of both third- and second-order states of awareness. Sounds in music functioning as timbre in other words do not *depend* on a wider musical context for their power to communicate. As we noted, the effect of a gospel singer's voice can be immediate. However, sounds functioning in this manner *do* nonetheless occur within wider contexts whose character may be constituted through various combinations and permutations of pitch, duration, timbre and inflection. The fundamental affect created by sounds acting as timbre in music can therefore be inflected and mediated by 'relations of *equivalence* across segments' constituted *both* timbrely (the sounds sound the same or nearly so) and through other syntactic elements (each syntactic context has to be different by virtue of the manner in which music functions as a structure). Similar observations can be made with respect to inflection itself.

It also has to be noted that difference in opposition can survive within this syntactic mode of musical articulation. Although Reti, for example, is at pains to demonstrate motivic connections by transformation between all the themes in a particular piece of music, the demonstration at times seems strained in its capacity to convince. 'Opposition' as well as 'equivalence' between motivic, thematic, timbrel and inflectional material can obtain, thus underpinning 'difference' as well as 'equivalence' in processes of musical articulation. The difficulty here, of course, is in deciding when variation and transformation cease to be variation and transformation (whether with respect to pitch, duration, timbre or inflection) and become opposition or 'difference'. Further, syntactical opposition at one level may be subverted or contradicted by equivalence (attraction) at another. Finally, given the multidimensional and multifaceted character of the sonic saddle, no one musical moment need be given over entirely to either 'opposition' or 'attraction'. Given this complexity of articulation through music it might be concluded that the fundamental reference point for all these possible relations of 'difference' and 'equivalence' is, in fact, equivalence. Even with 'opposition' and 'difference', the relations seem to be ones of 'attraction' and 'comparison', not 'repulsion' and 'immanence'. That is how music functions as a structure.

It is at this point that the real difference between language and music as structures of articulation becomes clear. This difference lies not in a difference between 'difference' and 'equivalence', or in a difference between 'opposition' and 'similarity' of elements of signification. It lies within a different order of differences. Difference in language is based on a principle of repulsion which results in the order of relations obtaining between elements of signification deploying components of meaning in an exclusive, consistent and, as a consequence, 'immanent' association with sounds recognized as discrete. Difference in music is based on a principle of attraction which results in the order of relations obtaining between similar and different elements of signification deploying components of meaning throughout concatenations of sounds recognized as discrete in a manner which has the potential to become infinitely complex. It is this basic difference in the character of how music and language function as structures which ultimately clarifies the somewhat confusing use of terminology in the discussion of these issues. We might therefore conclude by saying that, if there were no differences *between* segments – differences, that is, constituted by relations of 'equivalence' or 'opposition' *across* segments rather than relations of difference as contained *within* segments (whether these differences *between* segments are articulated through nearly identical *or* significantly unrelated syntaxes, timbres or inflections *or* through 'identical' syntaxes, timbres or inflections deployed in different contexts – bearing in mind that genuine re-identification with sound is not possible) – *if* there were no differences *between* segments as opposed to differences *within* segments, then there would be no music. It may be for this reason that Middleton argues that, with music, 'relations of *equivalence* are just as important [as relations of *difference*, and] *perhaps more so*' (1990, p. 183, last italics ours).

As we noted earlier, the principle of syntactical articulation (which we can now understand to include timbre and inflections as well as pitch and duration) is no different from that obtaining between individual moments of musical experience. Subsegmental, segmental and suprasegmental relations still involve – in accordance with the principles of how music functions as a structure – a process of mutual gathering and revelation. And since each musical moment carries with it not only the motion uniquely imparted through its particular location in a syntactical segment but also the motion imparted through the segment's segmental, subsegmental and suprasegmental relations to other segments, each musical moment within a musical structure still remains unique. The importance and true complexity of the saddle should never be underestimated. It is only in being able to move beyond considerations of 'relations of equivalence *across* segments' to consider the character of the actual moment of the articulation of significance through the sounds of music that the character of musical affect will be understood.

In our discussion of musical matter considerable emphasis was placed on the way in which timbre in music can be involved with second- and third-order states of awareness. This capacity is not, however, restricted to timbre alone. It applies also to syntactical segments. Various constellations of pitches and durations of musical sounds can become 'concretized' into formulae and 'themes' traditionally associated with various second-order states of awareness. Stolidly rising triads can thus evoke 'heroism' or 'chauvinism', as in the case of the opening of the 'Marseillaise'. Rather more vacillating movement by open fifths can evoke 'the character of wide open spaces', as in some of Aaron Copland's music. Two points need to be made here. Firstly, syntactical or thematic formulae can only work in this way by entering processes of the musical articulation of meaning at the level of primary signification. In this, the formulae are unlike timbres, which can enter also at the level of 'denotative', third-order awareness. Secondly, such formulae cannot evoke third-order states, even indirectly. While concrete elements of external reality can be embedded in second-order states as evoked syntactically through the additional, complementary use of timbre (for example, the use of brass in the opening of the 'Marseillaise' invoking the sounds of a military band and so a second-order state of awareness of 'militariness' commensurate with the second-order state of awareness of the 'heroic' achieved syntactically), or simply through arbitrary association, neither of these procedures matches the ability of timbres to evoke concrete elements of external reality in the ways previously described (see figure 1). It should, however, be noted that the possibility of arbitrarily associating third-order states of

awareness with second-order states of awareness as evoked syntactically only exists *because* of the homologous relations obtaining between the first-order states of awareness *necessary* for such
evocation *and* the second-order states evoked. The totality of
relations involving syntax and timbre is set out in figure 3. The
complexity of the sonic saddle and the grounding of this complexity in sound as the medium of music is set out in figure 4. In
figure 4 the character of the interpenetration of the complexities
of the medium as *sounds* with the saddle as *sound-image* (in reality, *only* timbre) should be noted in the context of previous
remarks on the impossibility of creating levels of analysis whose
status matches that of moments of musical articulation in
reality.

The presentation of sonic matter recognized as musically significant cannot help but evoke states of awareness whose degree
and manner of affectivity are related to the characteristics of the
sounds presented. The sounds of music cannot help, in other
words, but reaffirm the present existence of the individual, and
reaffirm it with a concreteness and directness not required for
reaffirmation through the sounds of language. The material
character of sound in music speaks directly and concretely
through its technology of articulation to the individual's awareness and sense of self, an awareness and sense, it should be
remembered, that is pervasively social and discursive in its
mediation and constitution. However, the sonic saddle achieves
more than this. Through its material presence, it reveals syntactically the character and condition of the musical universe which
contains the individual and which the individual inhabits.
Extension, dimension, structure and context are in this way
revealed and articulated within the individual. The versatility
and dimensional complexity of the sonic saddle is thus instructive in the sense that the individual, as a social and discursive
being, inhabits a social and discursive world, a social and discursive universe that likewise evidences features of extension,
dimension and structure, and provides the context necessary for
existence as a social and discursive being. The concept of the
sonic saddle, constituted as a complex technology of articulation, is suggestive in terms of the manner in which the relationship between the most massive social structures, the most
extensive and powerful discourses *and* the most powerful yet
intimate and idiosyncratic instances of individual awareness

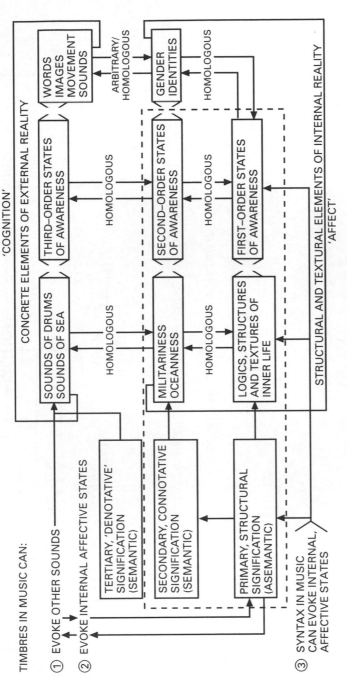

Figure 3 Syntax and timbre in music

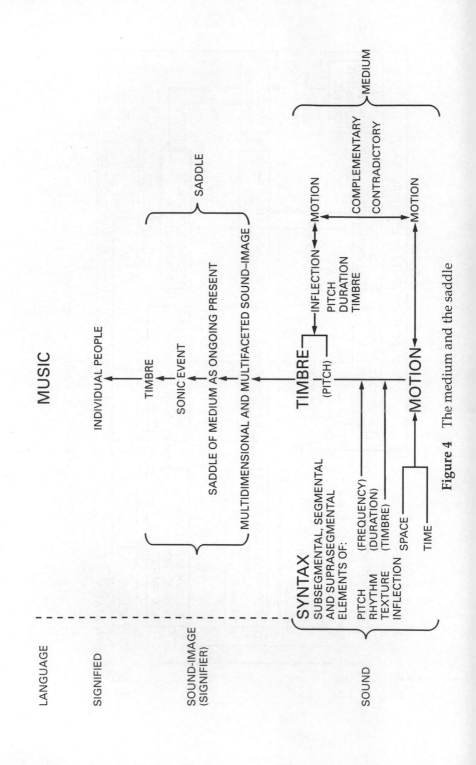

Figure 4 The medium and the saddle

might be theorized. A *prima facie* case can thus be established for the simultaneous evocation through music's sonic saddle of the internal and external social and discursive worlds specific to the individual at any particular moment.

The sonic saddle is instructive in one further regard. In arguing for the simultaneous articulation through the sonic saddle of the internal and external social and discursive worlds, an argument is at the same time being made for the simultaneous evocation of a world that is immediately and intensively affective (the internal world) and a world (the external world) which, in everyday life, is known less immediately, less intensively. In everyday life, the external world is a world into which people are capable of projecting themselves through language and vision. It is a world where cognition (apprehension *not* involving a technology of articulation) tends to precede affect. The internal world, on the other hand, is a world in which affect (apprehension which *does* involve a technology of articulation) tends to precede cognition. The sonic saddle is thus further instructive in that these complex interplays of the affective and cognitive, which occur between as well as within the internal and external worlds, are revealed to us *symbolically* through a primary affectivity, the primary affectivity of music. However, the technology of articulation of this primary affectivity displays, as we have seen, different 'levels'. While it is timbre which connects directly and immediately to the affective core of the individual, it is, on the whole, syntax which evokes symbolically the external world into which individuals may project themselves through language and vision. Although the analogy should not be carried too far, it could be said that, within Western cultures at least, if timbre appeals to the 'heart', syntax appeals to the 'head'. This complexity and versatility of articulation throw light on the articulative processes of music in the functional tonal tradition. In foregrounding and prioritizing syntax to the degree that it does, music in this tradition puts as much stress *as is possible through music* on the external, cognitive world, and this at the expense of the internal, affective world. There is a tendency for the internal world to be known through the external world when, in reality, it is the external world that is being articulated musically through the internal world. These alliances between the internal, timbrel and affective world on the one hand, and the external, syntactical and cognitive world are, it should be noted, different from those obtaining between timbre and cognition, *and* syntax and affect as set out in figure 3. At the same time as emphasizing the substance of self in relation to the contexts of the external world, timbre can evoke concrete elements pertaining to that world. Equally, at the same time as evoking the structures of the external world as marked out in reality by concrete elements, syntax can *only* speak directly in its presence as pure structure to the logics and structures of the inner life. The relations between affect and cognition in music as articulated through a primary affectivity are, indeed, complex.

The complexity and versatility of articulation *through* the sonic saddle enable an understanding of why it would be thought that 'the problem [with music] is . . . that the structure of the content plane is . . . probably ambiguous and amorphous' (Middleton, 1990, p. 179). It also enables an understanding of why, with a medium of expression that uses both 'difference' and 'equivalence', and in which 'units and their constituents often relate to each other as variants, transformations or repetitions, rather than [just as] oppositions', substitution techniques, in the words of Middleton, 'will mislead or provide only partial results' (1990, p. 183). The complexity and versatility of the sonic saddle demonstrate the ultimate futility of using concepts such as the 'signifier' or the 'museme' to explain primary signification in music and, *through that*, secondary signification (although Tagg's notions of 'museme stacks' does point in the direction of the 'sonic saddle'). Beyond this, however, it must not be forgotten that music does not function by 'association' or 'pure convention'. It evidences a technology of articulation. It is for this reason that all concepts derived from linguistics must ultimately be dispensed with in analysing signification through music. Semiology (or at least a first semiology) has little to offer in understanding music as a signifying practice. Tagg's work does not explain signification in music. It describes its effects at the level of secondary signification. If, in the language of Volek, there is to be a 'semiotics of music', then this semiotics must be what has been termed a 'second semiology'.

8

Music: A Performative Semiological Model

The task that was set for us at the end of chapter 4 was to understand how music, in evidencing a set of formal yet asemantic properties, could act as a structure in a manner matching yet distinct from that of language. In drawing a distinction between 'differences through attraction' and 'differences through repulsion', and in arguing that music encompasses rather than deploys the world, we believe that we have established that distinction. Through syntactical processes involving timbre and inflection as well as pitch and duration, *how?* each musical moment gathers up within itself the condition of the universe of which it forms a part, and reveals that condition in a manner unique to itself. Each musical moment thereby constitutes a particular phasing or charging of that universe which simultaneously has folded within it timbrel and inflectional elements of direct material relevance to individual states of awareness. As we have seen, sounds as the medium of music and, flowing from that medium, the sonic saddle as sound-image, manifest a potential for considerable complexity in respect of both affect and cognition in constituting music's technology of articulation. It is the sonic saddle, constituting a technology of articulation, which, through its various dimensions, facilitates different levels of signification through music. It is the sonic saddle which, as music's technology of articulation, takes us from the world of structuralism into the world of semiology: a world constituted through the connectedness of the sounds of music acting structurally to individual subjects. It is to this world that we now turn.

Terms and Relations

In chapters 5, 6 and 7, we argued that music as a social medium is constituted through structured and structuring sounds and matrices of sounds that give rise to a continually unfolding 'sonic saddle'. Through its multidimensional and multifaceted structural character, this saddle is capable of offering up possibilities and potentials for the investment in it of various states of awareness flowing from and sustaining the structures of the human world. However, the arguments presented in these chapters made it clear that the relationship between music as a social medium and the structures and states of the human world were of a considerably more complex character than those obtaining between the sounds of language and the meanings of the world. In the case of music, the idea of 'individual' sounds as supporting meaning has been replaced by the notion of the medium as structured and structuring sounds presented to us by the external world. The signifier has been replaced by the concept of the 'sonic saddle' as the continually unfolding sound-image derived from the medium and *experienced* as the material ground and pathway for the investment of meaning. This distinction between the medium as belonging to the external world and the saddle as belonging to the internal world therefore replicates Saussure's distinction between the material fact of the sounds of a morpheme in language and the psychological imprint or image of the sounds (sound-image) as they constitute the signifier in awareness. The concept of the signified has been replaced by the rather more general notion of 'elements of signification', a term which, in its generality and possibility of application outside the realm of music, may also subsume the concept of the signified.

As they are invested in the sonic saddle, elements of signification are derived from states of awareness and are coextensive with them. Elements of signification cannot occur independently of states of awareness, in other words. However, states of awareness are capable of existing independently of elements of signification in the sense that the particular configuration of elements of signification coextensive with states of awareness *depends* on the actuality *and* the particular form of the *material* and *public* articulation of meaning in any particular instance. Elements of signification depend as much on the actuality of public articulation, in other words, as they do on internal states of awareness. This is so whether the articulation is being presented to an individual, or being uttered by an individual. However, while it remains true that no state of awareness can come into being independently of social processes, the communication that makes social processes possible, and thus the material and public articulation of meaning (socialization *precedes* a sense of identity, not the other way round), it is nonetheless the case that states of awareness *can* exist independently of the material and public articulation of meaning in the *presence* of the here-and-now. Individuals can, in other words, experience states of awareness without rendering them public and therefore giving them material existence in the external world. In thus differing from elements of signification (which depend on public articulation to come into being), states of awareness can exist independently of elements of signification. If this were not the case, it is difficult to see how the relationship between sounds as the material basis for signification and states of awareness could remain negotiable (this applies to both music and language), and how individuality and creativity could, within certain constraints, be maintained. This is a point to which we will return.

The term 'states of awareness' has been used to emphasize the corporeal and somatic dimensions of meaning construction through music, dimensions which we believe to be *fundamental* to meaning construction through music. However, the term as it applies to music covers cognition as well as affect, and can therefore subsume the complex interplays between cognition and affect in music. To this extent, the term may subsume also the notion of the 'mental concept', the mental concept supporting and giving rise to signifieds in a manner similar to that in which states of awareness support and give rise to elements of signification. In giving rise to elements of signification, states of awareness are experiential in character and in this regard match the experiential character of the sonic saddle. As we argued previously, it is not however legitimate to separate this particular experiential world into distinct levels in a manner similar to that in which the experience of the signifier and the experience of the signified may be kept legitimately separate as orders of experience in language. The most that can be argued is that, in constituting an onset of affect (and subsequently – but not always – cognition), the experience of the sonic saddle and the experience of its 'associated' state of awareness constitute but one experience evidencing different aspects.

This distinction between the experience of the sonic saddle and that of its 'associated' state of awareness is thus *only* of analytic or heuristic relevance and application. This distinction is one that is not present in *actual* instances of meaning construction through music. This is because there is a technology or instrumentality of articulation operating in music that is not present in language, a technology of articulation that results in a material binding at the moment of the onset of affect which is likewise not present in language. It is for this reason that it is not legitimate to talk of an 'association' between the sonic saddle and states of awareness. It is for this reason also that the slippage which can occur – and necessarily so – between the sounds of the medium in music and individuals' states of awareness occurs between the sounds of the medium as presented to us by external reality and the sonic saddle as the experience of those sounds at each particular moment of their occurrence, as well as between states of awareness fixed in relation to elements of signification which *are* instigated through the presentation of a medium and 'associated' sonic saddle, *and* similar although somewhat changed states of awareness *not* immanent in the materiality of public articulation. The distinction between the sonic saddle and states of awareness (elements of signification) as aspects of one experiential moment nonetheless remains important, therefore, because it permits a more general theorization of internal states (which may be 'free' of music) in relation to the external, objective world. States of awareness (from which elements of signification flow in actual instances of the material and public articulation of meaning) may be thought of as the subjective dimensions of an ontology of which states of being are the objective constitution. There is a sense in which states of being as the internalized forms of external structures with which they nonetheless remain in a continuing dialectical relation become states of awareness as the experience of those states of

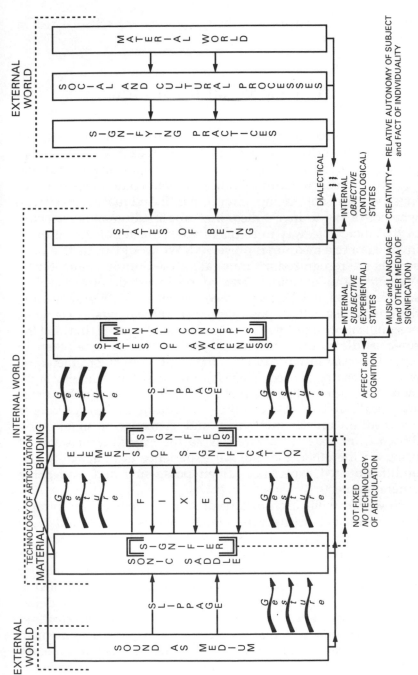

Figure 5 Semiological model

being. All these terms and their relations are schematized in figure 5.

Fixity and Negotiation in Music

It is now possible to argue that the generation and investment of meanings in a medium is not a matter of free choice *at the level of primary signification*. While it is not being claimed that the sounds of music determine, cause or even communicate meanings, we are not saying either that individuals can choose whether or not to invest meanings in a medium *once presented*, or that there is leeway in terms of the character of the meaning invested once a medium *is* presented. We would argue that once sounds are recognized as 'musical', a medium is automatically presented and meanings *have* to be invested (otherwise the sounds would not be recognized as 'musical'). Consequently, there is *no* negotiation possible between meanings as elements of signification and states of awareness on the one hand, *and* the sonic saddle as the *experience* of the medium on the other. In every *particular* instance of meaning creation in music, therefore, *primary* meaning is fixed. This claim is consistent with our argument that, although a distinction can be drawn for heuristic, analytical purposes between the sonic saddle as the *experience* of the medium on the one hand, and elements of signification drawn from states of awareness as the *experience* of states of being on the other, the musical experience is in actuality *one*, undifferentiated experience, albeit possessing and evidencing different aspects.

However, while each instant of primary musical meaning is fixed in relation to its experiential aspects at *each* and *every* moment, this does not mean that negotiation of meaning between individual instances and locations of primary meaning construction becomes impossible. This is because the character of the medium as structured and structuring sound presented to individuals through the *external* world cannot completely determine the character of the sonic saddle as the *constructed* and *internal* experience of that medium at any particular moment (although it can certainly proscribe it). The character of the sonic saddle is arrived at through an editing and interpretation of the medium which in turn is determined in part by the states of awareness (and their configuration) which are brought to bear on and elicited by the medium as presented. The identical medium can thus give rise to different (although probably similar) saddles in different individuals and in the same individual at different times.

The negotiation of the saddle as a product of awareness is thus made possible also by the way in which states of awareness may develop and change in individuals once they are free of their fixing in elements of signification as these elements are brought to life through instances of the public and material articulation of meaning. The fixing of meanings that nonetheless remain 'negotiable' in relation to the medium is a product of the technology or instrumentality of articulation exercised by the medium (structured and structuring sounds by definition recognized as 'musical') through the sonic saddle. In this way, the sounds of music *grip* the body with an instantaneous firmness whose character and significance nonetheless remain negotiable from person to person and from moment to moment. There cannot be significance in music without sounds as a structured and structuring medium, since without sounds there can be no experience and thus no fixing of awareness through the calling forth of the elements of signification coterminous with the saddle. Conversely, there cannot be significance in music without states of awareness on which the medium can act through its technology of articulation. Media and states of awareness have material circuits that are quite distinct. However, their encountering displays a *material* binding and fixity that is immediate and can be powerful. Although this statement may as a consequence seem self-evident, it is worth making in view of the tendency within musicology and commonsense understandings of music to reduce music to the condition of its sounds: without sounds – no music; without people – no music.

Music positions individuals, and with a material binding and instrumentality that is inescapable and can be powerful. However, positioning is, in our submission, distinct from 'speaking'. Firstly, sounds which some people recognize as musical may not be recognized as musical by others. In this latter instance, music does not occur and neither, consequently, does any positioning or 'speaking'. Secondly – although this is becoming increasingly difficult in a world of muzak – people can on the whole choose which music they wish to listen to and experience. In other words, people may choose whether or not to be positioned in particular ways by certain musics. They may choose not to be positioned by certain musics because the experience may be dissonant and fracturing to an uncomfortable or even painful degree. While music in some situations may not be recognized as music in others – with the consequence that 'music' does not occur – some music, while remaining recognizably musical, may be sufficiently distanced from an individual culturally or biographically that the moment of material binding and instrumental articulation displays little harmony or synchrony. The internal world of the individual can thus be confronted, twisted, brutalized and insulted to a degree that is unacceptable. This is an experience that parents not uncommonly have with the music of their children. This musical 'generation gap' has been experienced between those who loved Frank Sinatra and hated Elvis Presley, loved the Beatles and hated Heavy Metal, and loved rock but hated techno. This pattern of affective response towards various genres of popular music has a long history. For example, *Musical America* complained in 1913 that ragtime 'exalts noise, rush and street vulgarity. It suggests repulsive dance-halls and restaurants.' In 1901, the president of the American Federation of Musicians ordered his members to stop playing ragtime. 'The musicians know what is good', he said, 'and if people don't we will have to teach them' (quoted in Shepherd, 1982b, p. 37). In 1926, a Baptist minister wrote in the *New York Times* that 'I have no patience with this modern jazz tendency, whether it be in music, science, social life or religion. It is part of the lawless spirit which is being manifested in many departments of life, endangering our civilization in its general revolt against authority and established order.' A Princeton University professor went so far as to say that jazz 'is not music at all' (quoted, Shepherd, 1982b, p. 64). It is interesting to note that the sounds of music which cause such negative reactions are categorized as 'noise' or 'not music at all', and, because of the jarring effect they have on individual subjects, as having a deleterious effect upon individual and cultural identities. This dissonance and fracture also explains strong and negative reactions to some twentieth-century music in the modernist and avant-garde traditions (the case of the première of Stravinsky's *Le Sacre du printemps* in Paris in 1913 is a well-known example of this phenomenon). We would argue that, although a certain attempt at positioning occurs in cases such as these, little 'speaking' is achieved.

Thirdly, a person's response at one moment to a set of sounds recognized as musical may be significantly different at another. Identity and personality are not fixed. They are, within certain constraints, continuously negotiable, and, in this sense, the states of awareness in play at one moment may be changed at another. Although, at each instant, a person may be positioned musically (either willingly or unwillingly), this positioning cannot therefore be equated with 'speaking'. Finally, the question of the intensity of the technology of articulation and of the material binding that occurs at each moment of musical affect must be raised. In some cases, music can be experienced in a highly intensive manner. In others, it may be experienced, but only, perhaps, as a vague background presence. The focusing of intensity is something, we would submit, over which individuals retain an appreciable if not high degree of control.

These arguments contrast markedly with those of poststructuralism. While it is *not* being claimed that elements of signification have an existence prior to the sonic medium in and through which they have life, it is not being accepted, either, that discourses unilaterally speak subjects. The character of the intersection between elements of signification and the medium of music is thus taken to be iconic, but *not* fixedly so. The element of *symbolism* (a symbolism guaranteed through the 'move' of medium to saddle) remains, as we saw, an important one. There is, from *moment to moment*, a constant dialectic in process which requires that the negotiation of meaning remains possible. People may, on the one hand, be easily positioned by familiar music that they desire. In this kind of situation, little more than the reaffirmation of previous patterns of awareness may be at stake. However, in other situations, the individual may make a conscious choice to engage in a dialogue with new and unfamiliar musics that require a readjustment of the self. In other words, individuals may choose to extend themselves, to 'grow' in a biographical sense by *allowing* themselves to 'get into' and thus be positioned by new and unfamiliar music (Ellis, 1985). Although meaning in music is fixed at every moment of its articulation, the negotiability of this fixity illustrates that meaning in music originates *ultimately* with the individual.

Music and the Body

We complete our account of how it is that music imparts affect to individuals by exploring the relationship between music and body in the light of the semiological model we have described in the previous two sections. As an auditory phenomenon music offers up a material ground in and through which individual subjects can invest and map their own meanings, their own experiences. Music is meaningful to individuals inasmuch as the inherent characteristics of its textures and structures are suitable to the investment in them of the meanings – themselves coded and experienced through the rhythms, textures and structures of the body – that such characteristics may call forth. But because of the *relatively* tight iconic intersection between music as a medium in sound and the meanings called forth from individuals, not all music can receive all possible 'intended' meanings, and not all possible 'intended' meanings can be successfully invested in all musics. There cannot be a fixed, one-to-one relationship between music and meaning, in other words. But, on the other hand, not all meanings are possible in all musics. Middleton has put this contrast eloquently in pointing to the mutual advantages and disadvantages of culturalist and structuralist analyses:

> Whatever the position, it seems likely that in practice there are, inscribed in the musical form and its cultural history, *limits* to the transmutation of meaning and hence to the re-construction of homologies; 'culturalist' social actors are not free to express themselves by inventing or interpreting *ab novo*, and 'structuralist' texts are not free to wander infinitely away from the cultural contexts in which their meanings have been defined. It seems likely, too, that in the relationship of form and ... 'experience' ... the two must 'dock' – rather than the one completely producing the other or the conjunction being purely one of juxtaposition. The docking may be relatively loose; but the parties must meet within certain *limits of tolerance*. (1990, p. 154)

The sounds of music in other words remain relatively autonomous in relation to the processes of subjectivity that they call forth in individuals, and individuals remain relatively autonomous in relation to the musical sounds that they utter and internalize.

The internal dispositions and configurations of bodies that find expression in externally perceptible bodily movement affect fundamentally the dynamics of sound production from the most basic and inalienably human of all musical instruments, the human voice. The voice, says Middleton, is 'the profoundest mark of the human'. An unsounding human body, he continues, 'is a rupture in the sensuousness of existence'. Undoubtedly, he concludes, 'this is because vocalizing is the most intimate, flexible and complex mode of articulation of the body' (Middleton, 1990, p. 262). It is also, presumably, because the voice, as the most intimate, flexible and complex mode of articulation of the body, is fundamental to the creation of human societies. Johan Sundberg discusses the relationships between body movements, human emotion, and the physiology of voice production:

> There is a close correlation between body movements observable with the naked eye and hidden body movements. Examples of normally invisible body movements can be found in laryngeal cartilages, most of which are involved in the regulation of voice pitch. If it is true that a particular pattern of expressive body movements is typical of a specific emotional mode, then we would expect a corresponding pattern of, for example, voice pitch in speech produced in the same emotional mode. In other words, it is likely that expressive body movements are translated into acoustic terms of voice production. (1987, pp. 154–5)

The way in which internal states, somatically experienced, become the source of externally uttered movements, and the way in which this dialectic affects the physiology of voice production, is mirrored in the production of instruments as extensions of the human body and voice. Here there is an external, technological manifestation of sound production thoroughly implicated with the movements of the human body. John Baily has developed this theme in arguing that players' movements affect musical structures in fundamental ways. The motor patterns which are implicated in a particular kind of music result, in Baily's view, from interaction between the morphology of the instrument and the player's sensorimotor capacities. Equally, there has grown up an intimate relationship between instruments as imitators of the human voice, and the human voice as an imitator of instruments. Middleton discusses *this* dialectic with specific reference to African-American music:

One of the importances of Afro-American music lies in the fact that often the voice seems to be treated more as an 'instrument' (the body using its own resources to make sound) ... From work-song grunts through 1930s jazz styles (Louis Armstrong singing 'like a trumpet'; Billie Holiday 'like a sax') to the short phrases of funk and scratch textures (used like percussion, bass or synthesizer), we hear vocal 'personality' receding as the voice is integrated into the processes of the articulating human body. Of course, at the same time, instruments in this tradition often sound like voices. But the often noted importance of 'vocalized tone' is only part of a wider development in which 'instrumental' and 'vocal' modes meet on some intermediate ground: while it is true that the instrument-as-machine (technological extension of the body) becomes a gesturing body (the 'voice' of the limb), at the same time the voice-as-a-person becomes a vocal body (the body vocalizing). (1990, p. 264)

Whatever the complexities of the dialectics between body, voice and instruments, we may nonetheless conclude, with Baily, that 'music can be viewed as a product of body movement transduced into sound' (Baily, 1977, p. 330).

As a consequence we find it difficult to agree with Barthes that, in music, 'the body speaks, it declaims, it redoubles its voice: *it speaks but says nothing*: because, as soon as it is musical, speech – or its instrumental substitute – is no longer linguistic, but corporeal; it only says and nothing else: *my body is put into a state of speech: quasi parlando.*' We would argue that, as corporeally and somatically manifest, music is both structured and structuring. As such, it resonates powerfully within the lived, corporeal and somatic experience of the listener. To hear a voice, a musical sound, is to 'have knowledge' of the corporeal and somatic state which produced it. The reaction is both sympathetic and empathetic. 'Listeners', says Middleton (1990, p. 243), 'identify with the motor structure, participating in the gestural patterns, either vicariously, or even physically, through dance or through miming vocal and instrumental performance.'

The principle of symbolism remains important, however. For all Barthes's talk of music as 'madness' (1985d, p. 308), as only saying, and nothing else, he does, in his claim that 'the body passes into music without any relay but the signifier', point towards an alternative semiology. As Middleton concludes:

Barthes is writing of an extreme; but anyone who has participated actively or vicariously in intensely 'executed' performance – who has felt the polyrhythmic interplay of hands in boogie-woogie piano, resonated with the intricacies of a bluegrass texture, played along with a B. B. King guitar solo or the bass-line in Billy Ocean's 'When the Going Gets Tough' – will recognize what he is pointing towards. At this extreme, we would indeed find 'a second semiology, that of the body in a state of music'. (1990, pp. 265–6)

We are back with the concept of the auditory ground of music as a structured and structuring medium speaking directly to the world of gestures and gesticulatory forms. However, it remains important to maintain a certain conceptual distance between music as a medium in sound, corporeally and somatically immi-nent, and individual subjectivity as corporeally and somatically mediated. 'The body – the "real" body – ', says Middleton (1990, p. 266), 'cannot actually be grasped in music but only by the *hands*; in music, it is necessarily represented, positioned, analo-gized, (its movements) traced.' There is an absence as well as a presence, he concludes, 'and the body in a state of music is not the same as – and must coexist with – the music in a state of psychic-somatic cathexis'. The experience of music in other words manifests two dimensions (sonic saddle and elements of signification) which, while existing indissolubly and simultane-ously *at any particular moment*, cannot, for the purposes of analy-sis and understanding, be legitimately reduced the one to the other (because they remain different aspects of one nonetheless undifferentiated experience, one pointing outwards to the exter-nal world of the music as medium and one pointing inwards to the internal world of states of awareness).

This mode of signifying distinguishes music radically from language. Language makes an appeal that is initially cerebral and cognitive at the point of its articulation of significance. The form of this appeal is entrenched by the exclusively and doubly *indirect* character of the only relationship that it is possible for the sounds of language to have with the materially embodied structures of the human world that they inevitably and ulti-mately evoke (this relationship is doubly indirect because the material structures of the human world can only be accessed by language through reference to the objects, concepts, qualities and processes that demarcate and articulate such structures, and because there is no possibility that the relationship of the inher-ent characteristics of sound to denoting these objects, concepts, qualities and processes as visually or cerebrally identified be anything other than purely conventional). Taking to its limits the capacity of thought to be independent of the world on which it operates, *hegemonic* forms of language eschew any tactile awareness, any direct awareness of the material world. Sound, the sense of touch 'at a distance', as Murray Schafer (1977, p. 11) has called it, is effectively eradicated. In its hegemonic forms and manifestations, language does not wish to bring the body into play *directly*, either as a site for utterance or as a site for political struggle. Indeed, as we have seen, there is a strain of thought within poststructuralism that says that experience has meaning only when retrospectively located within the symbolic order – that is to say, retrospectively rationalized through language. The experience, knowledge and meanings of the body cannot, according to this view of signification, speak *directly*, be spoken *directly*, or constitute *directly* the site of a politically efficacious awareness. There are resonances of this way of thinking in Middleton's comments on Baily's understanding that 'music can be viewed as a product of body movement transduced into sound.' This, says Middleton, 'is moving us close to the limits of a semiotic approach'. To some degree, concludes Middleton, 'the correlations or correspondences here seem so direct . . . that they have less to do with meaning than with processes in themselves, less with signs than actions' (1990, p. 243). Middleton seems to feel that if music leads us away from the world of signs and closer to the world of actions, it necessarily leads us away from the world of meaning in bringing us closer to the world of processes *alone*. This is a view which we will now contest.

9

Music and Language in the Constitution of Society

If language has a special capacity to map and denote discrete phenomena in the external world and, through that, to facilitate the conceptual and cerebral dimensions of people's lives, then it has been responsible, through the particular way in which it functions, for shaping important aspects of the social worlds that people mutually create. Language, through its fundamentally arbitrary functioning and its ability 'to disengage thought from reality', has enabled people to develop spectacular technologies and complex and extended forms of social organization. However, we can also make a similar claim for music. Its special capacity to evoke and symbolize the emotional and somatically experienced dimensions of people's lives and, through that, the external social relations with which they are intimately involved, has equally been responsible for shaping important aspects of the social worlds that people mutually create. Music can emphasize the relatedness of human existence with a directness and concreteness that language cannot easily reproduce. Through its fundamentally iconic and concrete functioning, music can foreground the character of people's involvement with their biographies, their societies and their environment.

In making these arguments, we have continued to insist on a point made by Langer, namely, that the world that music invokes and the manner in which it invokes it are inherently and unavoidably symbolic. We have argued that, in being deployed in the commonsense spatio-temporal framework of the everyday world (as the particulars and structures of that world have been produced *in part* through language), *the sounds of music move to supplant that framework in creating their own*. In acting in this manner symbolically, the sounds of music and their framework become synonymous, *and synonymous in a manner of consequence to the world in which we live* (which is why the commonsense spatio-temporal framework of the everyday world is produced *only* in part by language). Music is in this way distinguished from the sonic communication of animals. However, whereas the basis and necessity of language's capacity to act symbolically if human worlds which are quintessentially symbolic are to be constructed seem clear, the basis and necessity for the parallel capacity in music seem less so. More locally, while it is clear how language can assist in the creation, storage and dissemination of music, it is far from clear what music can lend to language. If music *is* to be distinguished from the sonic communication of animals in the ways in which we have indicated, then questions concerning the character of its symbolic capacity remain. If the basis of affect and meaning in music is to be completely and properly understood, therefore, it is necessary to explore further what it is that music gives to the world, including language. This understanding cannot involve simply an analysis of how music brings the world to us, which has so far been the emphasis of this book. It must involve also an analysis of how music constitutes the world, and thus affects in a fundamental manner the world it then brings to us, including language. This analysis is nothing if not consistent with the view that the social character of music cannot be reduced to the condition of other social processes. Music manifests no less a degree of relative autonomy than other social institutions. Developing an understanding of the fundamental and constitutive role music plays in human societies will lead to the fulfilment of the second purpose of this book, namely, to gain from such an understanding insights into processes of affect and meaning as they operate in cultural contexts other than those which are specifically musical. It is the desire to gain such insights which now leads us away from an examination of the relations between cultural theory and an understanding of music towards the broader undertaking of the development of a sociology of sound.

The Material Basis of Signifying Practices

It is axiomatic that individuals, whether of the human or other animal species, can only gain a sense of themselves and their place in the world through an imaginative encountering of the external material environment. In the case of the higher mammals (other than humans), it would seem that individuals rarely manipulate the external environment for the *specific* and *sole* purpose of acting symbolically. Symbolism seems to occur through the mimetic and therefore imaginative extension of actions which are in any case required in relations with the external world. Gregory Bateson illustrates this principle by reference to the behaviour of wolves. Bateson refers to the method by which female wolves wean their young. 'When the puppy asks for milk', he says, the mother 'presses down with her open mouth on the back of his neck, crushing him to the ground. She does this repeatedly until he stops asking' (1973, p. 335). Bateson then recounts an incident in which a young male transgressed a pack norm by establishing coitus with a female, a privilege usually reserved for the pack leader. Locked into the female, the young male was helpless. 'Anthropomorphism would suggest', says Bateson, 'that [the pack leader] would tear the helpless male to pieces.' Instead, he simply 'pressed down the head of the offending male four times with his open jaws and then simply walked away' (p. 336).

This, it would seem, is a clear case of behaviour, defined as deviant, being disconfirmed symbolically. The pack leader would seem to be engaging in an imaginative and mimetic use of a form of behaviour customarily engaged in by female wolves weaning their young. However, this latter form of behaviour would seem to be mimetic in the sense that a larger, stronger wolf pressing down firmly with its open jaws on the back of the necks of smaller and weaker individuals would seem to carry a clear implication of another action rarely, if ever, carried out. An important point here is to understand that all symbolism rests upon real actions in the external world, actions which cannot occur without the exercise of force. Another is that animals other than humans can engage, or so it would seem, in symbolic behaviour facilitated through the imaginative creation of the mimetic, a mimeticism which has clear homologous and material connections to other actions in the world. Although it might be argued that the distance various higher mammals can travel in imagination from elements of signification created in response to relations with the external world (actual, concrete images) is severely constrained, it would nonetheless seem that sufficient space exists for these animals to manipulate states of awareness sufficiently for identical or near identical elements of signification to be recontextualized in significantly different states. As Bateson has observed in another context (1973, pp. 150–66), it is difficult to know how dogs distinguish between fighting and playing, because the behaviour seems to us so similar and the line between the two so thin. However, the distinction is drawn, and without the use of denotative symbolism.

We argued earlier that elements of signification can occur only in relation to the public and material articulation of symbols. Images of actual triangles, for example, can only be derived in the first instance from actual triangles as they exist in the external world – these images facilitating the generalized and abstracted mental concept of 'triangle' which forms a part of states of awareness. However, once in existence, the mental concept 'triangle' can be developed and manipulated to create an image of a triangle approaching the condition of a signified, an image which is more real than that of the mental concept in the sense that it is an image of an 'actual' triangle with specific and concrete characteristics, but not real in the sense that no such triangle may yet exist in the external world. We might say that such a triangle is 'symbolically imminent', symbolically imminent in the sense that it *approaches* the condition of an element of signification which translates immediately and unproblematically into a public and material utterance. The relation between triangle and utterance is in this case a little different from the relation between utterance and triangle in the case where an element of signification flows from a real triangle in the external world, in the sense that in the first case a real triangle does not exist and in the second it does. However, the *order* of relation in both cases remains close.

The point is that the urge to act on the world, an urge that gives rise to elements of signification, is an urge on which we are not *compelled* to act. The capacity for the mimetic and the symbolic does not, in other words, imply *necessary* changes in the external world. Wolves may conceptualize pressing down with open jaws on the neck of a smaller and weaker animal, but may decide not to follow through on this action as conceived. People, in a parallel fashion, may decide to 'bite their tongues'. In developing tools in a more extensive and open-ended fashion than other animals, and in developing the capacity to *map* through drawings or words the implications and consequences for the environment of the actions made possible by the development of tools, people in fact *made possible the mapping of their imaginings in relation to the external world* through the manipulation of that same world. In this sense, *and in this sense only*, signifying practices developed solely for the purpose of the articulation of imaginings in relation to the external world may be thought of as having *indirect* relationships with this world by virtue of the prior and direct relationships they have with states of awareness through the exercise of imagination. Nonetheless, these processes of mapping are *still* constituted as actions on the world involving the exercise of force. They may, however, be conceived of as *meta-actions* conceived in relation to actions. They are, in other words, actions about actions. To the extent that actions about actions convey their symbolic character to the actions they symbolize, no actions in the human world can be symbolically 'innocent'. All actions come, in one way or another, to be actions about actions and thus endemically symbolic. Yet this way of thinking about the creation of a *distinctive* form of symbolism within human worlds allows a critical distinction to be made between this symbolism and that of animals other than humans. While there remains a sense in which the mimetic and symbolic actions of wolves are actions about actions, they are not customarily actions about actions *whose focus is the possible (let alone probable) implementation of the latter*.

People thus created *for themselves* through the exercise of imagination aspects of the external world whose intended 'foci of attention' were not *in the first instance* aspects of the external world, but states of awareness as these states existed in imaginative and dialectical but not necessarily articulated relations with those aspects. While the actions about actions had as their *ultimate* intended focus the possible if not probable implementation of the latter, this line of intentionality could only be achieved *through* the manipulation of states (this line of intentionality is similar with animals to the extent that states of awareness are *always* implicated in actions, but different in the sense that states of awareness are, for animals, more likely to be coextensive with actions than instrumental in their implementation). So, while the ultimate focus for people was clear (the possible or probable implementation of 'first-order' actions), 'first-order' actions as a consequence of 'second-order' actions could only be achieved *indirectly* through the mediation of states of awareness. If the space for imagination with higher mammals other than humans is quite severely circumscribed through the character of their typical relations with the external world, then the range for imagination with humans is significantly increased because of the creation of mapping devices, of actions about actions whose order of effectivity on the latter can *only* be indirect, mediated, indeed, through human imagination. However, the scope created for imagination is different given the different inherent characteristics of various signifying practices. The scope with iconic forms of signification is very significantly limited compared to the scope with language. It is language's ability to mediate so easily the highly prescriptive potential of imagination which has rendered it of fundamental and constitutive importance to human societies.

Language, Music and Imagination

The basis of language's importance to the constitutive characteristics of human societies lies first of all, therefore, in the arbitrary relationship that can exist between signifier and signified. The mapping of the objects and properties of the external, material world in a manner which does not require that there be any necessary – which is to say materially homologous or iconic – relationship between the material character of words and internal yet material states of awareness (in this case, mental concepts as elements of signification) means that words can be manipulated *without there being any necessary or immediate consequence for these internal states as corporeally and somatically constituted*. Conventional semiological wisdom dictates that any significant consequence will occur *only* to the extent that individuals allow custom and convention to bind the signifier to the signified. This binding is not of a material character. Unlike the *material* binding of sonic saddles and elements of signification in music, it is as a consequence one which individuals *may* control. In practice, of course, it is rare for individuals to dwell on the character of this arbitrary connection, and to *this* extent, signifiers accepted as meaningful will have some consequences through the mediation of signifieds for the mental concepts embedded within states of awareness. However, it nonetheless follows from the arbitrary character of the connection or 'binding' between signifiers and signifieds that words can be likewise manipulated without any immediate or necessary consequence for the objects, properties and events, and thereby the relations of the external world to which they are taken to refer *despite* the fact that these objects, properties, events and relations are embedded in networks of actions and forces which *are* in materially iconic yet imaginative relations with states of awareness as corporeally and somatically constituted.

The second basis of language's importance to the constitutive characteristics of human societies derives from the first. It is, indeed, the ability of language to be involved through imagination in the *extensive* manipulation of the worlds it denotes – and without there being any necessary implication for change within those worlds. The possibility for imagination, it can be argued, rests in the ability of states of awareness to change organically in independence from elements of signification as called forth through the public and material utterance of symbols. If part of the materiality offered up by the external world is made up of sounds which have to bear no intrinsic relation to the internal states of awareness to which they are nonetheless taken to be highly relevant, then it would appear that the effectivity of this constraint is all but eradicated. The potential exists for the exercise of imagination in a manner which is *constitutionally* free of iconic material constraint.

It is nonetheless a constitutional condition of imagination that it can 'run free' of iconic material constraints under *all* circumstances. If this freedom did not exist, imagination could not play a part in the construction of the human world. The external, material world would have to be assumed to be 'free' of social processes and individual volition, and to be something that could only remain to be discovered when individual imagination, creativity and volition could be brought, so to speak, 'correctly' in line with it. However, when operating within iconic material constraints as presented by the external world, states of

awareness have first to divest themselves of elements of signification brought on by the public and material articulation of
symbols *before* organic change can begin and imagination can be
said to be in play. This initial divestment does not have to occur
in the same way with language, because no *material and iconic* constraint is operating, only constraint brought on by habit, by convention and custom. Imagination is initially free with language
in a way in which it can never be with iconic forms of symbolism. While individuals may not be aware of this – thus lending
power to convention and custom – they *can* be aware of it, and it
is this awareness which facilitates the creation of a linguistic and
cognitive world *imagined* to be free of the material and the corporeal.

Imagination working in relation to a world of material, iconic
constraints can be said to carry with it the burden of the changes
implied in the subsequent public and material articulation of
states of awareness thus changed. This burden may be experienced as a form of resistance, a struggle as imagination wrestles
with the corporeal and somatic changes implied as changes to
the external material world *of symbolism* are contemplated. Here,
the particular logics of forces and actions in the external world
which underwrite structures internalized as states of awareness
are being manipulated *symbolically* by individuals in as direct a
manner as is possible. It is thus not surprising that such manipulation encounters inertia. However, because *signifieds* need be in
no such relation with the external material world of symbolism
as internalized, the intensity of the burden, resistance or inertia
experienced can be reduced to the extent that individuals are
consciously or intuitively aware of this disjunction. Under these
circumstances, imagination can run 'more free'. It is easier,
because of the absence of a necessary, materially iconic connection between signifier and signified, for signifiers to be 'put on
one side' while imaginative, algorithmic manipulation of mental
concepts is under way. However, the signifiers are still there,
rarely unaltered in the intrinsic configuration of their sounds as
essential to meaning by virtue of being 'put on one side', an easy
and ready medium for public and material symbolic utterance
of the fruits of imagination. The character of the relationship of
signifiers to processes of imagination aids also in the comprehension of creativity or the fruits of imagination. While the algorithmic manipulation of mental concepts may cause some initial

difficulties in comprehension, the signifiers or 'words' individually – and within an accepted community of vocabulary – will likely remain meaningful. Furthermore, because the sounds of words as signifiers do not imply or require an immediate and direct, *significant* change in the states of awareness of those who hear them (since the material configuration of signifiers as sounds need not be in a materially iconic relation to such states of awareness), the implications of algorithmic manipulations in the imagination of another may be absorbed at a rate comfortable for the individuals who receive the fruits of such manipulation.

The same does not hold true in the case of music. By virtue of their very character, sonic saddles cannot be 'put on one side' while algorithmic manipulation of states of awareness occurs. There is one sense in which sonic saddles 'disappear' the moment states of awareness 'prise themselves free' from the elements of signification which are coextensive with the saddles. However, there is another sense in which material traces of the saddles remain within the materiality of states of awareness as they undergo their own, organic and non-algorithmic form of manipulation. That is why a sense of resistance and inertia *can* accompany processes of musical creativity in a manner different from that found with linguistic creativity. As the time approaches for the public and material utterance of musical symbols flowing from states of awareness as manipulated, new sounds in new configurations have to be found. These sounds and configurations will usually have much in common with other sounds and configurations within a particular genre or style, but for reasons that became clear in the discussion of Tagg's work, these sounds and their configurations can in no way be regarded as a consequence of the algorithmic manipulation of previous sounds within the genre or style in question *except in so far as language may be involved in musical creativity*. Further, it does not take much manipulation of states of awareness in relation to musical activity before this manipulation gives rise to sounds – within a recognizable formation of practitioners, listeners, genres and styles – that are offensive or meaningless. To 'change the sounds' of music is inevitably and inescapably to ask for the same *direct and immediate* order of change in the states of awareness that *receive* them as in the states of awareness that *produce* them. There is virtually no space for the distanced, 'rational' consideration that can be brought to bear in the face of language, *except* through the analysis of production which, as we argued, rests importantly upon discourses themselves constituted linguistically.

The Material and the Symbolic

We have so far argued that people created signifying practices for the specific purpose of mapping 'imaginings' in relation to the world by bringing imagination to bear on various aspects of the material universe. In the case of language and music, signifying practices were constituted as such through the use of sounds. We then argued that these signifying practices of language and music bore a different order of relationship to the exercise of human imagination. Actions carried out in relation to the material world whose focus is the possible (and probable) implementation of other actions – that is to say, language – thus encapsulate in the trajectory from the creation of second-order actions to the possible implementation of first-order actions varying potentials for the exercise of imagination. It is within this trajectory, this distance from second- to first-order actions that the principle of symbolism *for language* resides. It is the character of the mode of symbolism implicit in various signifying practices which, as we have seen in the cases of language and music, sets the parameters for the exercise of imagination. In order to grasp the character of the relations between *these* parameters and the constraints proffered by the actions and forces of the *material* world, it is necessary to consider first the character of the relations obtaining between the material and the symbolic more generally.

To the extent that forms of communication such as language and music have been implicated in human relations with the material world, it can be argued that people's grasp of the character of these relations in lived reality comes to be mediated in perception and conceptualization through the states of awareness and elements of signification (which *may* be constituted as mental concepts or signifieds) brought into play by various signifying practices. It should be further noted that these states of awareness or elements of signification can themselves only be given expression through a materiality *which is specific to them* and whose particular configurations may be thought of as flowing (through principles of convention, homology and iconicity) from the intentionalities invested in elements of signification by internal states of awareness. With human communication – and in cases where significance is not *subsequently* being attached to already existing material phenomena, as in the case of a 'glorious sunset' – there is a sense in which material configurations flow dialectically from the logics of symbolism. Symbolism cannot in a literal sense be *in* such configurations. It is therefore clear that elements of signification and states of awareness are not and cannot be constituted through the material dimensions which flow from and are therefore specific to them, although they can ultimately have no life independent of these material pathways and grounds of articulation which are in turn coextensive with the material world as humanly created. The symbolic cannot in other words be reduced to the material. As we have seen, music cannot be legitimately reduced to the material condition of the sounds that make it possible. However, the symbolic cannot occur without the material.

Conversely, since human worlds are created *in their entirety* by people, the materiality of such worlds is likewise *always* laden with a symbolism which is irreducible to it. In this sense, 'first-order' actions in the world – which include 'actions of perception' such as viewing a 'glorious sunset' – are no less symbolic than 'second-order' actions created with a specific symbolic intention in mind. As a consequence of this, signifying practices must be thought of as being constituted by *all* those actions – and not just those that we customarily think of as constituting 'communication' – through which people interact with the material world in creating their own worlds. It can therefore be concluded that *all* actions are inherently symbolic and that *all* symbolism is given life through actions.

It nonetheless remains the case that there are *two* orders of constraint and facilitation brought into play through this *one* world of human actions and forces. One resides in the character of the materiality involved in the world of human actions *tout court*, notwithstanding the symbolic character of all those actions. This order of constraint and facilitation speaks to the external world as we might imagine it to be independent of the world of human volition, but nonetheless implicated inescapably – where people are concerned – in the worlds of humans. The other order of constraint and facilitation resides in the character of the material dimensions which underwrite all instances of symbolism, it being understood that all actions are symbolic and that all such symbolism inescapably invokes the human world of actions. Because all action is symbolic and all symbolism is unavoidably articulated through action, we may conclude that the varying degrees of constraint and facilitation put in place through the inherent characteristics of the material dimensions of the actions of symbolism are in intense dialectic relations with the varying degrees of constraint and facilitation put in place through the inherent characteristics of the material dimensions of actions *tout court*. Although the symbolic can never be reduced to the condition of the material, the material in these ways nonetheless retains a high degree of effectivity in and through the symbolic.

Music and Language in the Constitution of Society

It is clear that people as individuals can survive only by acting on the material environment within which they live. Only through such actions can people provide themselves with food, shelter and clothing. However, it is equally clear that individual people can only survive in this manner by acting in concert and by co-operating with each other. It is because of this that we can say that people reproduce themselves materially (that is, con-stantly constitute and reconstitute themselves as material or bio-logical beings) by entering into relationships with one another. Within such relationships actions become significant, not only in terms of their effects on the material environment and their con-sequences for material reproduction, but also for the order and significance of relationships which make material reproduction possible. Material reproduction is only possible as a conse-quence of the ability of people to enter into relationships. And relationships between people are only possible because of the ability of individual people to engage in actions which are mutually of consequence and which as a result lend order and coherence to relationships within the context of material repro-duction. Material reproduction is in other words only possible through human relationships, and human relationships are only possible because of that aspect of actions and those sets of actions which we think of as constituting signifying practices. These relationships do not occur in isolation, however. They occur in the context of other human relationships. Networks of relationships are thus established through the actions of individual subjects who are involved, as individual subjects always are, in more than just one relationship. It is the totality of these networks of relationships which constitutes society.

It is these implications of totality – of the regularity in diversity of relationships in networks – which facilitate the concept of the social structure as a category of understanding. However, it is important to understand that the logical status of the concept of the 'social structure' *is* restricted to that of a category of understanding. As Pierre Bourdieu observes, 'Only by *constructing* ... objective structures ... is one able to pose the question of the mechanisms through which the relationship is established between structures and the practices ... which accompany them, instead of treating these "thought objects" as "reasons" or "motives" and making them the determining cause of the practices' (1977, p. 21, our italics). Only through the recognition of the concept of the social structure *as* a category is it possible 'to escape the *realism of the structure*, which hypostatizes systems of objective relations by converting them into totalities already constituted outside of individual history and group history' (p. 72). The concept of the social structure is nonetheless one which allows for an acknowledgement of the massive consequences for lived reality of the order and coherence which can be discerned in networks of relationships, consequences whose massivity is underwritten through the material embodiment of relationships and their constitutive actions.

The actions and forces of the human world come to be ordered as a consequence of the constraints for action proffered by the material world. It is therefore easy to think of the structures of the human world deriving or flowing from such ordering. However, while this ordering may be implicit in the constraints of the material world, *it comes into being and is maintained by people acting in relationships*. The human world is thus *not* produced by the material world, and the inescapably symbolic character of human worlds cannot be reduced to the character of the material conditions which make them possible. If the principle of the ordering of human actions and of the forces which flow therefrom is implicit in the constraints of the material world, therefore, *it is an ordering which has to be realized and maintained symbolically*. We would argue that while language can denote and assist in the manipulation of the isolatable and isolated elements of the material world, and thereby establish *one* of the conditions fundamental to the creation of human and thereby symbolic worlds, *there is no evidence that language, in and of itself, can supply the principle of structuring necessary for the symbolic maintenance of the structures of human worlds*. That is why music is so important and, in its own way, *itself* so fundamental to the constitutive features of human societies.

In order to understand why music is in this way so important and fundamental, it is necessary to reflect once more on the conditions which make human manipulation of the material world possible. Although vision is fundamental to this capacity in making possible the precise identification and location of objects in the material world, it is not sufficient. Although it may be surmised that images evidence and betray the structures in which the material world maintains the objects thus identified and located, there is nothing intrinsic to images which itself facilitates *their* manipulation. The sense of vision, it will be remembered, inheres in the world it identifies. Sound, on the other hand, lifts off and away from the surface of the objects of the material world which are its source. It is this disjunction which facilitates the creation of human worlds.

The characteristics of the sounds of language, it will be remembered, can bear no intrinsic relationship to the characteristics of the objects thus denoted, since the characteristics of sounds are aural and those of images visual. It is this cross-sensory use of sounds which makes possible and guarantees the arbitrary character of the use of sounds in language. In using sounds to create language, people in this way use a signifying potential which focuses attention outside sound onto the visual characteristics of isolatable elements of the world. In perceiving visually an isolatable element of the material world, the element is simply identified. Perception is at one with its 'brute existence'. It is only in assigning to this element thus *identified* a sound whose own, intrinsic characteristics can bear no relation to the visual characteristics of identification that the element becomes susceptible to conceptual *isolation* and, as a consequence, manipulation and recontextualization within a people-made world. Such isolation is only *potential*, however, because it rests *in actuality* in the element *being* decontextualized from its present location within the structures of the material world. The potential for isolation which facilitates recontextualization in the structures of a people-made world can in other words only be realized *through* the construction in actuality of such a world. The manipulation in and through people-made structures of elements of the material world thus identified visually and *potentially* isolated in and through the sounds of language is something which the sounds of language cannot on their own achieve.

One of sound's signifying potentials is that it can evoke other sounds which possess intrinsic characteristics capable of being *perceived by people* as identical or nearly identical. It is this principle of the mimetic, which applies to vision as well as to hearing, which facilitates structuring in human awareness. People seem capable of identifying or, perhaps more accurately, constructing *relations between* items of perception whose characteristics are perceived as at least being similar. Because the object of vision is the material world in which the characteristics of images thus perceived inhere, the *structuring* of the world of vision is, in this sense, and in this sense only, *given* by the material world. However, because the object of hearing is not the visually identifiable elements of the material world, but the sounds this world gives off, the structuring 'intrinsic' to such sounds *is a structuring of the world of sounds alone and not those of the material world as identified visually*. Because of this, the sounds used to identify and *potentially* isolate elements of the material world as identified visually will of necessity evidence relations of a quite different order and potential logic in structuring from those of the elements of the visually identified material world as maintained in structured relations by that world. *Linguistically speaking*, however, the sounds of language can have no relations 'intrinsic' to themselves, because their task *is* to 'point outside themselves' in an arbitrary fashion to isolatable elements already maintained in structured relations by the external material world as identified visually. A semiological arbitrariness *is in this way matched by an arbitrariness 'in structure'* dictated by the conditions of the external material world as identified visually.

If people were to be able to use this new, denotative practice made possible by sound to manipulate the world effectively and render the potential, conceptual isolation of elements actual – if people were to be able to use this new, denotative practice to create a full-blown signifying practice capable of structuring the isolatable elements of the material world into a human world – *then* they would have to find a mechanism, a technology through which to relate and manipulate the sounds of language. This mechanism could arise *only* as a consequence of the capacity of people to perceive identical or nearly identical characteristics in different sounds, and thereby to derive or create relations on the basis of such similarities. The characteristics of sounds used to support the creation of such structures in awareness need not (although they can) be the same characteristics of those sounds to be found in language *as* these *particular characteristics are implicated in language in an arbitrary fashion*, since the relations and structures obtaining between *these* characteristics of sound are those supplied by the external material world as identified visually. The characteristics used would as a consequence *have* to be those capable of creating and supporting structures in human awareness that could *subsequently* be transferred and visited onto the characteristics of the 'individuated sounds of language' as used arbitrarily. That, it can be surmised, is how 'music' arose as a signifying practice *independent of the actualities of the material world as visually identified* while at the same time remaining of the greatest consequence for the manipulation and interpellation of those actualities into worlds that were people-made. It is important to realize, however, that sounds 'as found in language' *do* themselves display characteristics capable of creating and supporting structures in human awareness (that is to say, characteristics which can be the same as or other than those 'involved in language') in the same way, indeed, as sounds 'as found in music' can themselves display characteristics utterly capable of being 'used linguistically'.

While sounds in language do not *necessarily* have to display characteristics incapable of being perceived as similar, therefore, and while sounds in language *are* as a consequence capable of supporting the creation of structures in awareness, their structuring 'as supplied by music' does not *have* to have anything to do with the structural relations, if any, made possible by the intrinsic characteristics of their sounds *as used arbitrarily*. Certain characteristics of sounds in language *must* be capable of being perceived as 'different' – even when perceptions of similarity are possible between the same sounds – *if*, indeed, these characteristics are to support the sounds as sounds 'acting in language'. If sounds in language are to be capable of 'mediating' between structures 'as given' and structures as 'people-made', then certain of their characteristics must be capable of being structured *through an external agency* (be it the structures of the world as given, or the structures made possible by the characteristics of sounds acting 'intra-sonically') in terms of *differences through repulsion* (because the sounds must be capable of *disjunction from and therefore resistance to* any *particular* structuring, be it the structuring supplied by the material world or that 'supplied' through their own inherent characteristics). Sounds 'in music' are, however, structured in terms of *differences through attraction*, because it is the perceived similarities of characteristics which facilitate and support structures in awareness and not a 'foreign' structure which is being imposed on 'unwilling' sounds.

It is important to realize, however, that music (as well as language) does not structure itself. It is structured by people in terms of their capacity to perceive in the sounds of the material world similarities or regularities capable of sustaining the action of *a purely symbolic structuring in awareness* (that is, a form of structuring which in principle – and in principle *only* – is independent of the actualities or inherent structurings of the material world as identified visually). The action of structuring in awareness is itself required through the character of individuals' dialectic relations with the ordered actions and forces of the external world, a form of ordering which *in itself* severely constrains the exercise of imagination and therefore the ability of individuals to create human worlds. The structuring imparted to language as a consequence of the capacity of people to engage in a 'purely' symbolic structuring in awareness 'through music' is therefore a structuring imparted by people. It is in this sense that music as a signifying practice is always in an *indirect* relationship with the actualities of the material world as identified visually, and therefore *always* in a dialectical relationship with this external material world as it is manipulated into a human world *by people acting together* in part through language. Since it is these human relationships – people acting together through language *and* music to reproduce themselves materially – which constitute societies, music, as well as the subjectivities of individuals, is social in character. Music is social, therefore, not *only* in being produced through the *material* world, and not *only* in being *produced* through the social world. It is social in providing the facility for structuring in 'independence' of the material world as identified visually which in turn facilitates the *human* structuring of this material world and so the constitution of the social world. Music is social also in its capacity to symbolize the external world, the external world of the material and the social *as thus structured*.

Conclusion

It is thus music (sounds 'in conversation' with sounds) which facilitates in human awareness a 'purely' symbolic structuring that is asemantic as a consequence of its 'independence' from the material world as identified visually and thus the world of language. It is this role of music in human life which goes a long way to explain the difficulties faced by Lacan and Kristeva in developing their theoretical schemes. Lacan never discussed music. Because, as we have seen, language cannot structure itself – something which Lacan recognized – he had to posit a purely theoretical concept by way of compensation. The concept of the phallus *as primary signifier* can in this way be understood as a compensation for the role of music. Kristeva, as we know, did discuss music, but always in terms of concepts drawn from the analysis of language. While Kristeva's attraction to music in her later work may have been fuelled by its apparent difference from language, she could never – as a possible consequence of the influence exercised over her work by that of Lacan – displace language from its central position in her theoretical scheme. While as a woman Kristeva felt a need to reinterpret other Lacanian principles of psychoanalysis in order to introduce a place for 'difference', she could not conceive of that 'difference' in terms of music as a signifying practice fundamentally different from that of language. That is why the concept of the *chora* was introduced as the location of 'the semiotic', the basic ordering principle of difference (through repulsion) in language. It is hardly surprising that, in providing a compensation for the role of music in human life and awareness, the *chora* subsumed some of its characteristics.

In contradistinction to the work of Lacan and Kristeva, it is *our* argument that the infinite free play of imagination and signifiers in language that is permitted by language's 'semiotic moment' is ultimately constrained by the structural *and* iconic principles according to which music articulates affect and meaning. The principle of *structuring* applies to the external world of 'the actions of language' as put in motion and internalized by people. The principle of *the iconic* applies to the internal world of states of awareness which gives rise to *and absorbs* elements of signification as an aspect of people's dialectical relations with the external world. It is the abstract yet embodied *structures* of states of awareness, created and maintained as structures through the material iconicity of music's 'semiological moment', which 'play host' to the structures of signifieds and their mutual relations as they absorb them as mental concepts. If the manipulation of the structures of music as forms that are *symbolic* is made possible through language's capacity to denote particulars, then the maintenance of language as a structured and symbolic form *and* its consequent capacity to manipulate particulars is made possible through music's endemic character as an iconic structure.

A critical point in all this is that language is *not*, in the final analysis, independent of the world on which it is made to operate. Language itself has grown from the exigencies of people acting, and acting with force, on the world around them. The ability of people to be in constant dialectical relations with aspects of the external material environment – language as sound and vision – that they have created for themselves to facilitate the widest range of imagination in the easiest possible manner in relation to this environment reinforces the fact both of people's *necessary* connectedness to the material world and the absolutely fundamental character of that connectedness. The ability to create and identify particular and abstracted concepts (signifieds) and generalized and abstracted concepts (mental concepts) in relation to aspects of the external world *perceived as displaying pattern, shape and regularity*, and to create these concepts in a further, *arbitrary relation* to certain, other aspects of the external world in a manner which facilitates the easy, algorithmic manipulation of signifieds is, indeed, a massively impressive achievement. But the character of this achievement should not be allowed to seduce us into the illusion (as well as delusion) that language is somehow context-free, unrelated to the materiality of the external world or our bodies. Propositional symbolism is important and powerful, and appropriately so. But it is not the end of the story. It is only the beginning, as Mark Johnson indicates:

> I am perfectly happy with talk of the conceptual/propositional content of an utterance, *but only insofar as we are aware that this propositional content is possible only by virtue of a complex web of nonpropositional schematic structures that emerge from our bodily experience.* Once meaning is understood in this broader, enriched manner, it will become evident that the structure of rationality is much richer than any set of abstract logical patterns completely independent of the patterns of our physical interactions in and with our environment. Any account of the 'logic' of a chain of reasoning thus would have to make reference to such schematic structures and to figurative extensions of them. The inferential structure of our abstract reasoning is a high refinement upon orderings in our bodily experience, a refinement that ignores much of what goes into our reasoning. (1987, p. 5)

As we left the world of semiology at the end of chapter 5, it manifested two possibilities: that of a first semiology, grounded in denotation and tied to processes of ideology, and that of a second semiology, grounded if at all in 'basic difference' (the basic difference of Kristeva's *chora*) and tied to a state of purity beyond ideology (as in the later work of Barthes). It will be remembered that whereas a first semiology can be used to analyse both primary (denotative) and secondary (connotative) signification in language and representational images, it can be used to analyse only secondary signification in music. It is for this reason that Barthes invoked the notion of a second semiology in relation to music: to acknowledge the existence of a primary and non-denotative level of signification in music. In the hands of a scholar such as Tagg, a first semiology ignores processes of primary signification and is lifted immediately to the level of secondary or connotative signification in exposing ideology through music. Valuable though this work might be in a substantive and empirical sense it did, however, give rise to significant theoretical and methodological problems. These problems are symptomatic, we would submit, of a serious error in drawing a categorical distinction in the manner of Barthes between a first and second semiology.

Having bought into this distinction, Tagg works with a first semiology, Barthes with a second. While exposing ideology, Tagg decontextualizes musical elements relevant to the connotative from their structural and syntactic ecology. In retaining a strong sense – albeit intuitive – of music's non-denotative primary mode of signification, Barthes seems unable to move towards meaning and ideology. The analysis of musical experience in which we engaged in chapter 6 in drawing on the work of Zuckerkandl and in particular in chapter 7 in discussing the concept of musical matter demonstrates that no aspect or level of musical signification can be separated legitimately from any other for the purposes of analysis. In this, music is no different from any other mode of signification. All media of human expression and communication are capable of several levels of signification, none of which is 'innocent' or free from ideology, and none of which is free of the influence and mediation of others. In the case of music, meaning and ideology have to be reconciled with non-denotative and asemantic modes of articulation that are fully formal and structural in character. This surely requires a transcendence of the two semiologies, rather than their maintenance as distinct methodologies.

It is because of this that *language*, as well as music, requires a third semiology which transcends a first and second semiology as identified in chapter 5. This requirement for a transcendent, third semiology flows from the fact that language, like music, is in a dialectic relation with the body, and thus *affect* as well as cognition. As we have seen, it is a consideration of the processes through which music affects people that has forced the issue in developing a third, transcendent semiology. It is nonetheless the character of the *total* set of dialectic relations obtaining between music, language, society, the body, cognition and affect which requires the third, transcendent semiology that we have developed in this and the preceding chapter.

10

Towards a Sociology of Sound

In the previous chapter we argued that language and music lend to each other in a symbiotic fashion those elements fundamental to, necessary for, and constitutive of the defining characteristics of human societies. In so doing, we acknowledged that language and music could invoke the *same* sounds, whose identical or different characteristics could be used by people to create both a form of auditory symbolism arbitrary semiologically and structurally in its relations to the external material world as identified visually, and a form of auditory symbolism iconic and homologous in its relations to this world as identified structurally and asemantically. The symbiosis and intimacy of this relationship does, however, raise a question which we have so far left unaddressed. This question has to do with how far it is possible to define adequately the constitutive characteristics of language and music as forms of human expression, communication and knowledge. In implying that the arbitrary signifying potential of sound is somehow fundamental to the constitution of language and the iconic signifying potential of sound somehow fundamental to that of music, the problem is raised of essentializing both language and music, of giving them an existence in objective reality that they have never had. Because of this, we need to look beyond the conceptual categories of 'language' and 'music' to understand the real basis upon which the arguments in this book have been mounted. That basis has, in fact, been the different signifying potentials of sound as recognized by people and put, in a wide variety of ways, into the service of the symbolic creation and maintenance of societies. It is as a consequence important to acknowledge these potentials, the manner in which they flow from sound as an aspect of the material universe, and the way in which they can be variously combined into the forms of human expression, communication and knowledge which have subsequently come to be categorized *discursively* as 'language' and 'music'.

The Signifying Potential of Sound

Sound displays three distinct potentials in acting as a ground and pathway for the generation of meaning and significance in human societies. First, sounds can imitate and thus, in a certain sense, refer to other sounds. In order for sounds to achieve this manner of signification successfully, the relationship between the sound of evocation and the sound of reference must be homologous. That is, there must exist some perceptible and recognizable similarity or parallel of structure between the two sounds. If there were no elements of necessity obtaining between the sound of evocation and the sound of reference, then the sound of evocation simply would not evoke its referent. One sound cannot therefore be completely arbitrary, that is to say, unconnected in terms of its inherent sonic qualities, in its relationship to the other. It does not follow, however, that there has to be a total congruence between the characteristics of the two sounds. One sound, in other words, does not have to be a precise copy of a second sound in order to evoke it successfully. The cuckoo calls in Beethoven's Sixth Symphony, for example, are hardly precise copies of actual cuckoo calls. However, their relationship to actual cuckoo calls is sufficiently homologous for there to be a successful evocation. Second – and this potential of sound as a ground and pathway for processes of signification in all probability derives from the first – sound can act as a homologous and iconic means of signification in relation to phenomena which themselves are *not* comprised of sound (this is the potential which has been the object of considerable discussion in this book). These first two potentials together seem to provide the basis for the phenomenon or range of phenomena that have come to be understood as 'music'. Third, sound can act as a material mapping or notational device in a way which completely elides its inherent sonic qualities. That is, the relationship between the sound and the phenomenon evoked is established and determined purely by convention. There is no necessary relationship between the inherent characteristics of the sound and the inherent characteristics of the phenomenon evoked or 'referred' to. This particular potential of sound is fundamental to the way in which significance in language is customarily taken to be generated.

'Music' and 'Language' as Discursive Formations

It is necessary to dispel any illusions that 'music' is constituted exclusively through the homologous or iconic signifying potentials of sound, and that 'language' is constituted exclusively through sound's arbitrary signifying potential. To make such claims would be to essentialize both music and language as separate, ahistorical phenomena and to assign them a status and substance in external reality which, frankly, they do not have. 'Music' and 'language' are intimately bound up with one another in the manner in which they can use the identical or different characteristics *of the same sounds* in their different signifying potentials to 'lend symbiotically to one another' those elements fundamental to the constitutive characteristics of human societies. Human worlds and human societies are created through *one* universe of sound, albeit manifesting different characteristics and signifying potentials. It is for this reason that affect and cognition are but different and integrally related aspects of *one* universe of human awareness. These different aspects can then be fixed differentially by the different signifying potentials of sound, but, because they are but different aspects of one universe of human awareness, they are always involved with one another, as Bierwisch points out:

> Cognitive processes – including their linguistic articulation – always have a more or less structured emotional aspect; emotions always have a more or less clear skeletal content of cognitive connections to reality ... That cognitive and emotional factors are mutually depen-

dent is a general condition. However, the connections obtaining between them are determined respectively by the actual contexts in which they occur, not by the logical structure of the thoughts and also not by the character of the emotions. Cognitive and emotional factors stand out from each other as separate components the more they are structured and fixed within this unity by respective and specific systems of signs. (1979, p. 53)

Systems of signs therefore 'pick out' from aspects of meaning elements or components that they are capable of encoding, thereby giving expressive shape to them:

> One of the central features of my thinking is contained in the assumption that processes of musical encoding are related to the world of emotions by fixing aspects of it which as gesticulatory forms become the meanings of musical signs – in the same way as logical forms represent the encodable aspects of cognitive processes. Gesticulatory forms are therefore defined – as are logical forms – by two sets of relations: they form distinct aspects of the multilayered entirety of emotional processes and thus the meaning of a certain type of sign among which musical signs allow the greatest degree of differentiation. The proposition as the central category of the logical form corresponds here to the gesture as the central category of the gesticulatory form. (p. 55)

Systems of signs do not therefore have to be 'purely' linguistic or 'purely' musical. Indeed, they cannot be. In this sense, 'saying, which depends on convention and showing, which is structurally motivated, are the mutually dependent poles of a continuum. Between these two poles are intermediary forms . . .' (p. 60).

The flexibility that Bierwisch's thinking allows in terms of the relation of the notions of 'language' and 'music' to concrete instances of signification, and in terms of the relation of concrete instances of signification to what is being signified is itself significant. If Bierwisch's work betrays precise notions of what constitutes music and language in their 'pure' forms – as poles of a continuum – then there is no hint of the assumption that there exist precise and delimited areas of meaning which equate exactly and exclusively with these notions. Rather, Bierwisch's work could be interpreted as setting up ideal types of signification (together with an understanding of their relatedness) through which it is possible to theorize and understand complex articulations of complex and contradictory realities. There is little sense in Bierwisch's work that the poles of his continuum are in any way privileged. This being the case, it would appear that assigning the linguistic and epistemological categories of 'language' and 'music' to the poles of the continuum is, in a certain sense, an arbitrary act. This act is of considerable use in highlighting the capacity of both the homologous and iconic, and arbitrary potentials of sound to fix and structure certain areas of meaning, but, in and of itself, it may throw little light on the frequently contradictory ways in which the terms 'language' and 'music' are used by people in the everyday world. This is not to detract from the value of Bierwisch's work. On the contrary, its level of sophistication aids rather then precludes an understanding of the complex character of most sonically based utterances. The only point at issue here is the precise scope and application of the terms 'language' and 'music'.

The position we therefore adopt is that there can be no easy equation between the different potentials that sound displays as bases for signification, and the phenomena that are customarily understood to constitute 'language' and 'music'. The question of 'what is music?' is an extremely complex one, and one that cannot be addressed usefully in terms of the love affair with definitions that seems to pervade the worlds both of academic and commonsense knowledge (Shepherd, 1985). 'Music' itself is a discursively constituted category. For this reason, the meanings invested in it are not consistent, but contested. As Grenier has observed, the term 'music' is 'highly polysemic' (1990, p. 28). Further, this word (and its near equivalent in some other modern Western European languages) is not to be found in a significant number of other cultures in the world (see, for example, Keil, 1979). The linguistic and epistemological category it invokes lies outside the cultural landscapes of such cultures and is not relevant to them. The same series of observations can be made in respect of 'language'. What, then, *is* 'music'? And what *is* 'language'? What *do* we mean by the 'linguistic' and epistemological categories that they invoke?

On reflection, it seems clear that no language, not even the most arid of academic language, is completely and purely arbitrary, without any allusion or reference to sound's homologous and iconic potentials. Language clearly contains phenomena that could loosely and imprecisely be referred to as 'musical', as, for example, in the case of onomatopoeia. More generally, all language, to be evocative, has rhythms and textural properties, the more so when it seems monotonous and flat. Equally, it seems clear that no music – not even the most rhythmic, the most textural on the one hand, or the most abstract, the most 'syntactical' (Meyer, 1959) on the other – is without a range of meanings that have become conventional, traditional, and to a certain degree arbitrary in relation to the homologous potentials and possibilities of the sounds through which it receives articulation and life. The work of Tagg has demonstrated the way in which sounds in music can act in ways that seem to have something in common with the 'referential basis' of 'language', although how far this is an 'arbitrary' function of 'music' in eliding sound's homologous and iconic potentials is, as we have seen, heavily problematic.

All human societies use sounds to communicate, and they use sounds – in various and different social and cultural contexts – in ways which draw in different degrees and combinations on the various signifying potentials of sound as a material phenomenon (as well as on these signifying potentials in relation to the various signifying potentials of vision and movement). These different and complex modes of sonically based signification and communication then come to be grasped and categorized in various cultures in relation both to the immanent characteristics of these modes as socially and culturally constructed, and in relation to the 'linguistic' and epistemological categories that come to be discursively constituted in relation to them. 'Music' does not have to be 'purely homologous' or 'purely iconic' any more than 'language' has to be 'purely arbitrary'. Indeed, the ability of 'music' to go beyond the homologous and iconic signifying potentials of sound in constituting itself as a performance event through words, images and movement is paralleled in the ability of 'language' to go beyond the arbitrary potentials of sound in constituting itself as a performance event through the 'paralinguistics' of rhythm, inflection, image and movement. In this context it is interesting to note that Kristeva's discussion of music follows a discussion of gestures and paralinguistics which, she says, 'studies the *accessory* phenomena of vocalization and, in general, the articulation of discourse' (1989, p. 308, our italics). Such studies, she continues: 'while they are still far from grasping all the complexity of daily gesturality, and even less the complex universe of ritual gesturality or dance, are the first step towards a science of complex practices, a science for which the name "the language of gestures" would not be a metaphorical expression' (p. 308). An understanding of music which pays due attention to the specific qualities of its signifying processes would clearly constitute another important step towards the development of this science. It would, in fact, demonstrate that the world of gestures and paralinguistics is rather more fundamental to the world of language than intimated by Kristeva.

Actual and concrete practices of sonically grounded human signification and communication are always couched within an understanding, categorization and formulation of these practices in terms of the ways a society or culture may reflect on them through an extension of these very same practices. The actual, concrete practices and their discursive categorization and formulation are powerfully and indissolubly linked in the sense that they emanate from the same, related modes of communication and metacommunication. However, it is important to understand that, in acting on practices to render them susceptible to the exercise of power, discourses are in a certain sense distinct from them. As Middleton has observed in relation to understanding 'popular music', it is essential to understand how knowledge comes to be discursively constituted, controlled and established as a basis for the exercise of power. 'Much recent historical work, notably Foucault's', says Middleton, 'has stressed the importance of investigating the discursive formations through which knowledge is organised. If we do not try to grasp the relations between popular music discourses and the material practices to which they refer', he concludes, 'and at the same time the necessary distinctness of levels between these, we are unlikely to break through the structures of power which, as Foucault makes clear, discursive authority erects' (1990, p. 7).

It is all the more essential to develop such understandings because discursive formations come to render the world as 'natural' and unexceptional, given rather than constructed. In this sense it is crucial to understand that neither 'language' nor 'music' are given *as such* in reality. There are no such 'things' or processes as 'language' and 'music' in the sense of there existing in the objective, social world sets of cultural practices which may be consistently, uncontestedly and definitionally subsumed under these categories. While the practices which these discursively constituted categories gather up, grasp, control and present to us as 'natural', as 'given in reality' are, indeed, given to us in the sense that they constitute a very important aspect of the *constructed* objective reality of the external social world, the way in which they are *discursively* formulated is not. This is precisely why Bierwisch is correct to draw a distinction between areas of meaning and the characteristics of those areas of meaning which are susceptible to certain kinds of coding and are so fixed and structured in certain ways through this coding. In this sense, then, 'language' and 'music' are themselves discursively constituted categories (that is, each term in itself can give rise to multiple, incommensurable and contested categories) which have come into being at particular points in history and which have, since then, been used to exercise a certain kind of political power, albeit contested.

Within the context of this history, it is not difficult to understand why Bierwisch would have focused on 'ideal types' of music and language as the poles of his continuum. Within European, post-Renaissance societies and the cultures which, in one way or another, these societies have come to control or influence, a discursively constituted notion of 'language', and of a certain form of language at that (Barthes has characterized this notion of language as *écriture classique* (1967) and as constituting 'readerly texts' (1976)) has come to be regarded as socially of consequence, of fundamental importance to the development, management and perpetuation of a world mediated through increasingly spectacular technologies, and increasingly dependent on sophisticated industrial and information networks. Within this world, 'music' has had to be very carefully managed. On the one hand, it has seemed dangerous to established political and cultural orders in representing the polar opposite of this dominant notion of language. On the other, it could not and cannot be ignored because it exists and is frequently present in publicly if not spectacularly efficacious ways. While the discursive constitution of this dominant, powerful and controlling form of language has pushed 'language', in *its* discursive constitution, as far as is possible in the direction of including the arbitrary and excluding the homologous and iconic signifying potentials of sound, 'music' has been pushed as far as is possible in its dominant discursive constitution in the direction of maximizing the homologous (if not the iconic) and minimizing the arbitrary – but of maximizing the homologous in a way which plays down, as far as is possible, sound's rhythmic and textural possibilities, those possibilities which constitute sound's inherent characteristics. There is a real sense in which the music of the established Western canon has, through the very technical musical parameters it foregrounds – those of pitch and duration, of abstract relations *between* sounds, of the 'syntactical' (Meyer, 1959) – played down as far as is possible the importance of sound's inherent characteristics to the concrete practices of 'music'. While remaining *structurally* homologous and therefore quintessentially 'musical', this music has at the same time approximated as closely as is possible to the preferred condition of 'language' by involving the inherent characteristics of sound as little as possible in processes of meaning construction (for a discussion of the parallels between Barthes's notions of *écriture classique* and readerly texts, *and* the discursive constitution of 'classical' music according to the parameters identified here, see Shepherd, 1991b , pp. 159–64). This tendency to 'feminize' and 'control' music has been noted by McClary (1991) and Brett (1994).

It is not perhaps without coincidence that those forms of 'music' and 'language' which draw attention away from the inherent characteristics of sound and from their 'multi-media' constitution (all uttered forms of language and music are ultimately performance events) are highly valued by those with political and cultural power as 'good music' and 'proper English'. Those forms which, however, draw attention to these characteristics in their constitution, and so to the lived, concrete and contradictory realities that they so successfully and powerfully evoke (for example, various forms of 'popular' and 'traditional' musics, and various 'dialects' of English such as 'black' English) are downgraded and downvalued by the politically and culturally powerful precisely in terms of their 'difference' from 'good music' and 'proper English' (in respect of language see especially Labov, 1969). The question of why a stress within signifying practices on the inherent characteristics of sound and on the multi-media potentials of sound acting together with vision and movement should prove threatening to a degree where it calls forth attempts at social control has been addressed elsewhere (Shepherd, 1993).

Power in 'Music', Power in 'Language'

We would argue that the basis of power in signifying practices – the basis of their capacity to position rather than speak subjects – rests in the material character of the iconic connections that *can* and *must* exist between the signifying potentials of the external world as taken up and used by people and the states of awareness with which they are in a dialectical relation. We would in addition argue that – apart from the sense of touch and the actual material placement of bodies – music *as discursively constituted* is *fundamental* among signifying practices in its ability to exercise precisely this kind of power. This is not to say that 'music' is necessarily any more or, for that matter, necessarily any less important than other signifying practices. It is simply that 'its inherent characteristics', its use of the iconic and non-denotative potentials of sounds, provides it with a special capacity to exercise power in a direct and concrete fashion. It can speak directly, concretely *and with precision* to the states of awareness which constitute our subjectivity, our very being.

Other signifying potentials of sounds are equally as important as that which appears to have dominated the discursive constitution of music in terms of what their own 'inherent characteristics' can bring to the world of signifying practices. However, there always appears to be a trade-off which flows from the quality of these characteristics. It is in this sense that many of the insights offered by the work of Marshall McLuhan (1962 and 1964) remain relevant to understanding signifying practices and their implications for individuals and society. The *'form'* of a communication, the material in which it is embedded and through which it is articulated, is at least as important as its syntactical and semantic disposition (crudely put, its *'content'*) to the character of its effectivity. Thus, with music, its capacity to position subjects directly, concretely, and with precision is, if we can put it this way, bought at a certain cost, namely, its inability to denote objects, events and properties in the external material world. Conversely, language's massively impressive capacity to map the objects, events and properties of the external material world and to allow for their algorithmic and frequently spectacular manipulation in consciousness through the easy mediation of the highly prescriptive potential of human imagination is also bought at a cost. Language's capacity to position subjects with any significant degree of *directness* and concreteness is severely circumscribed. Language has little *intrinsic* power.

Language's power, which in practice *is* considerable, rests upon two attributes. The first is the character of its embeddedness in states of awareness, its consequent embeddedness in the external world of force and actions, and so of its embeddedness more generally in the fluid and dynamic contexts of the human world. This power of 'language', we have argued, is a power which in effect is 'underwritten by music' through 'music's capacity to structure language'. Like music, language possesses elements of signification which only come into existence as a consequence of the public and material articulation of symbolic, which in this case is to say linguistic, utterances. The signifier 'triangle', in bringing into play the signified 'triangle', can lead to the production of images of specific triangles with concrete characteristics. However, once the moment of signification is past, the signified 'triangle', bereft of any concrete characteristics of real triangles, recedes to the realm of states of awareness. The mental concept in other words dissolves in terms of pure structure into states of awareness. This structure is nonetheless maintained as identifiable in organically *and* algorithmically dialectic relations with other concepts flowing in a like manner from other media and elements of signification through the purely textural character of states of awareness as embodied. It is in this way that 'host' states of awareness can provide contexts for the various kinds and qualities of mental concepts which constitute them, and can facilitate the kind of 'cross-sensory' communication within themselves *without which imagination and creativity would not be possible*. It is in this way also that signifieds as mental concepts carry with them the embodied, structured and textured force of states of awareness.

However, despite the material embeddedness in states of awareness of mental concepts flowing from language, despite the force in language of embodied, structured and textured states of awareness, and despite the consequent but indirect material relatedness of language to the external world, a significant degree of effectivity between signifier and signified remains to be achieved and guaranteed if language is, in fact, to exercise the power it does. This effectivity is achieved and guaranteed *to an extent* through custom and convention themselves.

There is, of course, one sense in which custom and convention are more easily negotiated, transgressed and repudiated than can be the case with the material binding of iconic symbolism. However, the spectacular and open-ended manipulation of the world which the customs and conventions of language have made possible has resulted in certain relations with the world – relations experienced by people as ordered actions and forces and thus embedded as social structures – which, if we can put it this way, have a vested interest in the maintenance of the linguistic customs and conventions in question. *Constantly* to transgress custom and convention is to render custom and convention irrelevant, to challenge their desirability or necessity, and thus to challenge the ordered actions and forces *and* consequent social structures in which they are at any particular time embedded, a challenge not likely to be tolerated to any significant extent. Signifieds contextualized as mental concepts within states of awareness thus guarantee a certain power for words, because not to would be to threaten the states in question. The power that flows from signified to signifier is not one that is supplied *at the semiological moment*, therefore (as is the case with the equivalent transaction in music), but one that operates by constraint, *the same order of constraint that underpins the limits of tolerance within which media in music and states of awareness can 'dock'*. This is the second attribute upon which the power of language rests. Beyond this, however, the power that flows from signified to signifier is achieved and guaranteed to the extent that people misrecognize in language a signifying practice that unproblematically names the world. In this way, language is inappropriately empowered to create the world for us and to render processes of imagination and negotiation impotent.

It may be concluded that language is *in this way* fundamental – through its mode of signification – to the constitutive characteristics of human societies and that in this way it exercises very considerable power. However – given the capacity of language to separate as far as is possible thought from the world on which thought operates – *the power of language flows from processes which are extrinsic to the processes through which it generates meaning*. If this were not the case, the relationship of signifier to signified could not be arbitrary in character. With music, on the other hand, the processes *through* which meaning is generated and power exercised are identical. *Meaning is power and power meaning*. To put it another way, we can only really understand the character of the exercise of symbolic power through language having understood the character of the exercise of symbolic power – and thus the character of the generation of meaning – through music. 'Music' and 'language' as discursively constituted are in principle equals, although different in their relations to processes through which meaning and power are effected.

'Language' and the Conscious, 'Music' and the Unconscious

Notwithstanding this mutual equality of 'language' *and* 'music', the clear and undoubted importance of 'language' to human societies has nonetheless resulted in language being assigned a priority among human signifying systems that is not warranted in all its aspects, and music being assigned an inferior and peripheral status that is also unwarranted. Given the commonality that can be observed between the iconic principles of music on the one hand and the analogic principle of animal vocalizations and pre-linguistic (and pre-musical) vocalizations on the other, there has also been a strong temptation to locate the roots of this 'inferior' and 'peripheral' signifying system in the very early stages of infantile development – in the stages *before* language and 'rationality' are established. The historical and ontological priority of metaphor and analogy over the linguistic sign results, quite unjustifiably, in music being assigned to a world that is 'pre-linguistic', 'pre-symbolic', 'pre-rational' and 'pre-logical' – to the world of each individual in the earliest stages of development. This world is assumed to be 'material' or 'metamaterial'. Music is assumed to originate from the 'metamusical processes' of this world – 'either innate or connected with very deep levels of psychological development', says Middleton (1990, p. 189). And this origination is assumed to be unconscious in character. Processes of music production, Middleton claims, are 'unconscious'. They involve 'the level of "unconscious iconicity" or "inner gesture" which underlies more culturally conventionalized relationships [and which] may be rooted in fundamental patterns of neural activity' (p. 226).

While there are good reasons why 'language', through the predispositions of its mode of signification, may tend to latch onto the world of the conscious, and why 'music', through its specific modes of evocation, may tend to attach itself to the world of the unconscious, *such tendencies are contingent rather than given*. They do not depend on the fixities evident in different ways in post-Freudian and post-Lacanian psychoanalysis. *They are contingent upon the exigencies of everyday life and interaction*. However, they are contingent upon more than that. They are contingent also upon a more deep-seated politics of perception and understanding which privileges language and represses and mystifies the importance of music as a signifying practice. *There is, in fact, nothing given in the relations possible between 'language' and 'music', the 'conscious' and the 'unconscious'.* Within the constraints evident in each instant of human life, constraints which facilitate its continuation, everything remains possible. We would argue that 'consciousness' can be articulated 'linguistically' *or* 'musically'. *Awareness does not have to be capable of verbal explication in order to be assigned the status of 'consciousness'.* In this respect, it is fitting to end with the words of the late John Blacking:

> if there are forms intrinsic to music and dance that are not modelled on language, we may look beyond the 'language' of dancing, for instance, to the dances of language and thought. As conscious movement is in our thinking, so thinking may come from movement, and especially shared, or conceptual, thought from communal movement. And just as the ultimate aim of dancing is to be able to move *without* thinking, to *be* danced, so the ultimate achievement in thinking is to be moved to think, to *be* thought ... essentially it is a form of unconscious cerebration, a movement of the body. We are moved into thinking. Body and mind are one. (1977a, pp. 22–3)

Bibliography

Adorno, T. W. (1984) *Aesthetic Theory* (tr. C. Lenhardt) (London: Routledge and Kegan Paul)

Althusser, L. (1969) *For Marx* (London: Allen Lane)

Althusser, L. (1971a) 'Ideology and Ideological State Apparatuses (Notes towards an Investigation)', in Althusser (1971b), pp. 127–86

Althusser, L. (1971b) *Lenin and Philosophy and Other Essays* (London: New Left Books)

Althusser, L. and Balibar, E. (1970) *Reading Capital* (London: New Left Books)

Anzieu, D. (1976) 'L'enveloppe sonore du soi', *Nouvelle Revue de psychanalyse*, no. 13 (Spring), pp. 161–79

Baily, J. (1977) 'Movement Patterns in Playing the Herati *Dutàr*', in Blacking (1977b), pp. 275–330

Barthes, R. (1967) *Writing Degree Zero* (trs Annette Lavers and Colin Smith) (London: Jonathan Cape)

Barthes, R. (1973) *Mythologies* (tr. Annette Lavers) (St. Albans: Paladin)

Barthes, R. (1976) *The Pleasure of the Text* (tr. Richard Miller) (London: Jonathan Cape)

Barthes, R. (1977) *Image, Music, Text* (tr. and ed. Stephen Heath) (London: Fontana)

Barthes, R. (1985a) *The Grain of the Voice: Interviews 1962–1980* (tr. Linda Coverdale) (New York: Hill and Wang)

Barthes, R. (1985b) 'Music, Voice, Language', in Barthes (1985d), pp. 278–85

Barthes, R. (1985c) 'Rasch', in Barthes (1985d), pp. 299–312

Barthes, R. (1985d) *The Responsibility of Forms: Critical Essays on Music, Art, and Representation* (tr. Richard Howard) (New York: Hill and Wang)

Barthes, R. (1989) 'One Always Fails in Speaking of What One Loves', in *The Rustle of Language* (tr. Richard Howard) (Berkeley: University of California Press), pp. 296–305

Bateson, G. (1973) *Steps to an Ecology of Mind* (St. Albans: Paladin)

Berger, P. L. and Luckmann, T. (1967) *The Social Construction of Reality* (Harmondsworth: Penguin)

Bierwisch, M. (1979) 'Musik und Sprache: Überlegungen zu ihrer Struktur und Funktionsweise', in Klemm, E. (ed.), *Jahrbuch Peters 1978* (Leipzig: Edition Peters), pp. 9–102

Blacking, J. (1967) *Venda Children's Songs: A Study in Ethnomusicological Analysis* (Johannesburg: Witwatersrand University Press)

Blacking, J. (1973) *How Musical is Man?* (Seattle: University of Washington Press)

Blacking, J. (1977a) 'Towards an Anthropology of the Body', in Blacking (1977b), pp. 1–28

Blacking, J. (1977b) (ed.) *The Anthropology of the Body* (London: Academic)

Bourdieu, P. (1977) *Outline of a Theory of Practice* (tr. Richard Nice) (Cambridge: Cambridge University Press)

Bradley, D. (1992) *Understanding Rock 'n' Roll: Popular Music in Britain 1955–1964* (Milton Keynes: Open University Press)

Brett, P. (1994) 'Musicality, Essentialism, and the Closet', in Brett, Wood and Thomas (1994), pp. 9–26

Brett, P. (1995) 'Piano Four Hands: Schubert and the Performance of Gay Male Desire', paper given at an international symposium, 'Border-crossings: Future Directions for Music Studies', Carleton University and the University of Ottawa, March 1995

Brett, P., Wood, E. and Thomas, G. C. (1994) (eds) *Queering the Pitch: The New Gay and Lesbian Musicology* (London: Routledge)

Capek, M. (1961) *Philosophical Impact of Contemporary Physics* (Princeton: Van Nostrand)

Chambers, I. (1985) *Urban Rhythms: Pop Music and Popular Culture* (London: Macmillan)

Chion, M. (1982) *La voix au cinéma* (Paris: Éditions de l'Étoile)

Cohen, P. (1972) 'Sub-Cultural Conflict and Working Class Community', *Working Papers in Cultural Studies*, no. 2 (Spring) (Birmingham: University of Birmingham Centre for Contemporary Cultural Studies)

Coriat, I. H. (1945) 'Some Aspects of a Psychoanalytic Interpretation of Music', *Psychoanalytic Review*, vol. XXXII, no. 1, pp. 408–18

Cusick, S. G. (1994) 'On a Lesbian Relation with Music: A Serious Effort Not to Think Straight ', in Brett, Wood and Thomas

Cusick, S. G. (1995) 'On Musical Performances of Gender and Sex', paper given at an international symposium, 'Bordercrossings: Future Directions for Music Studies', Carleton University and the University of Ottawa, March 1995

Dahlhaus, C. (1985) *Realism in Nineteenth-Century Music* (tr. M. Whittall) (Cambridge: Cambridge University Press)

Duncan, H. D. (1968) *Symbols in Society* (Oxford: Oxford University Press)

Ehrenzweig, A. (1953) *The Psychoanalysis of Artistic Vision and Hearing* (New York: Julian)

Ellis, C. (1985) *Aboriginal Music: Education for Living* (St Lucia: University of Queensland Press)

Engh, B. (1993) 'Loving It: Music and Criticism in Roland Barthes', in Solie (1993), pp. 66–79

Feld, S. (1982) *Sound and Sentiment: Birds, Weeping, Poetics and Song in Kaluli Expression* (Philadelphia: University of Pennsylvania Press) (second edn, 1990)

Feld, S. (1984) 'Communication, Music, and Speech about Music', *Yearbook for Traditional Music*, vol. 16, pp. 1–18

Feld, S. (1988) 'Aesthetics as Iconicity of Style, or, "Lift-up-over-Sounding": Getting into the Kaluli Groove', *Yearbook for Traditional Music*, vol. 20, pp. 74–113

Frith, S. (1987) 'Towards an Aesthetic of Popular Music', in Leppert and McClary (1987b), pp. 133–49

Frith, S. (1990), 'What Is Good Music?', in Shepherd (1990), pp. 92–102

Frith, S. and McRobbie, A. (1979) 'Rock and Sexuality', *Screen Education*, no. 29, pp. 3–19

Giles, J. and Shepherd, J. (1988) 'Theorizing Music's Affective Power', *Arena*, no. 85, pp. 106–21

Goodwin, A. (1992) *Dancing in the Distraction Factory: Music Television and Popular Culture* (Minneapolis: University of Minnesota Press)

Gorbman, C. (1987) *Unheard Melodies: Narrative Film Music* (Bloomington: Indiana University Press)

Gramsci, A. (1971) *Selections from the Prison Notebooks* (trs and eds Quentin Hoare and Geoffrey Nowell-Smith) (London: Lawrence and Wishart)

Grenier, L. (1990) 'The Construction of Music as a Social Phenomenon: Implications for Deconstruction', in Shepherd (1990), pp. 27–47

Grossberg, L. (1984) 'Another Boring Day in Paradise: Rock and Roll and the Empowerment of Everyday Life', *Popular Music*, vol. 5, pp. 225–60

Grossberg, L. (1987) 'Rock and Roll in Search of an Audience', in James Lull (ed.), *Popular Music and Communication* (Newbury Park: Sage), pp. 175–97

Grossberg, L. (1993) 'Is Anybody Listening? Does Anybody Care?: On "The State of Rock" ', in Andrew Ross and Tricia Rose (eds), *Microphone Fiends: Youth Music & Youth Culture* (London: Routledge), pp. 41–58

Hall, S. and Jefferson, T. (eds) (1976) *Resistance through Rituals: Youth Subcultures in Post-War Britain* (London: Hutchinson)

Hawkes, T. (1977) *Structuralism and Semiotics* (London: Methuen)

Heath, S. (1977) 'Translator's Note', in Barthes (1977), pp. 7–11

Hebdige, D. (1979) *Subculture: The Meaning of Style* (London: Methuen)

Hofstein, F. (1972) 'Drogue et musique', *Musique en jeu*, no. 9 (November), pp. 111–15

Johnson, M. (1987) *The Body in the Mind: The Bodily Basis of Meaning, Imagination, and Reason* (Chicago: University of Chicago Press)

Kaplan, A. E. (1987) *Rocking Around the Clock* (London: Methuen)

Keil, C. M. (1979) *Tiv Song* (Chicago: University of Chicago Press)

Kerman, J. (1985) *Contemplating Music: Challenges to Musicology* (Cambridge, Mass.: Harvard University Press)

Knepler, G. (1977) *Geschichte als Weg zum Musikverständnis: Zur Theorie, Methode und Geschichte der Musikgeschichtsschreibung* (Leipzig: Reclam)

Kohut, H. and Levarie, S. (1956) 'Some Psychological Effects of Music and Their Relation to Music Therapy', in E. T. Gaston (ed.), *Music Therapy 1955* (Lawrence, Kan.: Allen Press), pp. 17–20

Kohut, H. and Levarie, S. (1957) 'Observations on the Psychological Functions of Music', *Journal of American Psychoanalysis*, vol. 5, pp. 389–407

Kristeva, J. (1989) *Language the Unknown: An Initiation into Linguistics* (tr. Anne M. Menke) (New York: Columbia University Press)

Labov, W. (1969) 'The Logic of Nonstandard English', *Georgetown Monographs on Language and Linguistics*, vol. 22, pp. 1–31

Lacan, J. (1977) *Écrits: A Selection* (tr. Alan Sheridan) (New York: W. W. Norton)

Lacan, J. (1979) *The Four Fundamental Concepts of Psycho-Analysis* (tr. Alan Sheridan) (ed. Jacques-Alain Miller) (Harmondsworth: Penguin)

Lacan, J. (1982) *Feminine Sexuality* (tr. Jacqueline Rose) (eds Juliet Mitchell and Jacqueline Rose) (New York: W. W. Norton)

Langer, S. (1942) *Philosophy in a New Key* (Cambridge, Mass.: Harvard University Press)

Leppert, R. and McClary, S. (1987a) 'Introduction', in Leppert and McClary (1987b), pp. xi–xix

Leppert, R. and McClary, S. (1987b) (eds) *Music and Society: The Politics of Composition, Peformance and Reception* (Cambridge: Cambridge University Press)

Lévi-Strauss, C. (1966) *The Savage Mind* (London: Weidenfeld and Nicolson)

Lévi-Strauss, C. (1969a) *The Raw and the Cooked* (trs John and Doreen Weightman) (New York: Harper and Row)

Lévi-Strauss, C. (1969b) *Totemism* (tr. Rodney Needham) (Harmondsworth: Penguin)

Lévi-Strauss, C. (1971) 'Boléro de Maurice Ravel', *L'Homme*, vol. 11, no. 2 (April–June), pp. 5–14

Lévi-Strauss, C. (1972) *Structural Anthropology* (trs Claire Jacobson and Brooke Grundfest Schoepf) (Harmondsworth: Penguin)

Lord, A. B. (1964) *The Singer of Tales* (Cambridge, Mass.: Harvard University Press)

McClary, S. (1991) *Feminine Endings: Music, Gender, and Sexuality* (Minnesota: University of Minnesota Press)

McLuhan, M. (1962) *The Gutenberg Galaxy* (Toronto: Toronto University Press)

McLuhan, M. (1964) *Understanding Media* (Toronto: New American Library of Canada)

Margolis, N. M. (1954) 'A Theory on the Psychology of Jazz', *American Imago*, vol. 11, pp. 263–91

Masserman, J. H. (1955) *The Practice of Dynamic Psychiatry* (Philadelphia: Saunders)

Mendel, A. (1962) 'Evidence and Explanation', in *Report of the Eighth Congress of the International Musicological Society* (Cassel, London and New York: Barenreiter), pp. 3–18

Meyer, L. B. (1956) *Emotion and Meaning in Music* (Chicago: University of Chicago Press)

Meyer, L. B. (1959) 'Some Remarks on Value and Greatness in Music', *Journal of Aesthetics and Art Criticism*, vol. XVII, no. 4, pp. 486–500

Meyer, L. B. (1973) *Explaining Music* (Los Angeles: University of California Press)

Middleton, R. (1990) *Studying Popular Music* (Milton Keynes: Open University Press)

Moi, T. (1986) (ed.) *The Kristeva Reader* (Oxford: Basil Blackwell)

Molino, J. (1975) 'Fait musical et sémiologie de la musique', *Musique en jeu*, no. 17, pp. 37–62

Molino, J. (1978) 'Sur la situation du symbolique', *L'Arc*, no. 27, pp. 20–5, 31

Moore, A. F. (1993) *Rock: The Primary Text* (Milton Keynes: Open University Press)

Nattiez, J.-J. (1975) *Fondements d'une sémiologie de la musique* (Paris: Union générale d'éditions)

Nattiez, J.-J. (1987) *De la sémiologie à la musique* (Montréal: La Presse Université de Québec à Montréal)

Nattiez, J.-J. (1990) *Music and Discourse: Toward a Semiology of Music* (Princeton: Princeton University Press)

Noy, P. (1967a) 'The Psychodynamic Meaning of Music – Part II', *Journal of Music Therapy*, vol. IV, pp. 7–23

Noy, P. (1967b) 'The Psychodynamic Meaning of Music – Part III', *Journal of Music Therapy*, vol. IV, pp. 45–51

Noy, P. (1967c) 'The Psychodynamic Meaning of Music – Part IV', *Journal of Music Therapy*, vol. IV, pp. 81–94

Palisca, C. (1963) 'American Scholarship in Western Music', in Frank Lloyd Harrison, Mantle Hood and Claude Palisca (eds), *Musicology* (Englewood Cliffs, NJ: Prentice-Hall), pp. 87–214

Payne, M. (1993) *Reading Theory: An Introduction to Lacan, Derrida, and Kristeva* (Oxford: Basil Blackwell)

Pfeifer, S. (1923) 'Problems of Music and Psychology', *International Journal of Psychoanalysis*, vol. IV, pp. 380–1

Piaget, J. (1971) *Structuralism* (tr. Chaninah Maschler) (London: Routledge and Kegan Paul)

Pratt, C. C. (1952) *Music and the Language of Emotion* (Washington: Library of Congress)

Racker, H. (1951) 'Contribution to Psychoanalysis of Music', *American Imago*, vol. 8, pp. 129–63

Reti, R. (1958) *Tonality, Atonality, Pantonality* (London: Rockcliff)

Rosolato, G. (1974) 'La voix: entre corps et langage', *Revue française de psychanalyse*, vol. 38, no. 1, pp. 75–94

Saussure, F. (1966) *Course in General Linguistics* (tr. Wade Baskin) (New York: McGraw Hill)

Schafer, M. (1977) *The Tuning of the World* (New York: Alfred A. Knopf)

Schwichtenberg, C. (1993) (ed.) *The Madonna Connection: Representational Politics, Subcultural Identities, and Cultural Theory* (Boulder, San Francisco and Oxford: Westview Press)

Seeger, C. (1977) *Studies in Musicology 1935–1955* (Berkeley: University of California Press)

Shepherd, J. (1977) 'The Musical Coding of Ideologies', in Shepherd et al. (1977), pp. 69–124

Shepherd, J. (1982a) 'A Theoretical Model for the Sociomusicological Analysis of Popular Music', *Popular Music*, vol. 2, pp. 145–77

Shepherd, J. (1982b) *Tin Pan Alley* (London: Routledge and Kegan Paul)

Shepherd, J. (1985) 'Definition as Mystification: A Consideration of Labels as a Hindrance to Understanding Significance in Music', in David Horn (ed.), *Popular Music Perspectives*, no. 2 (Göteborg, Exeter, Ottawa and Reggio Emilia: International Association for the Study of Popular Music), pp. 84–98

Shepherd, J. (1990) (ed.) *Alternative Musicologies/Les Musicologies alternatives*, special issue of the *Canadian University Music Review/Revue de musique des universités canadiennes*, vol. 10, no. 2 (Toronto: Toronto University Press)

Shepherd, J. (1991a) 'Middleton's *Studying Popular Music*: A Review Essay', *Worldbeat: An International Journal of Popular Music*, no. 1, pp. 150–70

Shepherd, J. (1991b) *Music as Social Text* (Cambridge: Polity Press)

Shepherd, J. (1993) 'Difference and Power in Music', in Solie (1993), pp. 46–65

Shepherd, J., Virden, P., Vulliamy, G. and Wishart, T. (1977) *Whose Music? A Sociology of Musical Languages* (London: Latimer)

Silverman, K. (1983) *The Subject of Semiotics* (Oxford: Oxford University Press)

Silverman, K. (1988) *The Acoustic Mirror: The Female Voice in Psychoanalysis and Cinema* (Bloomington: Indiana University Press)

Solie, R. A. (1993) (ed.) *Musicology and Difference: Gender and Sexuality in Music Scholarship* (Berkeley: University of California Press)

Straw, W. (1991) 'Systems of Articulation, Logics of Change: Communities and Scenes in Popular Music', *Cultural Studies*, vol. 5, no. 3, pp. 368–88

Sundberg, J. (1987) *The Science of the Singing Voice* (DeKalb: Northern Illinois University Press)

Tagg, P. (1979) *Kojak – 50 Seconds of Television Music: Towards the Analysis of Affect in Music* (Göteborg: Skrifter från Musikvetenskapliga Institutionen)

Tagg, P. (1982) 'Analysing Popular Music: Theory, Method, and Practice', *Popular Music*, vol. 2, pp. 37–68

Tagg, P. (1987) 'Musicology and the Semiotics of Popular Music' *Semiotica*, vol. 66, nos. 1–3, pp. 279–98

Tagg, P. (1991) *Fernando the Flute: Analysis of Musical Meaning in an ABBA Mega-Hit* (Liverpool: The Institute of Popular Music, University of Liverpool)

Tailor, I. A. and Paperte, F. (1958), 'Current Theory and Research in the Effects of Music on Human Behavior', *Journal of the Aesthetics of Art Quarterly*, vol. 17, pp. 251–8

Taylor, J. and Laing, D. (1979) 'Disco-Pleasure-Discourse: On "Rock and Sexuality" ', *Screen Education*, no. 31, pp. 43–8

Volek, J. (1981) 'Musikstruktur als Zeichen und Musik als Zeichensystem', in H. W. Henze (ed.), *Die Zeichen: Neue Aspekte der musikalischen Ästhetik II* (Frankfurt am Main: Fischer), pp. 222–55

Walser, R. (1993) *Running with the Devil: Power, Gender, and Madness in Heavy Metal Music* (Hanover, NH: University Press of New England)

Weedon, C. (1987) *Feminist Practice and Poststructuralist Theory* (Oxford: Basil Blackwell)

White, A. (1977) 'L'éclatement du sujet: The Theoretical Work of Julia Kristeva', paper available from the University of Birmingham

Wicke, P. (1989) 'Rockmusik – Dimensionen eines Massenmediums: Weltanschauliche Sinnproduktion durch populäre Musikformen', *Weimarer Beiträge*, vol. 35, no. 6, pp. 885–906

Wicke, P. (1990a) *Rock Music: Culture, Aesthetic, Sociology* (tr. Rachel Fogg) (Cambridge: Cambridge University Press)

Wicke, P. (1990b) 'Rock Music: Dimensions of a Mass Medium – Meaning Production through Popular Music' (trs Regina Datta, Ernst Oppenheimer and Peter Wicke), in Shepherd (1990), pp. 137–56

Wicke, P. (1991) 'Middleton's *Studying Popular Music*: A Review Essay', *Worldbeat: An International Journal of Popular Music*, no. 1, pp. 135–40

Williams, R. (1965) *The Long Revolution* (Harmondsworth: Penguin)

Willis, P. (1977) *Learning to Labour* (London: Saxon House)

Willis, P. (1978) *Profane Culture* (London: Routledge and Kegan Paul)

Zuckerkandl, V. (1956) *Sound and Symbol: Music and the External World* (tr. W. R. Task) (Princeton: Princeton University Press)

Index